UN-COVERING THE CURRICULUM

UN-COVERING THE CURRICULUM

Whole Language in Secondary and Postsecondary Classrooms

KATHLEEN & JAMES STRICKLAND

Boynton/Cook Publishers
Heinemann
Portsmouth, NH

Boynton/Cook Publishers, Inc.
A subsidiary of Reed Elsevier Inc.
361 Hanover Street   Portsmouth, NH   03801-3912
Offices and agents throughout the world

The authors and publisher would like to thank the following for permission to reprint material from copyrighted work:

Excerpts from "The Voices We Hear" by Jeff Golub. In *English Leadership Quarterly*, May 1993. Reprinted by permission of the author.

Excerpts from "Whole Language: Implications for Secondary Classrooms" by Barbara King-Shaver. In *English Leadership Quarterly*, February 1991. Reprinted by permission of the author.

Excerpts from "No More Objective Tests, Ever" by Carol Jago. In *English Leadership Quarterly*, February 1992. Reprinted by permission of the author.

Excerpts from "Peer Dialogue Journals: An Ethnographic Study of Shared Reader Response to Holocaust Literature" by Kate Kessler. Unpublished doctoral dissertation, 1992. Reprinted by permission of the author.

Excerpts from "Contemporary Literature, Heterogeneous Style" by Eileen Oliver. Unpublished manuscript, 1992. Reprinted by permission of the author.

Acknowledgments continue on page 219.

Library of Congress Cataloging-in-Publication Data
Strickland, Kathleen.
    UN-covering the curriculum : whole language in secondary and
postsecondary classrooms / Kathleen and James Strickland.
        p.   cm.
    Includes bibliographical references (p.) and index.
    ISBN 0–86709–332–3
    1. Language arts (Secondary)   2. Language arts (Higher)
3. Language experience approach in education.   I. Strickland,
James.   II. Title.
LB1631.S824   1993   93–5801
428'.0071'2—dc20   CIP

Cover design by Phillip Augusta.
Printed in the United States of America on acid-free paper.
97 96 95 94   EB   2   3   4   5   6   7

To our parents, Fred and Lucille Paterson and Ken and Libby Strickland—our finest teachers.

Contents

Preface

Over the years, we have been fortunate enough to have friends and colleagues who have helped us to discover a philosophy of teaching born of a desire to understand how people learn. Between the two of us, we have had experience teaching in elementary school, middle school, high school, college, and graduate school. What we have found is that there are many tenets of learning that are common to every grade level and age.

Our beliefs about teaching and learning can be best explained as "Whole Language." To paraphrase Ken Goodman, whole language found us. Our belief that learning must be a transaction continues to be the basis for our investigation into how language is learned and how learners must be supported as they develop. In our work, we have found these questions addressed by many books seeking to explain whole language to elementary educators. There are even more books to explain the writing process, reader response, assessment and evaluation, special populations, and politics, but each book is detailed and only a part of the picture. What we have attempted to do in this book is to explain the term *whole language* to those who work with secondary school and college students, pulling together the many facets of learning commonly called whole language. We hope that those in secondary education will find whole language based on sound research investigating how people learn and will find it able to be implemented in any school at any grade level, once the philosophy is understood and accepted.

You may not be able to judge a book by its cover, but a good title never hurts. We wanted a title that would continue the metaphor of "In the Middle," but "The Far Left of the Middle" didn't seem right and neither did "At the Other End." It was Wendy Bishop who suggested that we reread our teachers' stories, listening for a phrase that would sound just right. We found it. The phrase was "covering the material" and "covering the curriculum." Late one afternoon in the Galt House East during the Fall NCTE convention, we played with the phrase and left Louisville with three variations: Uncovering the Curriculum; Recovering the Curriculum; and Discovering the Curriculum. Several days after the conference, we received a manuscript in the mail from Jeff Golub, and in it discovered a typographical twist on our title that he used: UN-Covering the Curriculum. It was perfect, but we had to promise to give Jeff credit so that his friends would not accuse him of stealing our title. Thanks Wendy and thanks Jeff.

There is never enough time or space to thank those who have had a nurturing influence on our lives; however, we would be remiss not to thank four people: Dr. Donald O'Brien, who opened our world in the early seventies with Frank Smith's first edition of *Understanding Reading* and Kenneth Goodman's early research; Dr. Patrick Hartwell, who taught us so much about style and grace; Dr. Donald McAndrew, who showed us so much about teaching; and Dr. Mary Agnes McKay, who encouraged us through long months of research and writing.

We would like to thank the teachers who were generous enough to share their stories of their classrooms with us: Brian Biemuller, South Brunswick High School, NJ; Esther Broughton, Mesa State College, Grand Junction, CO; Rick Chambers, Grand River Collegiate Institute, Kitchner, Ontario; Diana Dreyer, Slippery Rock University of Pennsylvania; Martha Dolly, Frostburg State University, MD; John Ferguson, Murphy Junior High School, Stony Brook, NY; Connie Fleeger, Slippery Rock University of Pennsylvania; Carol Jago, Santa Monica High School, CA; Kathy Kelly-Garris, Penn-Trafford High School, PA; Kate Kessler, Chambersburg High School, PA; Barbara King-Shaver, South Brunswick High School, NJ; Bill Murdick, California University of Pennsylvania; Eileen Oliver, Washington State University, Pullman, WA; Anne Picone, North Hills Senior High School, Pittsburgh, PA; Janine Rider, Mesa State College, Grand Junction, CO; Terrie St. Michel, South Mountain High School, Phoenix, AZ; Kathy Simmons, Hempfield Senior High School, Greensburg, PA; Herb Thompson, Emory & Henry College, Emory, VA; Amy Walker, Intermediate Unit IV/Mars Youth Home, Mars, PA; and, Terry Wansor, Hempfield Senior High School, Greensburg, PA.

We would also like to thank the following students for sharing their work with us: Preeti Advani, Carla Braun, Mya Breitbart, David, John Fuller, Greg, Steve Kelty II, Kim McCann, Karen Montoya, Stacey, Christopher Vaccaro, and Samantha Zyontz.

We would also like to thank our editor, Peter Stillman, for his belief in our ideas and his encouragement throughout the process. Peter feels as passionately as we do about this philosophy, as is evidenced by his statement in a letter to us: "Anyone *not* teaching from this stance should be summarily canned."

A word of thanks is also owed to some wonderful people at Heinemann, especially Melissa Inglis, our permissions editor, and Nancy Sheridan, our copyeditor.

Finally, we would like to thank Slippery Rock University for its generous support of scholarship in granting Kathleen the Dean's Scholar Award so that she might complete work on this book.

Chapter One

A Transactional Philosophy of Learning

[Teachers should] invite pupils to use language. Get them to talk about things they need to understand. Show them it's all right to ask questions and listen to the answers, and then to react or ask more questions. Suggest that they write about what happens to them, so they can come to grips with experiences and share them with others. Encourage them to read for information, to cope with the print that surrounds them everywhere, to enjoy a good story.

Whole language programs get it all together: the language, the culture, the community, the learner, and the teacher.

—Kenneth Goodman

Questions for Thought/Journal Entries

1. Think about classrooms you have been in during high school and college. What role did the teacher play in these classes? What was your role as student?

2. Can you describe how you learned in secondary school?

3. Why has whole language been accepted in elementary grades, while it has hardly been discussed in secondary grades? What are some things about secondary schools that you would like to see changed?

4. Describe the environment of high school classrooms. Is the environment conducive to learning? If so, in what way? If not, why not?

5. Think back to the class that was your most memorable in high school or college. What made this class special? What did it have that your other classes lacked?

Introduction

In this chapter, we will explain the term *whole language* by presenting the background and history of whole language, the tenets of its philosophy, and the differences between traditional and whole language classrooms. This chapter will "paint a picture" of a whole language classroom in order to reflect the roles of teacher and learner; the place of reading, writing, listening, and speaking; and the place whole language has in secondary classrooms.

What's So Different About Whole Language?

Two years ago, Kim, a student who had been a student in my (Kathleen's) Secondary English methods class the previous semester, called on the phone one Sunday evening, frantic about her student teaching. Kim was to teach a unit on *The Canterbury Tales* to ninth-grade students in a suburban high school, following a curriculum set by the district and her cooperating teacher.

"Mrs. Strickland, they hate it!" Kim lamented, speaking about her students and her lesson. "What can I do to get them interested? They lay their heads on their desks, gaze out the window, lose their place as we're reading. Last week I gave a short reading assignment, and over half the class didn't do it. I feel like such a failure!" Kim confessed.

I didn't feel I could tell Kim what to teach, but Kim and I talked briefly about why she thought the kids were bored. Kim admitted that even *she* hated *The Canterbury Tales*, but, after all, it was the required reading and she had to teach it. She further admitted that she had been approaching the unit lessons "kind of traditionally," since all the other teachers in her school seemed to teach that way. What Kim defined as a traditional approach was to ask the students to read the assigned text, answer the questions, prepare for the unit test, and write a critical analysis of the "theme."

Kim and I spent some time talking about whole language, a philosophy she had been excited about in her university methods course, but one she had not implemented in her teaching. Instead, Kim was teaching the way she had been taught in high school, a method that she perceived as safer, easier, yet quite unlike what she thought teaching would be. As a student taking methods courses,

Kim had hoped to make a difference, helping her students become readers, writers, and thinkers, and she was rightfully discouraged because it was not happening.

Fortunately, Kim had a cooperating teacher who was willing to let her teach in any way Kim felt would accomplish her goals. The next week Kim changed her approach. She asked her students to divide into groups. Their assignment was for each group to choose one of Chaucer's travelers and to read the section of *The Canterbury Tales* dealing with the tale of their traveler. Each group was then responsible for somehow presenting this tale to the class. Kim and her students brainstormed ways to accomplish this; their suggestions included role playing, choral reading, paraphrasing, rewriting the journey in contemporary language, and presenting it as poetry. Kim was honestly amazed at the change in the attitude of the class. They not only read *The Canterbury Tales*, but their response convinced Kim that they would never forget the experience. Her students dressed in costume; wrote soap-opera versions; wrote original poetry, which they put to music; and even told the tale through painted murals. As a final exam for the unit, the students each wrote their own Canterbury-like tale, telling stories of bus trips with the school choir and band, adventures shared with their families on vacations, and tales recounted years earlier around campfires at summer camp. Kim gave them time in class to work on their writing, and every student was expected to continue to work outside of class as well, returning to class prepared for participation and response. Every student was able to write a tale, and most were anxious to share their tales with the class.

Kim had accomplished her goal—the students had read *The Canterbury Tales*, enjoyed the experience, and all participated as readers and writers. What was different about how Kim approached this assignment?

Pamela Grossman (1989), in her research about teacher training, gathered some insights about the differences in approaches to teaching. Grossman tells the story of two secondary English teachers, Jake and Steven, one who taught in the way Kim described as traditional, and the other who believed in getting students involved and letting them discover as Kim did with her *Canterbury Tales* unit.

Grossman's characters both had undergraduate degrees in English and strong backgrounds in English literature. However, when teaching *Hamlet* to high school students, each teacher had completely different objectives. Jake, who had been trained in the traditional approach to teaching English with a heavy emphasis on textual analysis, spent seven weeks on the play. His primary objective in this unit was textual analysis in order to help bring students an understanding of the "power and beauty" of the play's language.

His students were required to do an in-class analysis of one solilo-quy, to memorize and recite a soliloquy, and to write a five-page paper on any theme in *Hamlet*. At the conclusion of the seven weeks of oral reading and critical analysis, the class was given a final exam that included a question requiring them to write a paragraph on the importance of language in the play.

Steven, on the other hand, spent only two and one-half weeks on *Hamlet*. His primary objective was to help students see the connec-tion between Hamlet's problems and some of the problems they might face in their lives. A second objective was to interest the stu-dents in the play. Steven began by motivating his students, creating an interest, and showing students that Hamlet's life was part of their "schema"—their background experience and knowledge. Without mentioning the name of the play, Steven asked his students how they would feel if their parents got divorced and their mother sud-denly started dating another man. Students were asked to write their responses to the situation, including how they would feel if they found out that their mother's new boyfriend had taken over their father's job and they suspected that the new guy had something to do with their father being fired. Steven also asked them to write about a point in their lives where they might be driven to murder someone. When Steven told students they would be reading *Hamlet*, he tried to introduce the plot by connecting the themes of divorce and mur-der to the play. Steven provided written summaries prior to watch-ing videotapes of *Hamlet*. Discussion of the play connected the plot with the students' own experiences, and instead of a final exam, Steven asked the students to write about a characteristic of Hamlet's that exists in people today, supporting their arguments with specif-ics from the play. The class used a week of class time to brainstorm and share ideas and to organize and revise their drafts.

What are the differences between the approaches of these two teachers? Which students will remember *Hamlet* long after the books are passed on to another teacher? Although both teachers taught the same piece of literature, only one connected it to the lives of the stu-dents and helped them see its reading as purposeful. The other edu-cated his students according to "sound" behavioral principles of learning, practices sanctioned by the educational psychologists.

Behaviorism in American Schools

Much of what is done in current traditional teaching and learning is based on the "taxonomy of learning" developed by Benjamin Bloom (1956), a follower of B.F. Skinner (1953), the founder of behavioral psychology. Educators who looked to behavioral psychology to explain the psychology of learning found a science that employed counting and measurement as the basis of experimental tests with variables under control. For early educational psychologists, simple observation of how learning occurs and inductive knowledge were not acceptable scientific methods. What was regarded as "scientific" was research in the behavioral sense, research based on the study of animals (not human children) in controlled laboratory settings (not in home settings or real classrooms).

According to Bloom's taxonomy, "stimulus-response" learning, or rote memorization, is the easiest type of learning, and applying and evaluating knowledge is the most difficult. In order for the rote memorization and recall to occur, which behaviorists call learning, motivation and reinforcement are necessary. Behaviorist theory holds that children learn to read by first making sense of the smallest components of language (letters) and then progressing to larger components (sounds, words, sentences). According to such a model of learning, children read by learning to decode the language; their understanding follows only after the code is broken and the component parts are mastered. In general, behavioral psychology supports the premise that learning takes place from part to whole. Such behaviorist orientation controls classrooms in high schools and universities in which students are expected to memorize information and regurgitate ideas and facts transmitted to them through lectures and textbooks. In the behavioral paradigm, an educated person is said to be one who has learned the necessary "facts," one who is culturally literate, one who knows what his or her culture has tacitly agreed are the important facts to possess.

For the past several decades, most American schools have followed traditional approaches to the teaching of language arts based on behaviorist principles. Students in English classes always seem to begin with lessons that focus on grammar, mechanics, spelling, and vocabulary lists, followed by numerous skills exercises, each having one correct answer. The text used in secondary and college English classrooms is often a grammar handbook, a classic such as *Warriners* or Strunk and White's *Elements of Style*, supplemented with workbooks and dittos for the practice of skills. When students write, they write essays on assigned topics, in prescribed formats such as "comparison and contrast," with a prescribed length assigned in numbers of words, and they write for a known audience—their teacher. If they read literature, it is what has come to be called the classics or what some deem the "Great Books," literature chosen for its historical, cultural, and traditional importance, literature commonly set out as "the canon." How and what to read and write are taught by English teachers in English classes, and the rest of the knowledge needed for life in the twenty-first century is handled by others, teachers of history, math, and science, who see themselves as responsible for the teaching of their own specific content area, and certainly not responsible for the teaching of language skills.

Kim found, as many a new teacher has before her, that not every student learns just because the curriculum says he or she should. Experiences such as the ones that Kim had as a student teacher have led many teachers to question the traditional ways they teach and expect their students to learn.

In 1963, Thomas Kuhn, a physicist, wrote *The Structure of Scientific Revolutions*, revealing how paradigms or belief systems shift due to unexplainable anomalies, inconsistencies between beliefs held and evidence uncovered in a particular field or academic discipline. Teachers teach in a particular way because of how they believe learning takes place, and the textbooks they employ reflect that model of learning. New teachers and preservice teachers learn the tradition from education courses, cooperating teachers who sponsor them during student teaching, and mentoring teachers who take them under their wing, guiding them through a prescribed curricula taught with prescribed textbooks. The system is self-perpetuating. In fact, we found in a study we conducted that students who leave the university without a strong personal philosophy of education quickly adopt the teaching methods and tacit philosophy of the experienced teachers with whom they work (Strickland, 1991). So great an influence does this assimilation process have that new teachers are all but told, "Never mind what you learned in college; this is the real world." Thus, the system remains stable until research presents overwhelming evidence to contradict accepted practice or presents enough shocks to the system to cause what was the traditional way of seeing things to become unreliable, unsatisfactory, and generally perceived as being out-of-date. It is then that a paradigm shift occurs.

Transmission Versus Transactional Models of Teaching and Learning

As educators were confronted by anomalies that could not be explained by behavioral psychology, they turned to other disciplines such as anthropology, sociology, linguistics, and developmental psychology. Cognitive psychologists made discoveries about how the human mind learns; developmental psychologists studied the importance of early childhood learning, development that takes place between birth and the beginning of formal schooling. Research by psycholinguists found important connections between thought and language, previously the domain of philosophers. Composition researchers looked at how actual writers compose and traced the relationship between the written and the spoken word. Frank Smith (1988b) suggests that educators who subscribed to the current traditional paradigm of teaching reading and writing faced problems they had trouble explaining due to a misguided reliance on behavioral psychology rather than on anthropology. Sociologists and sociolinguists probed the social aspects of learning and the influence of community on learning; similarly anthropologists examined society by entering communities and cultures for an insider's view.

As a result, over the past fifteen years, the paradigm has begun to shift in education—away from what Constance Weaver (1990) labels a "transmission" model of teaching, behaviorist-based instruction in which teachers are basically nothing more than "scripted technicians" who pass on a curriculum established by people outside the classroom. The paradigm has moved toward a "transactional" model of learning, a whole language philosophy of instruction in which learners actively engage with their teachers, their classmates, and their environment in order to create their curriculum (Holdaway, 1979; Hall, 1987; Cambourne, 1989; Smith, 1988c). The differences between transactional and transmission models of education can be illustrated by contrasting a traditional and a whole language classroom (see Figure 1–1).

A transmission model of learning fails to take several aspects of human learning into account—primarily those in the affective domain. Behaviorists fail to consider how students feel about the subjects they are learning and dismiss any notion that what students learn will change them as persons. Education, as much as other fields of inquiry, found itself questioning existing beliefs that had become unstable in the light of new findings.

Whole Language: A Philosophy of Language Learning and Teaching

Recent research and theories in psycholinguistics, together with supporting theories in sociolinguistics, have provided a research base that supports a shift in education away from the traditional model of learning, fueling the grassroots movement in education generally known as "whole language."

Unfortunately, no simple definition exists for the term *whole language*. As indicated earlier, the term does not refer to a methodology;

Figure 1–1

Contrasting Models of Education

Transmission Philosophy Traditional Classroom	Basis of philosophy	Transactional Philosophy Whole Language Classroom
1. Based on the behaviorist model—stimulus/response learning of behavioral psychology.	Basis of philosophy	1. Based on the cognitive/social model—based on research in developmental psychology, linguistics, sociology, anthropology
2. Teachers are dispensers of knowledge. Teachers lecture and give the impression that there is one correct answer or interpretation—the teacher's	Teacher-role	2. Teachers are facilitators. Teachers demonstrate what it means to be a reader and a writer by reading and writing in and out of the classroom and by sharing literacy experiences with students.
3. Students strive for "right" answers and see success and learning as high SAT scores.	Students' View of Learning	3. Students are risk-takers. They see learning as an exciting opportunity for open-ended response and critical thinking.
4. Literacy is a product of a prescribed curriculum. Emphasis is on skills such as vocabulary, spelling, and grammar that must be mastered before students can effectively read and/or write. Cultural literacy is the goal.	Literacy	4. Literacy is taught in a meaningful context. There is an emphasis on meaning and "making sense" in oral and written communication. Students' schemas help to connect to new experiences.
5. Reading and writing take place in the English classroom only. Reading is textual analysis, and writing is product centered. Teacher chooses reading selections and writing topics.	Reading and Writing	5. Students read and write every day. Students have opportunity to choose what they read and write about and choose from a variety of literature written by adult and student authors.
6. Part to whole language learning; spelling and vocabulary lists and tests; grammar exercises.	Skills	6. Whole to part language learning; skills are taught in the context of language.
7. Students work independently; often classes are grouped homogeneously.	Grouping	7. Students work cooperatively in groups that are formed for many reasons, including shared interests.

Figure 1–1 (cont.)
Contrasting Models of Education

Transmission Philosophy Traditional Classroom		Transactional Philosophy Whole Language Classroom
8. Desks in rows; texts are basis of curriculum. Teacher lecturing in front of room, bulletin boards empty or decorated with school schedule and fire drill rules. Students take notes, respond when called on.	Physical Environment	8. Environment is designed to promote literacy development. Variety of language materials are readily available for student use and student work in progress is displayed. Classroom becomes a clustering of literature and writing groups where peer groups work and teachers conference.
9. Teachers evaluate primarily by grading products or by giving tests. These tools focus on what students do not know. A successful teachers hopes for a bell curve.	Evaluation	9. Teachers are "kid watchers," evaluating and assessing student progress based on observation, focusing on what students can do.

whole language is a philosophy. Rather than a program to be followed, whole language is a set of beliefs, a major tenet of which holds that language is best learned in authentic, meaningful situations, ones in which language is not separated into parts, ones in which language remains whole. Whole language integrates reading, writing, listening, and speaking and defines the role of the teacher as one of facilitator and the role of the student as an active participant in a community of learners. To understand the place of whole language in today's educational system, it may be helpful to understand its origins.

The Roots of Whole Language

Whole language, as a transactional model of learning, has deep roots both inside and outside of education. While the term *whole language* may be relatively new, the philosophy upon which it is based is not. As early as the seventeenth century, educator John Amos Comenius believed that learning should be pleasurable and rooted in students' real lives. Whole language grows out of progressive education, a theoretical position that developed from Jean-Jacques Rousseau's romantic naturalism, John Dewey's (1916) pragmatism, and Russian psychologist Lev Vygotsky's (1978) convictions concerning the social aspects of learning. Progressive education opposes social conformity, classroom authoritarianism, and a set academic curriculum as restraints upon the natural curiosity of learners. Whole language embraces the progressive ideal of teaching students rather than teaching subject matter and respecting each student as an individual learner, each blessed with unique needs and abilities. Thus, whole language classrooms are student-centered with curriculum that is organic, growing with and out of teachable moments as they exist in the classroom. As a philosophy grounded in research studying how people become literate, whole language has revolutionized how reading and writing are taught and has changed educators' beliefs about the nature of reading and writing and learning as well.

As with any philosophy, the practices that are described as being "whole language" are actually concrete applications of theoretical arguments arising from research in such diverse fields as psycholinguistics, sociology, anthropology, child development, composition, literacy theory, and semiotics. From this combined research, whole language has come to embrace certain beliefs about language learning, such as:

1. Students learn by constructing meaning from the world around them, a view quite different from a behaviorist view of learning by imitation. In a behaviorist classroom, students are believed to learn by listening to lectures, copying notes, memorizing information, and reproducing the information on a test. In the real world, not the world of laboratories, people create meaning, learning what is worthwhile, useful, and easiest to learn, as Frank Smith (1988b) tells us in *Joining the Literacy Club*. Jeff Golub (1993), the 1991 winner of the State Farm "Good Neighbor" award for innovative teaching, believes that students can construct meaning in his English classes; he says, for example, "Literature, in an interactive classroom, becomes a vehicle for the constructing and negotiating of meanings and for making sense of English in ways which make sense to students." Jeff continues, "It is not presented as something to be taught or covered. When one must 'cover' items—and usually there are far too many items in the curriculum anyway to be covered adequately—one tends to focus on teaching content instead of teaching students" (pp. 2–3).

2. Language learning is not sequential; reading and writing skills develop simultaneously along with oral language skills. In a

behaviorist classroom, reading is taught through direct instruction as a progression of skills, objectively tested in order to be certain students are ready for the next skill. Regrettably, the teaching of writing has often followed this same behaviorist premise of learning from part to whole. The subskills of spelling, grammar, and sentence structure are taught through drill and practice before students are allowed to attempt real writing. Jeff Golub, as a teacher of junior and senior high school for 20 years, comments, "For years now, teachers have kept separate their lessons on grammar and usage from their writing activities, often working on editing skills *before* they allow their students to engage in extended writing activities. This practice is analogous to the idea of pumping the brakes while the car is still in the garage!" (p. 2).

The result is that students learn the wrong lesson:

> That matters of grammar and usage—the editing skills—are the most important part of writing. When a student brings me a rough draft to read, [Jeff says,] I routinely ask, "How well do you like what you've written here?" I want to get a sense of what the student was trying to convey in the writing and see how successful the student thinks the effort has been. Many times students will reply, "I don't think it's very good. My spelling's really messed up." Students have come to equate their spelling ability with their writing ability in general. Where did they get this notion? And why do students complain about a grade they received on an essay by saying, "Why did you grade it so low? I only made three mistakes in my sentences." They look for the circled words and the underlined sentence fragments when trying to figure out what's "wrong" with their papers. [The behavioral approach] taught them to do this by emphasizing the mastery of editing skills before teaching them to write fluently and honestly and creatively. (p. 3)

Judging by the intensity with which behavioral learning is taught in schools, it's hard to believe that Noam Chomsky in 1957 demonstrated, in *Syntactic Structures*, that language learning is too complex to be regarded as "habit learning" and that such behaviorist approaches trivialize language and learning.

3. Curriculum in a whole language classroom is not a prescribed course of study; instead, learning occurs when students are engaged and teachers are demonstrating. Jeff Golub remarks,

The pressure to "cover the curriculum" is perhaps the most direct and immediate pressure that teachers feel. Too often, the curriculum becomes divorced from the teachers who teach it, so that needed changes cannot be made by those who are most affected by it. In some areas of the country, for instance, the curriculum is set up county-wide; how does one go about making changes in *that*? Moreover, the very idea of "covering" items in a curriculum is an approach that is sometimes difficult to work with. (p. 2)

A whole language teacher "does not 'cover' *anything*. Instead, he or she works to 'UN-cover' the curriculum, to provide experiences that allow students to develop certain insights and an improved level of language competence" or content knowledge (p. 2). Unlike a behaviorist view of learning, one in which teachers assume that their students will perform within the limits of the teacher's own expectations, whole language teachers provide their students with an opportunity to demonstrate what decisions they, as language users, are interested in and capable of making.

4. Although error is inherent in the learning process, learning is best developed in an environment that encourages risk-taking. Learning occurs when students are given opportunities to transact with print; encouraged to think, to create, and to make mistakes as they move toward true discovery; and supported in their conception of themselves as readers and writers. All of this occurs in an atmosphere of respect and mutual engagement. Students are more apt to use reading and writing strategies if they are immersed in an environment in which they see people—both students and teachers—reading and writing. The development of reading and writing depends on strategies that characterize the literary expectations of proficient language users—text intent, negotiability, risk-taking, and the fine-tuning of language with language itself.

5. Reading and writing are context-specific and are reflections of each situation in which learning is taking place. Just as young children approach written language expecting it to make sense, students using reading and writing in secondary and post-secondary classrooms for real purposes and for real audiences continue this same natural functional approach to language learning. Whole language

emphasizes the importance of engaging students in authentic communication, speaking and writing experiences that have the students communicating to real audiences for real purposes. Directing students to write without an audience in mind is like asking them to talk into a "dead" phone with no one at the other end to listen and respond. No one talks into a "dead" phone. It's an artificial, unproductive exercise, leaving the speaker or writer unmotivated and uninterested. Authentic communication, on the other hand, invites engagement as students speak and write to persuade and inform and to describe and create. They are aware of their audience and adjust their language performance in response to the feedback they are sure to receive. This is a welcome change from traditional methods of writing instruction. (Golub, 1993, p. 2)

6. Whole language includes all aspects of language learning— students learn to read while they are writing and they learn about writing by reading. "Students' classroom talk is used as a vehicle for learning," Jeff adds. "Revising in small groups, for instance, allows students to try out their ideas on each other, to find out what works and what doesn't in their writing, to come to care about their classmates' communication efforts" (p. 2). Students may also learn about reading and writing while listening, but not when forced to listen exclusively to class lectures by their teacher. It's no wonder that students rarely pay attention during a lecture; that activity, after all, is designed to exercise the teacher's language abilities, not the students'.

The Teaching of Reading

A defining feature of the transactional model is the belief that learning—and the teaching that stimulates it—proceeds from whole to part rather than from part to whole. Students learn to read by reading, and reading is seen as a "creative and constructive activity having four distinctive and fundamental characteristics—it is purposeful, selective, anticipatory, and based on comprehension" (Smith, 1988c, p.3).

There is no one way to teach reading in secondary classrooms. Because of past experiences with texts in English classes as well as in content courses, students' reading abilities and interests are varied by the time they reach secondary school. Teachers, however, are responsible for teaching reading by providing students with opportunities to read, thereby providing opportunities for students to develop as readers. Although the teaching of literature has long been accepted as the teaching of reading, it often is not, as we will explain in detail in a later chapter. Literature is more often a vehicle for teaching literary conventions rather than a way to teach reading. In fact, many secondary teachers do not see themselves as reading teachers—at this stage of a student's education, they think reading is the responsibility of "remedial" teachers. In truth, all teachers who use the printed word are teachers of reading if, as Smith explains, they understand what reading is—"a creative and constructive" activity.

Barbara King-Shaver (1991), an English supervisor at South Brunswick High School in Monmouth Junction, New Jersey, sees herself as a teacher of reading as she provides opportunities for her students to construct meaning as they read classroom novels. Barbara, who uses a technique called "jigsawing" in her Honors III English class, has also seen the technique used successfully by a colleague to teach Mary Shelley's *Frankenstein* to a "low ability" English class. These students, because of their past difficulties with English, are often uninterested and discouraged when faced with the challenge of reading, and this novel is a particularly difficult one for these students to read. Barbara explains:

> Traditionally only the more advanced students were given this novel to read; however, this teacher felt that his basic English class should experience the novel, even though it would be difficult for them to read. In order to make the book more accessible to his basic English class, he divided the class into small groups, making each group responsible for two chapters in the novel.
>
> As each group read their assigned chapters, they kept a record of difficult vocabulary, reviewing the words in small group discussions, trying to understand the words' meanings by contextual clues, using classroom dictionaries when all else failed.
>
> Each group presented the plot of its chapters to the whole class, tying the story together, thus completing the jigsaw puzzle. Each group did a close reading and character analysis of their assigned chapters by reading carefully with an eye for potential scenes to script and film. After selecting these scenes, each group wrote scripts, including stage directions and dialogue, and enacted the scenes before a video camera. These scenes were later shown to the whole class.
>
> In this particular assignment, while participating in jigsawing group work, the students were using a variety of language skills. They were using the four language acts—reading, speaking, listening and writing—in a real situation and integrating

them in a natural way. In addition, on their own, they were making decisions, important language decisions, constructing meaning out of the novel as they read, discussed, scripted, and performed their scenes. (p. 5)

In traditional classrooms, when students are asked to respond to worksheets and take tests that assess "mastery" of minute skills such as prepositional phrases and direct objects, they are deprived of opportunities for active involvement in the reading process. In a transactional classroom, students are psychologically engaged in the process of actively reading and writing authentic texts that have meaning for them. Students simultaneously learn language and literacy in environments that permit them to read, write, listen, and speak for a variety of authentic purposes.

An important aspect of the transactional model of literacy is the reading of a variety of literature, both independently and in class, instead of reading only the Literature (with a capital L) prescribed by traditional reading lists. Literature (with a capital L) refers to a set of texts designated by the culture as having value above and beyond other texts in the culture—an authoritative, orthodox canon of texts. Each culture has its tacit understanding of what is included and excluded from the canon; for example, Charles Dickens would be included and Stephen King excluded, for reasons that are hard to explicate. Reading Literature is variously described as essential for the development of the mind as well as the acculturation of the young. And yet, instruction in reading Literature is a limited activity, one having much to do with cultural literacy (or Trivial Pursuit) and little to do with language development. Literature-based reading instruction, on the other hand, involves reading a variety of literature—classics, contemporary favorites, librarians' selections, articles in popular magazines, grocery-store paperbacks—reading that has a significant effect on language development. The more readers know of stories, the better they are able to predict what will happen next. This development of "story schema" helps readers adjust their expectations about characters and events in new stories and broaden their understanding of how the world works (Hickman & Cullinan, 1989). At every level, as students progress in their reading, experience with literature helps them build the story schema needed to be able to recognize the conventions and patterns of language.

Unlike traditional reading instruction, literature-based reading instruction does not look for "single readings" of a story. Charlotte Huck (1977), an advocate of literature-based reading, says that it is important to help students discover the ways authors create meaning rather than to superimpose a teacher's concept of literary analysis. Jean Piaget (1971) reminds us that to learn is to invent. Robert Probst (1988) would go further by suggesting that readers create meaning as they are reading and that neither literary analysis nor one-answer comprehension questions are appropriate responses to reading. Students as active learners don't need to be forced to memorize facts *about* literature; in a literature-based approach to teaching reading, students are afforded opportunities to work *with* literature. They discuss, discover, consider, represent, and reread in order to make their own meanings.

Carol Jago (1992), a teacher at Santa Monica High School in California, has changed her entire approach toward testing in her literature class because she is interested in how her students are creating meaning and connecting what they read to their schema. She tells us, "Instead of using an objective test . . . to assess a class of tenth graders on their reading of *The Odyssey*, I asked my students to write about a major character in the epic who was most like them and to explain the similarity using examples from their own and the character's lives" (p. 5). The exam answers confirmed Carol's belief that her students were indeed active learners. By way of example, she shared with us what one of her students, Karen Montoya, wrote in class that day. Not a word has been changed:

> Zeus-born, son of Laertes, Odysseus of many devices resembles me the most out of all the characters in *The Odyssey*. I can relate to him because in the whole epic his purpose is to see his family and someday reach sunny Ithaca. Like Odysseus, I am often sad because I know what it is like for one's family to be so far away, mine being in Mexico. I don't have to go through the dangerous adventures Odysseus experiences, but I do have to wait a long time before seeing them again.
>
> When in the land of Phaecians, a singer comes to town and relates the story of the battle at Troy, Odysseus' own story. Odysseus shed a tear, trying to hide it from the hospitable Phaecians. A couple of weeks ago I saw a television show about Puebla, Mexico, what I call my land. It showed the town's churches and schools and the town square. These things are part of my story and my life. It made me sad to be so far away, and I cried. Odysseus and I grieve when each hears his own story.
>
> Last year I spent Christmas in Mexico. To do so, I had to raise enough money for my plane ticket. I sometimes had to pass up going to the movies, and I walked straight through a store without buying that alluring black knitted sweater. I saw a wonderful new bike that called to me. I had enough money to buy it, but that was the money to go see my family. I passed up all these temptations in order to reach my goal. In Odysseus' journey back home, he confronts much

greater temptations. He wants to hear the Siren's song. He enjoys being in Circe's halls eating and drinking, drinking and eating. He also had a chance to taste the Lotus flower to forget all his troubles. He passes up all these temptations to reach his home.

If I ever met Odysseus, we would have much to talk about. When he was in Alcinoos' halls he had luxuries and was treated well. I also have luxuries and am treated well here, but like Odysseus, this doesn't matter to me. My family is a much greater "luxury" to have. Calypso holds down Odysseus in Ogygia for 8 years. Here I am held down by school, by my parents and many more things. If I were able to talk to Odysseus, the first thing I'd say would be, "Odysseus of many wiles, I know how you feel." (p. 5)

Reading Karen's exam adequately proved to her teacher that (1) Karen had read the book and (2) Karen had understood what she read. As well as achieving these primary assessment goals, the prompt provided her with an opportunity for further learning by inviting her to see the heroic dimension of her own life. "I do not believe this happens," Carol said, "when students match names with quotes or identify true or false statements" (p. 5).

Louise Rosenblatt (1978) explains her theory of response to literature as an active response—a transaction between the reader and the text. The words on the page are cues from the author, but the reader makes meaning through personal knowledge, associations, feelings, and experiences as she transacts with the text.

The Teaching of Writing

The teaching of writing in American schools has also been dominated by behaviorist theories for decades. The features of the current traditional paradigm for the teaching of writing have been characterized by Richard Young (1978) as: "the emphasis on the composed product rather than on the composing process; the analysis of discourse into description, narration, exposition, and argument; the strong concern with usage . . . and with style; the preoccupation with the informal essay and research paper; and so on" (p.31). In a landmark article, "The Winds of Change: Thomas Kuhn and the Revolution in the Teaching of Writing," Maxine Hairston (1982) added to Young's description that proponents of the current traditional paradigm believe that competent writers know what they are going to say before they write, that the most important task before writing is to organize content, and that the composing process is linear. Finally, and this is what has strongly dominated the traditional paradigm, adherents believe that to teach editing is to teach writing.

Hairston pointed out that challenges to the traditional paradigm became evident following the analysis by Noam Chomsky (1957) of the complex rules by which language is generated. At the historically famous Anglo-American Seminar on the Teaching of English held at Dartmouth College in 1966, educators, adopting a Chomskian perspective on language, "deemphasized the formal teaching of grammar and usage in the classroom and emphasized having [students] engage directly in the writing process in a non-prescriptive atmosphere" (Hairston, 1982, p.19).

Over the decades since Dartmouth, the adoption of a transactional philosophy has been evident in the teaching of language in the primary grades through postsecondary education. While the traditional paradigm is still very much a part of American education, the majority of recent research findings support a shift to a new paradigm. The research of scholars such as Mina Shaughnessy (1977), Janet Emig (1971), James Britton (1975), and Linda Flower and John Hayes (1980) continued to press for change in the dominant paradigm. Subsequently, educators such as Stephen Tchudi (1985), Steven Zemelman and Harvey Daniels (1988), and Nancie Atwell (1987) took what composition researchers had learned about how people develop as writers and about the process of writing and showed teachers how such research applies to the teaching of writing to students.

How Can Whole Language Be Implemented?

Whole language teachers use a variety of creative and innovative methods for facilitating learning. A cookbook approach to teaching whole language is not possible, because whole language is not a program or a method. Expensive elaborate materials are not needed when implementing whole language approaches. Students read texts that are familiar and meaningful, drawing upon familiar concepts and experiences to which they can relate. It is not necessary to purchase elaborate "units" designed by publishing companies, material that often controls the curriculum by failing to consider student need and input. The whole language teacher does not worry about a preordained sequence or hierarchy of skills; the curriculum becomes organized as teacher and students share planning. A whole language classroom becomes an environment where students' own needs and experiences provide the motivation for reading, writing, listening, and speaking activities. Areas of study evolve and develop as students identify areas of interest and as questions are raised through reading and investigation. Such areas of study are student centered and depend on the teacher to facilitate learning based on student need and interest.

Risk-taking is encouraged in a whole language classroom and students learn from experience. Unfortunately, many traditional teachers encourage "one right answer" types of questions and suppose that students absorb knowledge through lecture and the reading of textbooks. For example, Kate Kessler, an English teacher in a high school in Pennsylvania tells of a discussion with a group of students that she previously had in her English class, a group interested in learning and willing to work. One student said, "Ms. K., in our math class, eighteen of the nineteen people in the class are failing." Kate asked why, expressing wonderment at their inability to succeed. The student replied that in the beginning of the course everyone asked questions. "You know how we are," she said. "After a couple of weeks, our math teacher screamed, 'That's enough. The next person to ask a stupid question gets a detention slip.' So now, we don't know what's going on, but no one asks questions. We don't know if our questions will be considered 'stupid' or not, and none of us wants to risk a two-hour after-school detention."

Obviously, the math teacher saw the constant questions not only as a challenge to her teaching ability but as a classroom management problem as well. "Covering" the material was being prevented because of the constant interruptions, and the teacher perceived a loss of control in the class. The percentage of failure in the class should stand as an indictment of the teaching, yet from an external point of view, the teacher was moving through the curriculum at the scheduled rate, covering the required items, and the students were quietly taking notes at their desks.

Kate, as well as other whole language teachers, understands the importance of risk-taking in a whole language classroom. How would a whole language philosophy have helped this class? The teacher might have the students write down their questions while the teacher was explaining and demonstrating, so that new material could be presented. The teacher would still have to be willing to entertain the questions that remained unresolved and the new questions that arose. The traditional approach says that presentation of uninterrupted material is the purpose of education. It is not. Students must understand what is presented, processing the information and relating it to what is already known. At the point where one student is confused, the learning has stopped for that student and others in the class who may share the student's confusion. Whole language teachers recognize that questioning is an integral part of understanding and subsequent learning, and they work to establish an atmosphere in which students are comfortable taking risks.

What Does a Whole Language Classroom Look Like?

If you walked into a whole language classroom, what would you see? Because whole language classrooms involve a transaction between students and teacher, all people in the class are learners, and all classes are unique. No two whole language classrooms are alike because they do not follow prescribed models. There are, however, similarities in the structure, purposes, strategies, and atmosphere that are consistent with a whole language philosophy. Given the rich variety of whole language classrooms, many share common elements:

1. A whole language classroom designs an environment to promote literacy development; that is, a variety of language materials are readily available for students to use, and the classroom becomes a clustering of literature groups, writing groups, and discussion groups where peers work together or individuals work while teachers conference with them.

2. Students read and write every day, choosing what they read and write about and choosing from a variety of literature written by adult and student authors.

3. There is an emphasis on meaning and "making sense" in oral and written communication; literacy is taught in a meaningful context.

4. Skills are taught in the context of language rather than as isolated exercises.

5. Students work cooperatively in groups that are formed for many different reasons, including shared interests, and teachers act as facilitators rather than dispensers of knowledge, demonstrating what it means to be a reader and a writer by reading and writing in and out of the classroom, sharing their literacy experiences with their students.

6. Teachers are "kid watchers" (Goodman, Y., 1978), evaluating and assessing student progress based on observation, focusing on what students can do.

7. Students are risk-takers; they see learning as an exciting opportunity for open- ended response and critical thinking.

Let's look at two whole language classrooms—an English class and a Science class that, although very different, are both modeled on a whole language philosophy.

Whole Language in a High School English Class

When she taught English at Terra Nova High School in Pacifica, California, Eileen Oliver (1992) decided to offer a course for seniors called "Contemporary Literature." What was different about this course was that there were no prerequisites and that it was open to all students.

"And that's exactly what I got," explained Eileen.

There were college-bound students whose literacy experiences had been in the "classical tradition" mixed with other students who chose the class because, after struggling through the "lower" track courses, they still needed an English course to graduate. Still others enrolled, not particularly motivated to exert themselves, who figured that "just reading" did not sound too bad. In all, forty students enrolled because of the demand for the course and due to the fact that there were no other electives available at this hour. (p. 1)

Eileen says that her colleagues thought she was "nuts," yet she was willing to try it.

I knew from the beginning that neither the traditional approach to teaching literature nor unified units of study would work for this "mixed bag" of students. And I absolutely refused to consider tracking students within the class, partly because I felt that tracking is unrealistic—except in extreme cases—as I have yet to see a truly homogeneous group, and partly because experience told me that heterogeneous groups provide for much more interesting discussion. Furthermore, having spent several years teaching courses in all of the required tracks in our department, I knew that adolescent interests have less to do with intelligence than with age. To put it succinctly, teenagers are interested in adolescent issues no matter what predictions objective tests might make about their abilities to do so.

I began the class by spending the first few days talking about reading and contemporary writers and eliminating "the correct answer" approach that most of them believed was the proper way to read. It was difficult to get them to believe me, but some were willing to take the risks and others seemed surprised to find that I was genuinely interested in what they had to say, even if their opinions were different from mine.

I explained to the class that we would form "reading groups," but not in the way they were used to being in groups. We would form the groups much the way people form "book clubs" to discuss the literature they read and share opinions and ideas they have gotten from the books.

Next I presented the class with a number of books from which I expected each student to make a choice. During my "book talk," I spoke about each work, telling a little about the author, reading a few selected parts, and sharing my thoughts on why each book might be interesting to read. The books I selected were ones that I, or my colleagues, had had prior success with and ones that students had seemed to enjoy. They were also selections which I felt they had most likely not read on their own, providing me with the opportunity to open up their world a little. I made sure that the materials were accessible, no small task in a school where books are shared by a number of teachers. Finally, I chose a variety of novels which could be read by students who came with a variety of reading experiences. In general, the categories included science fiction, African–American experience, Native American experience, teenagers under stress, drama, and romance.

I reserved a large choir room for this class, so we would have enough room to spread out. We discussed reading schedules and each group chose a specific section of the room to read and work in. Every day students read for a few minutes while I went around to see how each group was doing. Sometimes I gave the groups questions pertaining to their novel in order to help get discussion going. They knew from experience that these questions were not display questions, ones which had a right answer, but were questions they could react to honestly, without fear of my evaluating their responses. At other times I suggested that they create their own topics for discussion, choosing a recorder to give me a summary of their discussion after they had met.

My students wrote book reviews, critiques, and "adaptations" of the novels. They made up questions to use to begin discussion with future groups. This strategy was particularly good for students who had had difficulty with the reading. Not only did they feel that they were contributing in a positive way to someone else's future reading experience, but it also helped with their own understanding of the story. Further, their questions revealed to me how well they were comprehending what they were reading.

At times groups discussed for half the class period and read for the other half. I required each student to keep track of their individual work. At various stages students wrote responses, both formal and informal. My role during this time was one of roving facilitator.

Very often some students finished their book long before the others in their group, and when this happened, they started another novel which was somehow related to the central book of the group. Then they shared information and impressions of the new book and offered recommendations to others during class meetings. After awhile, everyone was reading his/her own book and periodically brought to the class discussions some new aspect of the issues they had discussed previously.

Predictably, students found each other's recommendations of books more valid than mine, and the interchange among them was exciting to watch. Some students who had previously been in "lower ability" classes were recommending books to "college-bound types." Periodically we shifted groups, and I brought in new topics and books. What pleased me most was that the students at all levels became empowered to discuss the literature they read in a constructive way. They no longer looked for the "right" answers. Instead, they read their books and came to class ready to discuss their views and to listen to the views of others. Sometimes they argued, disagreeing in much the same way as adult readers do when they talk about books.

Most importantly, they were reading and these books became a very important part of their lives. My major goal for the class was to give the students the opportunity to develop a love for literature which they could take with them when they graduated. I wanted them to want to pick up a book at a book stand someday, even though they were not required to read it. I wanted to help them become readers. (pp. 1-4)

A Whole Language Science Class

The tenets of the whole language philosophy are applicable in science, math, social studies, and other learning situations in high school and college. Whole language is not content specific—that is, language is learned not only in English classes but in all other content areas where language is used in learning.

Barbara King-Shaver, introduced earlier, presented a whole language workshop for her high school faculty three years ago. After the workshop, a colleague from the science department, Brian Biemuller, approached Barbara about using different forms of writing to help students learn biology. As Brian and Barbara talked, they realized that not only writing but also reading, speaking, and listening were powerful tools for learning science. Based on common beliefs about language and learning, Brian and Barbara decided to explore different ways that language could be used in Brian's biology classes, and in the summer of 1991 they received a mini-grant from their district to implement language activities into the learning of biology.

Brian and Barbara's investigation led them to ask themselves what a secondary, discipline-centered science classroom would look like if many of the principles of a whole language philosophy were applied. During the summer, they developed a series of biology lessons that supported the integration of language modes, student-centered activities, and collaborative learning. Although the lessons were developed to help learn biology, Brian and Barbara believe that learning biology while engaged in language activities will also improve students' range of language skills. As students use language to learn content material, they learn to use language more effectively.

The students in Brian's biology classes represent a range of academic abilities, learning styles, and grades (9–12). One successful activity that allowed for student interests and student differences developed from a unit on cells. This activity, assigned near the end of the unit, helped students review a major concept about cells as well as think affectively about the scientific knowledge they acquired during the study of this topic. The following is Brian's explanation of the assignment to the students:

> All life is cellular, i.e. composed of cells; therefore, a commonality exists among oak trees, bacteria, yeast, dogs, people—all life. In fact, in the cellular sense all life is biologically related to all other life. (Imagine—you are biologically related to the crab grass growing in your lawn!)
>
> But the wonder of science continues. All chromosomes, as you know, are composed of the same nucleotides (letters) A–T and C–G. Just as in English, with its 26 letters, all words are related, in the DNA of chromosomes, with its 4 letters, all DNA is related. Yes, its true; we have the same chemical letters as crab grass. Only the sequencing of lettering is changed.
>
> Now, the scientific study of the cells is done. We've discussed organelles and osmosis. We've seen cells, stained cells, and studied mitosis and cell size. Our lesson, however, is incomplete. We're lacking the "awe," the wonder of the cells and their relationships. There are many students who are not as fortunate as you, who do not understand this relationship, this unity of life.

Brian asked his students to "communicate the wonder of the relationship of all cells, of all life," and he even allowed them to work on the activity with a partner of their own choosing. (We remember when this would have been considered cheating.) Many of the students wrote poems to convey their sense of wonder, and they shared readings of their poems with the class. The students were further encouraged to consider a larger audience by submitting their work to the school literary magazine.

Reading this assignment, you might ask, "Is this an English class or a science class?" Brian uses writing as a means of communication. He encourages students to work cooperatively to share their knowledge and ideas and to grow together. He also brings together the English classroom and the science classroom by demonstrating to students that they can learn biology and language at the same time and that often one depends on the other.

Did Brian's students learn about cells in biology, and how did they learn about written language in the process? The following examples of their poetry will argue that these students understand "the wonder of the cells" and, indeed, use language to communicate that wonder.

Cell Poem

Every cell must divide, it's the logical thing to do!
Every time a cell divides it goes from one to two.
It may seem pointless and not very fun,
But to stay alive, it must be done.

It happens in you, it happens in me,
It even happens in every tree!
Cells make your dog, cells make your cat,
Cells make you skinny, cells make you fat.

From people on land, to fish in the sea,
Cells reproduce asexually.
From the largest elephant to the smallest bee,
Cells work hard for you and me!

      —John Fuller and Christopher Vaccaro

Cell Poem

cell membrane
cellular, thin
diffuses, controls, contains
keeps the cell together
cell membrane

      —Steve Kelty II

Cells

Cells:
microscopic, complex,
Moving, diffusing, multiplying,
The center of life,
Corpuscles

—Samantha Zyontz

Mya Breitbart and Preeti Advani used the form of an "I AM" poem, explaining that they wrote the poem "as if we were the chromosome," and the poem expressed "some of the feelings that we think it would have if it were human."

Cell Poem

I am a chromosome who gives you all your physical traits.
I wonder if you're happy with your appearance.
I hear the nucleus giving orders.
I see your children's hair color.
I want to live forever.
I am a chromosome who gives you all your physical traits.

I pretend that I am as smart as the nucleus.
I feel important because I contain DNA.
I affect the lives of all living organisms.
I worry about the mitosis process.
I cry when people are unhappy with what I've given them.
I am a chromosome who gives you all your physical traits.

I understand my importance in your lifestyle.
I say whether you are a girl or a boy.
I dream that people would recognize my actions and set aside
 a day to honor me.
I try to be systematic in everything I do.
I hope that you understand me better now.
I am a chromosome who gives you all your physical traits.

—Mya Breitbart and Preeti Advani

What Whole Language Is Not

The term *whole language* has been misused a great deal in the last few years, and many people are confused by some of the myths that they have heard or read concerning whole language teaching and learning. Sometimes it's easier to understand a concept after clearing up misunderstandings and misconceptions. Although these misconceptions will be addressed in detail in subsequent chapters, it may help to mention some of the most common myths about whole language.

Myth #1

Whole language is a method for elementary grades. *Not true.* First of all, whole language is not a method; it is, as previously stated, a philosophy. Whole language teachers use a variety of teaching strategies consistent with a transactional philosophy to meet the needs of the learners in their classes. Because whole language is a philosophy based on how people learn, it is not just for elementary grades. It is true that whole language has been implemented more extensively in elementary grades, yet the tenets of whole language apply to all learners of all ages, at all stages.

Myth #2

Whole language teachers don't really teach; they let students run the class, doing whatever they please. *Not true.* Whole language teachers do a great deal of teaching, but the misconceptions occur because whole language teachers do not view lecturing and transmitting isolated bits of information to students as teaching. Rather than teaching skills and information in isolation, whole language teachers teach within the context of reading and writing and learning across the curriculum. They believe that students readily learn skills when they are engaged in authentic reading and writing activities.

Myth #3

Whole language classrooms lack structure. *Not true.* In a whole language classroom many things happen at once—people moving around, groups of students talking and working together, the teacher conferencing with one student or a group of students. What might seem unstructured to someone used to the straight rows of quiet students in a traditional classroom is actually the structure of a class that is student centered. As students work together, they are responsible for their learning, and their teacher is providing them with opportunities to interact as they think about what they are doing. Whole language teachers meet the needs of their students by providing a structure that includes the social aspects of learning; they do not adopt a structure for their classroom that is imposed by others outside the classroom who could not possibly be aware of the needs and interests of this particular group of learners.

Myth #4

Whole language teachers accept all work, regardless of quality, and refrain from evaluating students. *Not true.* Assessment and evaluation are important parts of a whole language classroom, yet they are not defined as stanines and percentile scores. Whole language teachers are observers who are constantly assessing students' strengths and needs in order to provide experiences that will build on those strengths, rather than concentrating on students' weaknesses. Evaluation is an important part of whole language teaching. The teacher evaluates as a result of ongoing assessment, and, in turn, students are taught to self-evaluate in order to set their own goals for further learning.

Myth #5

Being a whole language teacher is easier now that there are so many whole language packages on the market. *Not true.* Because whole language is a philosophy, not a program, it can't be packaged by a publishing company and imposed on a teacher or class. Buying a class set of novels or an integrated unit to use in social studies, science, and English classes does not, in and of itself, constitute a whole language situation. The materials alone are not what make a class whole language—the philosophy of the teacher and his or her understanding of student learning and his or her role as teacher are what make a class whole language. Whole language teachers use materials that suit the needs of the class, and the curriculum is, to a great extent, the product of interaction between the teacher and the students.

Myth #6

Whole language is a fad. There is no reason to change the way I teach when something else will take its place in a few years. *Not true.* Whole language certainly is not a fad. Whole language is based on years of research in cognitive psychology, psycholinguistics, sociolinguistics, language acquisition, and education. Teaching, like other professions, must change as research suggests ways to improve the way we teach, so that we might better reach all learners. When discussing whole language with parents and teachers, we often compare the practice of teaching to the practice of medicine. For example, consider eye surgery as practiced some twenty years ago. The patient was hospitalized, given a general anesthetic, and his doctor, widely recognized in the field, performed a lengthy operation. The patient remained hospitalized for several days to watch for infection, a common side effect of this type of surgery, and returned home to a darkened room to convalesce for several weeks. Although the operation was a risky one, with a 60 percent success rate, the patient recovered fully, due to the expertise and knowledge of that doctor.

Twenty years later, if his daughter needs that same operation, she might go to that same doctor, thinking what worked in the past is good enough. However, if her father's doctor has not remained current in the field, she would be better to choose a doctor who has learned through research and training how to perform laser surgery. She could to have the operation in the office, be given any necessary medications, and return to her home and job in a matter of hours. Both father and daughter will consider themselves fortunate to recover fully from the eye surgery, but the procedure need not be as painful and traumatic for the daughter as it was for the father twenty years earlier.

The same is true in the teaching profession. Twenty years ago teachers did a fine job educating millions, based upon what was known at the time about how people learn. Teachers worked hard, and though some students dropped out, many made it through school successfully. Yet there is no compelling reason to say that what worked in the past is good enough for our children. We have discovered a great deal about the learning process, thanks to extensive research in many and varied fields of inquiry. It is the responsibility of all teachers to stay current in their field and to base their teaching on what we know today.

For Further Exploration

1. Think about your experiences as a learner in high school. How did you feel about language learning—writing and literature? Would you consider your experiences to be traditional or whole language? Why?

2. Based on your experiences as a learner, how will you teach? What are your goals as a teacher of adolescents or young adults? What will your classroom be like?

3. Visit several secondary and college classes. What philosophy of teaching and learning are evident? What criteria did you use to label these classrooms? Did English classes differ from classes in other content areas?

4. Interview several secondary teachers. Ask them their views of whole language. How do they define whole language and how do they view its importance in their classrooms? In American education? If possible, observe these teachers teaching. Are their

views of teaching and learning consistent with what they articulated in your interviews with them?

5. Interview several secondary students. How do they view their role in the classroom? How do they see the role reading and writing plays in their learning? What have their experiences been in learning to read and write?

Related Readings for Further Thought and Exploration

Goodman, K. (1986). *What's whole in whole language.* Portsmouth, NH: Heinemann.
Characterizes the features of whole language and serves as an excellent resource to use in answering the question, "What is whole language?" Originally published as an introductory guide to whole language for teachers and parents.

Hairston, M. (1982). The winds of change: Thomas Kuhn and the revolution in the teaching of writing. *College Composition and Communication, 33,* 76-88.
Describes the paradigm shift in the teaching of writing and its importance in understanding the shift in thinking from a behaviorist approach to a transactional approach in teaching and learning—a landmark article.

Smith, F. (1988). *Joining the literacy club: Further essays into education.* Portsmouth, NH: Heinemann.
Argues the social nature of language learning. Frank Smith illustrates how learning is a matter of "joining a club" whose members include teachers in the classroom, peers, those in the world outside the classroom, and authors of what is read.

Vacca, R., & Rasinski, T. (1992). *Case studies in whole language.* Fort Worth, TX: Harcourt Brace Jovanovich.
Explains whole language philosophy through detailed description and narratives of various teaching strategies. A helpful book for teachers and preservice teachers who want to "see" a whole language classroom. Although this book uses elementary classrooms as examples, those in secondary classrooms will gain an understanding of the climate of a whole language classroom and the role of the teacher and learner.

Weaver, C. (1990). *Understanding whole language: From principles to practice.* Portsmouth, NH: Heinemann.
Clarifies the term whole language, *which is more and more often misused and misunderstood, by explaining its philosophical base.*

Other sections of the book include discussions of the development of literacy, implementing whole language in the classroom, and student assessment from a whole language perspective. An excellent book for teachers, teacher educators, and administrators.

Chapter Two

The Reading/Writing Workshop

Students adopt other writers' ways because they write and read in a classroom where they have plenty of time to do both, where they can choose what they'll write and read, and where they give, receive, and hear plenty of response to written texts. Every genre, topic, theme, and technique becomes fair game, both to read and write, because I finally dismantled two sets of barriers, those separating reading and writing and those separating literature and kids.

—Nancie Atwell

Questions for Thought/Journal Entries

1. How are reading and writing related? Are good readers more likely to be good writers? Why or why not?

2. How were you taught to read and write in secondary school? How does a teacher actually teach reading and writing?

3. How do you feel about yourself as a reader? As a writer? If a student is not a reader and writer by the time he or she is in high school or college, isn't it too late to make a difference?

4. In high school or college, how did teachers support your development as a writer?

5. Whose responsibility is teaching reading and writing? Has anyone other than an English teacher helped you grow as a writer? Who else might help students grow as readers and writers?

Introduction

Literacy can no longer be divided into separate compartments. The reading/writing workshop, an integral part of whole language classrooms, provides students and teachers with the opportunity to use literacy in real and varied situations. A workshop approach to teaching literacy provides students with opportunities to be responsible for their learning and provides teachers with opportunities to facilitate student learning by participating as a fellow reader and writer.

What Is a Reading/Writing Workshop?

A relationship between reading and writing is outlined by James Squire (1983) based on the premise that reading and writing place similar demands on a person's thinking skills. Before beginning both activities—comprehending and composing—readers and writers prepare for the act by establishing a purpose and recalling prior knowledge of the topic. During the act of comprehending, readers do much more than decode symbols on a page; readers are actively involved, both intellectually and emotionally, in constructing meaning. Writers, like readers, also construct meaning intellectually and emotionally, constantly reading and rereading what they have written during the act of composing. Robert Tierney and Margie Leys (1986) note, "Writers use reading in a more integrated fashion [than readers use writing] for . . . they are constantly involved in reading their own writing, reading other materials, and using understandings they have acquired from past readings" (p. 23). Reading during the composing process directly affects the quality of the written product (Birnbaum, 1982; Perl, 1979).

Reading/writing workshops are regularly scheduled, substantial chunks of class time, where students work at various stages of reading and writing activities. In the past, teachers have spoken of reading and writing workshops as if they were two distinct entities. Reading and writing are connected activities and are no longer taught as two distinct subjects. While it's true that at times the majority of the students are engaged in writing, it's also true that in that process they are growing as readers. Conversely, if students are reading during workshop time, they are being provided with the tools that writers need—ideas, ways of expressing themselves, and a sense of story. For these reasons, reading/writing workshops might better be called literacy workshops.

The term *workshop* immediately brings to mind images of a craft union or guild, a place where people work, create, and produce, a place filled with the noise of activity as artisans use the tools of their trade to create a product or work of art. Today, students in a vocational track still take "shop," a class where they learn to use their hands to produce an artifact. Sometimes the workshop is in woodworking; other times, it's metal-shop or rebuilding internal combustion engines. Those in the shop work through a process of construction until they have a finished product of which they can justly feel proud and which will be enjoyed as they share it with others. In the workshop, an expert artisan labors, an essential figure, producing and modeling so that those training in this art can learn through example, mentoring and guiding so that those with less experience gain training, experience, and expertise.

The same is true of the literacy workshop where students work at becoming artists of reading and writing, creating understandings while interacting with text, and creating written works in order to share their ideas with a reader. Teachers, the expert artisans in literacy workshops, labor alongside their students, modeling reading and writing as they share their expertise with their students, who in turn learn from their teacher's example and from each other through engagement.

According to Jane Hansen (1987), five components provide a framework for setting up and maintaining reading/writing workshops—community, time, choice, response, and structure.

Community

The building of community is essential to the success of a reading/ writing workshop. Teachers and students in a whole language classroom work together and share ideas through their discussion and their writing. We live in a very competitive society, one in which grading, homogeneous grouping, and standardized testing foster competitiveness in education. Students in a traditional classroom learn that another's success diminishes their own (someone always wrecks the curve). A traditional classroom is designed for isolated learners—doing their own work, keeping their eyes on their own papers, and talking to no one except the teacher when called upon. The straight rows of desks, all facing front, support this design, and students play "school," offering teacher-pleasing responses to their teacher's known-answer questions. In traditional classrooms, discipline is required to prevent cheating and disruptive behavior; the concepts of individual achievement and competition are sometimes unspoken but widely understood.

How then does a whole language teacher change this perception, building community in a literacy workshop? Building a community of learners requires that the teacher subscribe to the belief that literacy is socially constructed, a social activity that results from the need to communicate one's wants, needs, desires, hopes, and dreams—to communicate about life. The teacher needs to demonstrate an atmosphere of support and respect if students are to come to respect one another and become genuinely pleased by their classmates' accomplishments. When students are not asked to give one correct answer to teacher-generated questions, their ideas will not be regarded as property to be owned and protected, and cheating will not be a problem.

Reading and writing are not learned through the isolated practice of skills but through the use of reading and writing in purposeful activities. Zemelman and Daniels (1988) contend that "what students learn about writing depends more than anything else on the context in which they write" (p.50). This context includes how writing is used, the attitudes the teacher and students have toward literacy, the perceptions of the students about their purpose for writing and reading, and how the teacher and students in the classroom react to each other's ideas and beliefs.

An important component in building community in the literacy workshop is the teacher, who must be able to assume a variety of roles and adjust behavior to meet the needs of the group as well as the needs of individuals. A teacher must model all the roles that each will assume at some time in the community of a literacy workshop—listener, reader, writer, speaker, editor, responder, observer, and supporter. Students learn how to assume these roles by watching their teachers model and facilitate.

Sandra Gail Teichmann (1993) of Florida State University tells of the importance of a teacher becoming a part of a community of learners. Sandra's students entered her first-year composition class expecting a teacher who was an authority, one who had all the answers. Some were disappointed that Sandra, teaching this class for the first time, was honest enough to tell them they would all be learning together.

She shares the experience in the journal she kept in class along with her students:

> We started off: Essay #1—conduct an interview; write a profile. The number of students in the class was even, so I was left without a partner for interviewing (not good; at my desk alone, I was different, conspicuous, separate, not what I had intended). I decided to write about someone I knew—my dad—write about

his preparing to die. I got involved in the memories, but just to let my students know that I still existed as they went about their interviewing, I wrote a note on their third class handout that it was my daddy's birthday. I got no response from them, and when I told my dad on the phone, he laughed and said I probably had them wondering about my sanity, but I went right on working on my invention exercises and journal entries and lists, building my essay as they were building theirs.

Then I assigned a journal entry to do a clustering and a vignette from the word, "toothpicks." This broke the ice, humanized me as [my graduate professor] Wendy [Bishop] would say. The students and I started sharing our writing. They showed me and each other what they had surprised themselves with, and they wanted to see what I had written about toothpicks. We were on our way. We wrote, and then we responded to each other's essays, and we made revisions and more revisions. For me, the responses and revision suggestions from this first-year class were as interesting and helpful as any response I received from the advanced [writing] workshop I was taking [in graduate school], and I told the first-year class that their reactions were sharp and thoughtful. The students knew I was sharing my essays with the advanced workshop and wanted to help me make my writing the best that it could be, just as I wanted to help each of them write an excellent essay.

After writing a third draft of [an essay] I spent about ten minutes talking about the process I was going through writing this exploratory profile. I told my students that I thought there was evidence of a thinking process toward discovery in the essay, and they said, "yes, we understand; the idea is neat." I was modeling; I told them that this essay was an example of how they too could work through the process of writing.

Sandra's students learned from and with their teacher. If she had let her nervousness about her first year of college teaching paralyze her, the class would have quickly lapsed back into their old way of seeing writing teachers as dispensers of knowledge. Instead, Sandra showed the courage it takes to share her own imperfect works with those whom the traditional hierarchy labels as beneath her. Teaching in a workshop setting demands humility.

Sandra continues in her journal:

Because self-confidence is so important for exploratory writing, my intent was to propose no heroes in first-year writing: no published author held in awe over a student author, no student author held in awe over another student author, no teacher author held in awe over any student author. I did not and neither did the invited guests bring essays just for the students to read. All who brought drafts of essays did so for help in getting to the next draft, not for displaying accomplished work.

My reason for wanting to be a teacher/writer was to act as role model, but more importantly to gain entry into what could have been a closed circle of students. Through my second essay, I think I was accepted further as I wrote about me-as-I-see-myself through the subject of manners. I took a big risk; I exposed quite a lot of myself through the essay, not only to the students, but to myself.

To participate in a literacy workshop requires many things. It requires trust that knowledge can be discovered, not just passed down. It requires commitment since each member of the class is depending upon the other. It demands openness and requires risk-taking because writing means sharing our vulnerability. And most importantly, it means teachers and students alike must possess these qualities.

Sandra comments in her journal:

Recently [my graduate workshop teacher] suggested to me that perhaps it is enthusiasm, commitment and interest that make for a good teacher. I don't disagree with the value of these qualities, but think a teacher's experience can be that of ongoing innocence if he or she incorporates curiosity, risk and respect into each semester of teaching and writing.

[My teacher] may not have thought of herself as vulnerable as she shared her writing with the class, but as a student in that class, I felt she was as vulnerable as any of the students, and I treated her accordingly. I was curious about her and her ideas, and I hoped that she was as interested in me. By writing with the class and sharing drafts of essays, she had as much opportunity to risk exposure of self through her ideas as I did as a student in her class. She also had an opportunity to respect each student's individuality and ideas as each student had opportunity to respect her.

Perhaps if I had not been writing with my class, I would have felt separate from the students, above them, in control of them. I might then have acted more like the teacher [they originally] desired. . . .

As part of the larger community of language learners, we're glad she didn't.

Time

For many teachers who have been conditioned to think in traditional terms of material that must be "covered," time in a workshop setting is a difficult concept. Teachers are required to teach what has been established by districts as the curriculum and this takes time. Middle school and high school classes are usually organized into forty-to-fifty-minute periods, and teachers must plan what the class will be doing during each period, devising a course of study that will "cover" all the material in a ten-, fifteen-, or forty-week time frame. For example, if weeks three and four are devoted to mythology, then every class period and reading must be carefully scheduled because at the end of the two weeks the class must move on to English Literature.

In fact, the lesson-plan book itself is an interesting artifact in the traditional teacher's commitment to structured time. Rebecca Laubach (1990), a high school teacher in Mars, Pennsylvania, confesses that she became absolutely obsessed with her lesson plans as she prepared for maternity leave. She worked overtime creating a foolproof set of lessons for her substitute teacher to follow, thinking she was doing the sub a favor, taking the worry out of taking up the fight, as it were. Upon returning to her class, Rebecca discovered her lesson plans had made the substitute teacher so nervous about staying on schedule that she had alienated any feelings of collaboration and destroyed what rapport Rebecca had built up in the class as a community of learners. Everyone had become worried about being "on time."

Similarly, college teachers must create a syllabus before classes even begin, with every class period planned, every test date and every assignment decided upon before the class even meets. Operating within such a framework, the needs, interests, or experiences of the students have little bearing on what happens in the classroom. However, such is not the case in the whole language classroom where learning refuses to conform to this type of time constraint.

Whole language teachers are still responsible for covering the material, but they do so in ways that revolve around the students in the class. Just as no two students are the same and no two classes are the same, literacy workshops provide a structure in which every student can learn as an individual, while still adhering to the curriculum as set up outside the classroom.

So much reading and writing take place in a workshop classroom that curricular requirements are not only being met but often surpassed, with students reading and writing far more than their peers in traditional classes who are trying to learn to read and write while being lectured at and required to complete skills worksheets and grammar exercises. The students in whole language classes are also learning these skills, but they're doing so in the context of their own writing and reading. Thus, they're learning what they need and want to know, and they're using these skills in order to communicate ideas to other readers and writers. In addition to skills, they're learning about decision-making, goal setting, and personal responsibility. They're also learning about community, and they're learning about pride in their accomplishments as readers and writers. In reading/writing workshops, curricular requirements are satisfied in different ways and at different times.

In a workshop situation, scheduling is still important, but for different reasons. As mentioned earlier, students become better readers by reading and better writers by writing, not by listening to someone tell them how to read and write. Consequently, students are rarely lectured to. Instead, the majority of the class period is spent reading, writing, planning, discussing, thinking, and sharing, depending on the needs of the class as a whole and on the needs of the students as individual learners. Students are engaged in literacy activities regularly, every day, and they count on this scheduled time to accomplish their goals. This doesn't mean, however, that everyone must do the same thing at the same time. Each student in a literacy workshop has a personal goal; for example, to finish a draft by Tuesday, to read and respond to two novels by the end of the second week, to publish a final draft by the end of the unit.

Sharon Wieland (1991), a high school teacher in Sacramento, California, takes the time to teach her students how to set personal goals for themselves in her class. Sharon explains that for the first quarter of the year,

> I set the initial goals for the students, goals that will introduce them to the whole process of writing and get them started thinking as writers. I want them to find topics they care about, take risks by trying new techniques, topics, skills, and kinds of writing, write drafts, self-edit, make decisions about what worked and what did not work in their pieces, listen to and question other writer's pieces, and give thoughtful, helpful responses. In other words, I want them to begin making most of the decisions that real authors have to make and to make them within the context of a collaborative language workshop.
>
> Some of my students begin accepting much of the responsibility for their own writing by the end of the first quarter. When I ask them to set their own goals for the next quarter, however, some of them balk and want to keep receiving guidance. I remember a student who approached the subject diplomatically

during the first evaluation conference: "Could you just explain to me how you run the class?" And, another blurted out as I was preparing to write down each student's writing plan for the day, "Why isn't this like a regular English class, anyway?" These students had valid questions, deserving good answers. Because their teachers had always provided them with pre-established plans and time schedules, it was natural that they would expect it from me and would be confused when new rules changed the way they had always "played school". (p. 9)

In the workshop classroom, Sharon's students develop a new appreciation for time. Sharon tells us that when her students realize that good writing takes time—a significant amount of time—they begin giving themselves time as a goal for writing, the time that good writing demands for completion. Many of her students comment that they never realized before just how much time should be devoted to writing. Occasionally, setting a goal of more time means letting a piece of writing sit for awhile before returning to it. Previously, her students felt that writing was usually completed in one sitting. Now they had begun to see that papers from previous quarters could be returned to as viable pieces of writing. They echo their classmate's goal of wanting "to add more to my Russia story" with their own: "Continue with what I started this quarter and improve my skills"; "Go back to my poems"; "Finish my unfinished stories."

In a whole language classroom, students must be given time in order to accomplish goals. Writing takes time. Reading takes time. Readers and writers need time to share, listen, respond, ask for and receive feedback. Teachers need time to write with students, share their writing with students, respond to student writers, encouraging them and providing feedback. Literacy learning can't be rushed; whole language teachers avoid being trapped into thinking that reading and writing can be imposed on students or that reading and writing can be taught to all students in the same way in a certain number of weeks. Literacy learning is an individual and personal process that is supported by a community of learners who need time to learn.

Choice

In traditional English classrooms, teachers assign novels, plays, short stories, and poems according to prescribed reading lists determined either by the teacher or by an outside committee. The teachers in these classrooms also assign topics to be written about, determine a required length and form, and set a due-date.

In literacy workshops, students are expected to make choices, often based on who they are, what they want and need to learn, and their purposes for reading and writing. The teachers in these whole language classrooms don't have to abandon their goals or the district's curriculum any more than Kim and Steven did in Chapter 1 when Kim taught *The Canterbury Tales* or Steven taught *Hamlet*. One difference in these classrooms is that these two teachers provided students with opportunities to make choices. In both these examples, the teachers followed the prescribed curriculum, but the strategies they used for teaching reading and writing weren't traditional. Kim's students chose a tale to read, chose groups to work in, chose a mode to write in, and chose a strategy to use to retell their tale. They also chose the topic for their final exam paper, although all were about a journey, a theme they had had time to think about. Steven provided his students with similar choices. They all chose an act for which to be responsible and all chose a mode of writing as they presented their act to their peers. They also chose the mode of writing for their final exam, although all wrote on a theme of the play, comparing it with their own life experiences.

The students in Eileen Oliver's classroom, also described in Chapter 1, made many decisions about choice of topic or genre they wanted to read about, choice of novel they wanted to read, choice of questions they wanted to discuss, and choice of how to go about responding to each other's interpretations of the text. None of these were imposed by Eileen, and by giving them choices, she acted as a facilitator, providing opportunities, guidance, and support as they worked through their learning.

Traditionally, students are taught that they must finish every book they begin reading and hand in or publish every piece of writing they draft. But experienced readers and writers behave differently, and when appropriate, students should be encouraged to abandon a book and start another if the one they're reading does not meet their needs. The same holds true for writing. Every piece of writing that is started need not be developed into a piece to be shared with others or evaluated. In a workshop situation, the students do so much reading and writing that such choices are not only possible, they are preferable. Making these decisions helps students begin to assess and self-evaluate. They begin to think about *why* they may not like a book they are reading: the characters are dull; the author's organization is difficult to follow; the plot is too predictable; and so forth—reasons experienced readers give for putting down half-finished books. When making such evaluations, students are reading critically and learning about literary techniques, characterization, and story structure. The same holds true in writing. Sometimes writers begin a piece and soon find they have little of interest to say about it or not enough background to make it comprehensive. In making a decision to move on to begin another piece, a student is actually self-assessing, a necessary step in growing as a writer. Students need to be given the opportunity to make choices, guided by a teacher who models decision making while giving students the confidence to take risks. Students must learn to rely on themselves and make judgments based on experience. They must be given the choice to read and write about what is important to them, what touches their lives, and what they need to learn about. As adults, we read books about what interests us, what is part of our lives, and what we want to learn more about. Those of us who are writers know that our best writing concerns what we know about and care about.

In giving students opportunities to make choices, teachers must know their students well enough to help them and support them in their choices. High school teachers have to read adolescent literature, talk about teenage problems and concerns with their students, and know about and respect the culture of the students they teach. College teachers must go beyond the "Great Books" and read contemporary literature if they ever hope to be able to recommend literature that might touch the lives of their students. Teachers can do that only if they know who their students really are.

Response

I (Kathleen) was an observer in a classroom recently and spoke with a sixteen-year-old girl about her whole language class. The girl told me about what she and her classmates were reading, about the story she had written last week, and about how much she was enjoying her English class this year. When I asked about her teacher, the girl responded, "Oh, Miss Zimmerman? The great thing about her is that she listens."

Listening is a key element to effective feedback in a literacy workshop, where readers and writers turn to other members of the community for response. Students and teachers listen in a variety of roles: as part of a discussion or response group, as an audience for a student's writing, as a listener to ideas generated by students when brainstorming Before responding, teachers must learn to listen actively, a concept borrowed from nondirective therapy, grounded in the belief that people are able to solve their own dilemmas if a caring person helps them reflect by listening to their verbalizations. For example, a student might say, "I want to write about my grandfather, but I don't know what to say." A traditional response might be, "Describe what he looks like, how you see him in your imagination," or "Tell me about a time you two spent together." As helpful as that might seem to some, the response is imposing an idea that is not the student's own. A nondirective response might be, "Your grandfather was special?" The student will respond, affirming your statement, "Oh, he was the funniest man I know" or "He was the guy who taught me how to hit a baseball" or "He took me on a father-son campout when my dad had to work overtime." He might even contradict the statement with responses like, "Not really. It was seeing him in the funeral home that made me so uneasy whenever anyone dies" or "He frightened me, like when he pushed me into the pool and told me to learn to swim, laughing while I was choking on the water and trying to reach the edge of the pool." A nondirective written response would be to tell the student to brainstorm five words that come to mind and then create a web with *grandfather* in the center. The whole language teacher sees response as eliciting rather than imposing. This approach carries through to written responses as well.

In traditional classrooms, teachers frequently brag, in a complaining tone of voice, about the inordinate amount of time they spend responding to student writing. By response, these teachers usually mean critical response and evaluation. The teacher responds to a piece of writing by making the student aware of organizational problems, mechanical mistakes, and the overall weaknesses of the piece of writing, "red-penning" it to death. Occasionally content is commented upon, but more often it is not. Some teachers even use a double marking system, even though separating form from content is not possible. What usually happens to these papers that traditional teachers spend so much time "responding" to? Students immediately look for the grade at the top of the paper, scan the red marks in the margin (expecting a correlation between the amount of red and the grade), and ultimately, the papers end up in the back of a notebook or in the wastebasket. The student who received a high grade, with a large red A on the top of the paper but little else written in the margin, knows all one needs to know (to paraphrase Keats): the teacher liked the paper. The student never knows what exactly made it a good paper because the ultimate point of the exercise was whether or not the teacher liked it. Another student—one who had difficulty with the piece and will continue to have difficulties until someone offers meaningful feedback—also tosses the paper in the wastebasket because the response in red only told what was already known: the teacher didn't like it; it was a terrible piece of writing; and, the student cannot write. Neither student benefitted from the teacher's comments because red-penned criticism and grades aren't a constructive form of response.

Response in a reading/writing workshop is very different. First, in a whole language class both students and teachers are responders. Second, response is not criticism, but the vocalization of understandings, the offering of suggestions, and the giving of encouragement. Third, response is more than comments written only at the end of a process; it is guidance, support, and encouragement throughout the process.

Diana Dreyer (1992), an associate professor at Slippery Rock University of Pennsylvania, finds her first-year college composition sections with a higher-than-average enrollment of nonnative speakers, largely because of the success her reading/writing workshop approach has had with international students. Diana's workshop provides students with opportunities for teacher-student response as well as small-group peer response. One of Diana's students, Yuki, like many international students, found writing in a second language difficult. Though an avid writer in her native Japanese, Yuki worried all semester about what she perceived as her serious second-language flaws, primarily grammar and word choice: "I need to know more vocabulary and expression," she wrote (p. 263).

Early in the semester, during their first teacher-student conference, Yuki told Diana that the small reading/writing groups made her feel more comfortable. Yuki became an active member of her reading/writing group, not only receiving support and guidance from her classmates but offering it as well. Yuki's enthusiasm caused Diana to comment that Yuki was "indeed not shy about responding to others" about writing nor "in her one-to-one conversations with me" (p. 263). The understanding, support, and guidance offered by her teacher and classmates paid off, causing visible changes in Yuki's writing. By midterm, she wrote, ". . . writing is getting easier for me. If I didn't have to concern [myself] about grammatical mistakes, I could continue writing forever now. IN ENGLISH" (pp. 263–264). She also acknowledged the debt she owed her classmates and teacher for the help she received. She adds that the reading/writing workshop helped her learn "how to focus on specific topics . . . as well as [on her] writing skills" (p. 264).

By the end of the course, Yuki had lost her preoccupation with grammatical correctness, arguing "as long as we have a class named English writing, we should learn about writing. I mean grammar is a second[ary] concern for writing" (p. 264). She further recognized the social aspect of writing and gloried in the suggestions and encouragement that are so much a part of a reading/writing workshop: "I'm enjoying writing and reading [my writing] to my classmates," adding that she sometimes "even [has] argument[s] about [her] writing with them" (p. 265). She may not have always followed her peer's advice for revision, but she continued to seek their response throughout the writing process. Furthermore, Yuki hopes that other students in Japan will be fortunate enough to "realize how writing is enjoyable through contact with classmates and teachers . . ." (p. 265).

Structure

What might seem like loose structure in a workshop situation, or in some cases no structure, is actually at times a highly organized plan for teaching and learning. Again, the misinterpretation results from a difference in how structure is conceived by a traditional classroom and a workshop classroom. In a traditional classroom, structure means all or some of the following—desks neatly set in rows, with silent passive students facing forward, attentive to the teacher in the front who lectures, responding to teacher questions when called upon, which frequently happens when they don't raise their hand and it's obvious that they don't know the answer. (Our daughter once asked why teachers seem to do this; "Is it to embarrass students?" she wondered.) To those familiar with the traditional classroom, a quiet room signals a teacher in "control," with students focused on the teacher, listening and absorbing information, the prerequisite for learning.

In a whole language class, when students are learning in a workshop situation, structure means something entirely different. Instead of control, silence, and authoritarianism, structure in a literacy workshop means organization, planning, and responsibility. Donald McAndrew, who taught high school English in Buffalo, New York, before moving to Indiana University of Pennsylvania, tells a story similar to the experiences of many teachers who have taught in traditional settings. Don's classes were workshops where on any given day students could be seen writing, conferencing, and working in response groups. One day the school principal walked in for Don's scheduled yearly observation. Don knew he was coming, and business in the class was going on as usual—students were everywhere in groups, there was a low buzz of conversation as they discussed their writing with each other, and Don was in the back corner of the room at the conferencing table, talking with a student about a draft. When the principal walked in, he looked around the room for Don. When he finally saw him, he waved his hand and said, "Oh, Don. Sorry. I'll come back later when you are teaching."

To that principal, a workshop setting was not one where you could observe real teaching, classes where teachers give information and students absorb the information that is given. Because that principal did not understand the structure or purpose of the class, he couldn't see Don teaching and his students learning. He didn't have a workshop schema, an understanding of how that class was structured. Had he understood, he might have evaluated Don's teaching on his organization, planning, and responsibility.

While there is no one way to structure a workshop—different teachers organize workshops differently, depending on variables such as time, space, materials, and student needs—organization is the key to a successful workshop. And because the structure is different from traditional classrooms, students need to be aware of the structure of the workshop and the role they play as learners who are part of a community. Awareness does not happen overnight. Too many students, like the school principal, have no understanding of workshops, having never been in a whole language class, and they seek the comfort of the familiar traditional structure. When a whole language teacher explains that in a workshop environment all members of the class must be responsible for sharing, responding, supporting, and producing, it often takes time for students to feel comfortable.

Sharon Wieland (1991) says she remembers the discomfort that occurred when she first started asking her students to accept responsibility. They were alarmed, confused, and belligerent. "Why don't you just give us something to write about?" "What do you want, anyway?" "I can't think of anything to write about." One student even went to his teacher from the year before with his complaint: "I don't understand how she's grading. She wants *us* to say what we need to learn." As time passed and they found out that they could make a writer's decisions, Sharon's students became protective of their writers' rights, not wanting to go back to the old way. They said, "Why can't we write on our own topics?" whenever their teacher tried to assign "writing activities" (p. 9).

Given time, students will see for themselves that things happen in a workshop; they will see that they're writing and reading more, that the teacher is someone they can count on for support, and that their classmates are learners who are sharing the learning process with them. Students in a workshop become goal oriented. They know what they're doing and why they're doing it. Such structure gives the student responsibility but also security. They know what to expect and know that their needs as readers and writers will be met in such a class.

Managing a Reading/Writing Workshop

Amy Walker uses a reading/writing workshop approach to teach middle school adolescents in a small school in rural western

Pennsylvania. Amy's students, who spend the day in a contained classroom, know the routine. Their afternoons are spent with language—reading, writing, discussing, sharing. Amy builds a major portion of the curriculum around literature, believing that students who are readers use what they know as readers as they write. On any given day, Amy's students return to the classroom after lunch talking about the novel they're reading in class. On one particular day, the students entered the classroom talking about the Civil War, a topic they had been reading about in novels such as *Charlie Skeed-addle* and nonfiction accounts such as *Harriet Tubman* and *The Boys' War*. Tanya brought a book to class about Clara Barton that she found in the library, knowing that Shannon was reading about Clara Barton's life and her role in the Civil War. They are immersed in the subject—talking among themselves and to Amy about what they're reading, what they've discovered in their research, and what they plan to do in class. Involved in each other's reading and writing, they are a community of learners who support each other and respond to each other as fellow readers and writers. They are in the process of completing written projects, expository pieces of writing that will be published in a class collection. The students have each chosen a Civil War figure or incident that interested them in the novel they were reading as a class and have done research on the topic for the last couple of weeks. Working on self-selected topics, they are each confident that they'll be given time to complete their writing and reading without interruption, working at a rate that is comfortable for them, and given the opportunity to get response from both their peers and their teacher as they go through this process of learning.

Students will learn to be readers and writers if they use literacy for real purposes and in authentic situations as they do in reading/writing workshops. It is apparent from Amy's class that a reading/writing workshop requires some management skills in addition to an understanding of the reading and writing process. Kathy Kelly-Garris (1993), an English teacher at Penn-Trafford High School in Harrison City, Pennsylvania, has used a workshop approach in her classroom for several years and has developed management techniques that help with the organization of the workshop.

As Kathy observes, it isn't always easy to teach this way, especially when beginning a transition from a traditional approach to a workshop approach. Kathy explains the process and how she structures a whole language workshop in her classroom:

> When I first started using writing workshop, I thought I was going to lose my mind. The noise and confusion seemed overwhelming; however, I didn't give up. I turned to texts and colleagues who knew more. I finally understood that a teacher

needs to pick and choose items from the available information to make a system which works for that individual. The following is an explanation of what works best for me, a twelfth grade general English teacher.

Training. Before reading/writing workshop begins, the students are trained in a number of areas, such as process writing, courtesy to class members, conferencing, and record keeping. The initial training takes approximately a week of class time but is reinforced throughout the semester. Each of the preceding areas are introduced in what Nancie Atwell (1987) calls a "mini-lesson," a 5–10 minute explanation of an idea or concept that requires direct instruction followed by a period of time in which the students are asked to try out what was presented that day sometime during the remaining 32 minutes of class.

Beginning and record keeping. After training has been established, the students are ready to begin reading/writing workshop which is totally student-centered. The only time I talk in front of the class is during a mini-lesson. The first week of mini-lessons prepares the students for the workshop; the remaining lessons focus on a variety of matters such as grammar, style, tone, etc. Now the students know what is expected of them. When they enter the room, a modified version of Nancie Atwell's "Status of the Class" form is on each front desk in their row. Unlike the procedure in Atwell's system, my students, not the teacher, fill out the form in my class, telling me what they'll be working on that day [see Figure 2–1]. The range of work can be from drafting to conferencing to editing to finishing a final copy. If a student is peer conferencing that day, she must mark down who her partner will be. If a student wants a conference with me, she writes that on the form. I collect the form and keep it with me as I circulate the room. I add minor notes on the form, indicating whether or not the student was on task. I believe that giving the students the responsibility of choosing what they'll be working on for the day reinforces the student-centeredness of the classroom.

The students are free to move about the room during workshop and they may even leave the room to go to the Communications Center, our in-school writing lab. To leave the room, they have only to sign out on the Status of the Class form.

Another use of this form is to keep track of time on task. I keep the daily Status of the Class reports on file in order to see any patterns. To keep a record of academic progress, I use a steno pad to take notes about each piece of writing the student has been working on. Each class member has a page in the steno pad and it is in this pad that I make notes about an individual student's

Figure 2-1

Status of The Class   Week of 1/4

Period 1

NAME	Monday	Tuesday	Wednesday	Thursday	Friday
Jamye Hartman	*Literature Workshop*		Draft 1 Poem Death (worked entire period)	Peer Conf. JOY (said she got a lot out of her conference w/ Joy)	Final teach. Conf. (I helped edit piece for spelling)
Joy Ferenc			Draft 1 Poem "Gramma" (on task)	Draft 2 Teach. Conf. (we discussed punctuation)	Peer Conf. w/ Jamye + Lorie Final (OK)
Jason English			Brainstorming topic (we discussed possible topics)	Draft Short Story Squadron 1400	Draft 1 (worked on draft most of the period)
Lorie Alsop			Comm. Center Draft 1 S.S. To Save A Child (came back to class w/ printout)	Draft 1 Teach Conf. (Then went to Comm. Center)	Draft 1 (This short story is a's long one she's working a lot)
Jennifer Amour			Comm Center Poem Draft 1 Friends. (came back to class w/ print out)	Draft 1 + Peer Conf. Lorie. (conferenced for about 15 min)	Draft 2 + Final (we discussed piece after it was finished) (went to Comm Center both days)

Key:

Draft 1: rough draft first copy

Draft 2: revising rough draft 1

Final: finishing final draft

Peer Conf: working with other students on writing

Teach Conf: you want a conference with the teacher

Comm. Center: you want to go to Comm. Center for computers or tutoring

progress. I rate the effectiveness of the conference using a check, check plus, or check minus (✔, ✔+, ✔-). The rating is more of an assessment of my effectiveness during the conference as I try to determine how much I have helped the writer. Next, I make written notes about the writer's progress. I mark what the student does well, and I also mark what needs to be improved. In a later conference, I check to see if any progress has been made in that area. I never try to "fix" everything in the piece. I just give suggestions and ask questions.

Since it is difficult to remember each writer's work, the steno pad acts as a way for me to remember what each writer excels in or areas in need of support. The pad also gives me freedom since I am not tied to an excessive amount of record keeping; I am responsible for one record while the students are responsible for two. Besides keeping a Status of the Class report, the students also keep a writing folder, which they are responsible for updating. It must contain any prewriting, drafting, writing and editing work. On the inside flap of the manila folder, the student must write the title of the piece, date started and date completed. Consequently, the students keep the nuts-and-bolts records, and I keep the maintenance record. Giving students responsibility lessens my time filling out forms and gives me more time to spend conferencing with students.

Evaluation. At midpoint, I have an evaluation conference with every student. We talk about what has been accomplished thus far and set goals for the end of the nine weeks. At this conference, the student gives me the pieces she wants graded. I require a total of four graded pieces for the nine weeks. These are graded holistically which I later convert to a letter grade to conform to my school's grading scale. Writing more than the required amount counts toward the student's class participation grade. These pieces may be used for a graded piece for the next nine weeks if they have been revised during that grading period.

As the semester progresses, the reading/writing workshop, where students work on whatever writing they choose, is reduced to three days a week. The other two days of the week are devoted to reading literature. If, on a given day, a student does not feel like writing, that student is free to read a novel or literature book. Students realize that they will have to produce an updated writing portfolio at midpoint and at the end of the nine weeks. Having these two evaluation points makes the student responsible for time on task.

At the end of the nine weeks we have another conference, and at this time we work together to come up with a grade for the portfolio. This grade is in addition to the four grades for the individual writings.

The class is still noisy but it is no longer a mass of confusion; students are actively engaged in reading and writing and responding to writing. The students enjoy the freedom they are given to make choices about their writing, and they also enjoy the freedom of the workshop approach. The desks are arranged in pairs, but students are not limited to work with their partner; they may conference with whomever they choose. They may sit on the floor, in the hall, or at their desks.

The students accomplish much in the time they are given. The class goes quickly and often ends with the students clamoring for more time to finish a piece. Although I am still working on the management of the workshop approach to teaching, the students and I are satisfied that we are working together to produce pieces of writing of which we are all proud. (pp. 1– 5)

It's Never Too Late

While it's true that many students are now entering secondary schools from whole language backgrounds, it's also true that many students in high schools and colleges are still products of a very traditional approach to learning, especially in the area of writing. Janine Rider (1992), who teaches at Mesa State College in Colorado, asks students to recall their experiences when learning to write. Many of her students' responses were similar. Tina for example wrote,

> I used to write short stories all the time and was told that my short stories had some excellent ideas and imagination. Then I wrote my tenth grade teacher a seven-page short story and she flunked me. She said that my story was by far the best in the class, but she gave me an F because of my spelling and punctuation. Since then I haven't written a short story. (p. 2)

Unfortunately, this is not an unusual scenario. Michael wrote, "My past was tough at first. My writings seemed to always be questioned and marked in red. Either the topic wasn't strong enough, or my grammar or vocabulary seemed to be out of place" (p. 3).

"Dread, Pure, and simple," were the first words on Mark's paper (p. 3).

Secondary and postsecondary teachers do have their work cut out for them: Not only must they help students progress as readers and writers, but they must often do so in light of many such negative experiences and attitudes. Nevertheless, learning takes place throughout life, and learning to write can happen at any point in a person's education. Often teachers complain that they're unable to change years of negative attitudes and traditional beliefs about what writing is, but Esther Broughton (1992), also from Mesa State College in Colorado, tells of a personal experience, one in which her son became a whole language learner in college. As Esther points out, a whole language teacher's patience is often rewarded.

Esther's son Bryan attended an out-of-state university for his first two years of undergraduate work, and the experience was somewhat lackluster and uneventful. Bryan decided to move home, save some money, and get "this college business out of the way." Since he transferred to the college where Esther taught, she was able to watch a slow but obvious transition in Bryan's attitude and accomplishments.

Along with his mother's interest and encouragement, Bryan had the support of two instructors during his first year at the college, teachers who embraced a whole language philosophy in their teaching. One instructor taught a writing class—one in which students kept learning logs, worked on collaborative assignments, and read and responded to writing in helping circles. Grading was postponed until the end of the semester when students had individual conferences with the instructor to review their work for the semester. For the first time, Bryan worked hard on his writing, and his A in the course boosted not only his GPA but also his confidence as a writer.

The other teacher who made a huge impression on Bryan was a literature professor who probably didn't even realize he was a whole language teacher. However, he was grounded in current composition theory and was passionately committed to his field. He saw reading and writing as inseparable and didn't give long lectures to show off his expertise. Instead, students discussed literature in small groups, and their individual writing assignments called for personal reactions to what they had read, reactions that could be revised until satisfactory. This class was a perfect setting for Bryan to test his newfound writing wings.

After one semester, Bryan's life changed; in fact, he changed his major to English. Esther was justly proud when Bryan called her at her office and said, "Hey Mom, let me read you Dr. M.'s last comment on my Shakespeare paper: 'Get thee to a graduate school' " (p. 5).

For Bryan and many other secondary and postsecondary students, whole language has made a difference. It's never too late.

For Further Exploration

1. If you were a teacher implementing a reading/writing workshop, how would you begin the school year? What would you do to

help students feel comfortable and understand the purpose of literacy workshops?

2. Visit a classroom that functions as a literacy workshop. Become part of the class for a few days participating in all the activities the students participate in. How did you feel as a reader and a writer? Did you have a sense of community in this class? In what way? What was the teacher's role in this class?

3. Visit a traditional classroom where reading and writing are not taught in a workshop situation. What was the environment of the class like? What was the role of the students? Of the teacher?

4. Interview several teachers about their views of teaching reading and writing. Without making judgements, try to ask questions that permit teachers to articulate their philosophy of language learning. Compare these responses and draw some conclusions about whether the teacher follows a whole language philosophy or a traditional philosophy.

5. While observing in a reading/writing workshop, observe how the elements of time, choice, response, structure, and community are addressed.

Related Readings for Further Thought and Exploration

Atwell, N. (1987). *In the middle: Writing, reading, and learning with adolescents.* Portsmouth, NH: Boynton/Cook.
Traces Nancie Atwell's own process of discovery as she worked collaboratively with her eighth-grade students to change her classroom and her teaching style. Atwell describes how her students learn and what teachers can learn from and about their students to help themselves become more effective teachers. Based on sound theoretical principles, this award-winning book is rich with practical strategies such as descriptions of mini-lessons, classroom organization, conferencing techniques, and record-keeping suggestions.

Kirby, D., & Liner, T. (1988). *Inside out: Developmental stagies for teaching writing* (2nd ed.). Portsmouth, NH: Boynton/Cook.
Continues to offer, in the second edition, sound ideas to teachers of junior and senior high school writers. Dan Kirby and Tom Liner add authenticity to their fine work with discussions by high school teacher Ruth Vinz detailing how language-learning strategies work in the secondary classroom.

Newkirk, T. (1989). *To compose: Teaching writing in high school and college.* Portsmouth, NH: Heinemann.

Discusses the writing process and its place not only in the English classroom but across the disciplines. Chapters by notable educators and researchers such as Probst, Perl, Romano, Murray, Flower, Atwell, Fulwiler, and others make this a valuable book for those wishing to tie together the ideas of various contemporary experts.

Romano, T. (1987). *Clearing the way: Working with teenage writers.* Portsmouth, NH: Heinemann.
Discusses writing to learn, conferencing, evaluation, the reading-writing connection, and the place writing can have in students' lives by using examples from teenage writers. The strength of this book is that it was written by Tom Romano while he was a full-time secondary school teacher. After years of helping student writers, Romano can accurately and honestly discuss the problems and the celebrations of teaching writing.

Zemelman, S., & Daniels, H. (1988). *A community of writers: Teaching writing in the junior and senior high school.* Portsmouth, NH: Heinemann.
Discusses the writing process in all content areas from grades 6-12, stressing the importance of community and offering guidance for workshop organization, cooperative learning, conferencing, and responding constructively to writing. This book bridges the gap between the theoretical and the practical.

Chapter Three

More Than Great Books
Reader Response in a Whole Language Literature Class

When literature is read, rather than worked upon, it draws us into events and invites us to reflect upon our perceptions of them. It is not at that point a subject to be studied as an artifact illustrating an age or a product representing an artist; it is rather an experience to be entered into.

—Robert Probst

Questions for Thought/Journal Entries

1. Think back to any literature class you have taken. What books did you read? How did you feel about them? Who chose what you were to read? How did the course affect you as a reader?

2. What books should teenagers and young adults read? What is your role as a teacher in a class where literature is read?

3. Have you ever been in a course where you had to analyze the "meaning of the text," challenged to figure out what the author was trying to say? How did you feel about reading in that class? How did you feel about discussing the literature? Did you ever interpret a story or a poem differently from the way the teacher interpreted it? Who was correct? Did you state your interpretation? What was the reaction of the teacher and the others in the class to your interpretation?

4. How does reading in school differ from reading outside of school? Is one kind of reading more enjoyable than the other? Why?

5. What is the purpose of teaching literature?

Introduction

What constitutes good literature? Does the term *literature* refer to those works named to a list of "great books," the classics—ancient and modern—which the educated, privileged class consider as having excellence of form and expression, possessing universal truth, and upholding the standards of our civilization, or does the term refer to a body of writings that can have a place in every student's life. Are these two definitions of literature mutually exclusive?

A curriculum set by school systems is usually driven by a belief in the existence of a canon of literary masterpieces and the need for its perpetuation, an approach to reading grounded in theory derived from New Criticism. This chapter will show teachers how to move out of the trap of instructing students in a way which privileges the memorizing of plot outlines and capsule critiques and move toward a classroom where readers are encouraged to respond on an affective level to a variety of works.

What Is Reading?

When I (Kathleen) think back to my days in high school and college, I remember well-intentioned teachers impressing upon their students the importance of understanding "the meaning" of great works of literature. In those days I did a great deal of reading in and outside of school, but the experiences were very different. When I read in school, I was reading to uncover the right answer or to fulfill a requirement. I remember trying to figure out what the hidden meaning was when reading an assigned novel, story, or poem— *The Odyssey*, *The Scarlet Letter*, *The Great Gatsby*, *The Old Man and the Sea*, *The Red Pony*, *The Pearl*, and the poetry of Longfellow, Poe and Whitman; more to the point, I needed to know what would be the correct answers on Friday's quiz. I even resorted to using the infamous *Cliff's Notes* to help me interpret what I was afraid I had missed in my reading or—heaven help me—misinterpreted.

When I read at home after school, I did so for enjoyment or to learn more about a subject in which I was interested. I went through an Edgar Allan Poe phase, memorizing poems because I loved the way they sounded; I read Charlotte Brontë's *Jane Eyre* and then every Gothic romance I could get my hands on. Now, many years later, I remember little of what I read in school, but I have vivid memories of those works of literature that I chose to read on my own, those that I reacted to and thought about. They touched my life, without anyone to tell me if I was right or wrong. Why? Perhaps the paradox involves understanding what is meant by reading.

What Happens When We Read

Reading is certainly a physiological process; our eyes move across a text, with short, spasmodic jerks, pausing at intervals to process the information taken in—fixations (Smith, 1988c). Conventional wisdom would advise a reader having trouble understanding a text to slow down to increase the fixations, allowing more time to process the information received from the eye. Surprisingly, just the opposite is true. When we read, we attend to meaning, not to words. Meaningful sequences of words can be retained better than unrelated or isolated bits of information (Simon, 1974). When a reader slows down, the brain attends to isolated words or letters, a concentration that results in the loss of meaning. Poorer readers, slowing down to take in and hold only a word or series of letters in a fixation period, will be confused when they try to store isolated bits of information into memory. The truth is that when a reader is concerned with isolated bits of information, comprehension is difficult. In order for comprehension—for meaning—to be at its optimum, proficient readers must usually read at a rate somewhere between 200 and 300 words per minute (Tinker, 1965; Taylor, 1971). Slower reading actually interferes with comprehension, and therefore is inefficient.

While reading *is* a physiological process, in part, it is not just a matter of light images being received by the human retina and sent to the brain for interpretation. As we receive information, it is held in short-term memory— working memory. However, information in short-term memory is lost, forgotten, or becomes otherwise unavailable unless it is stored in long-term memory. Luckily, our long-term memory has ample storage space; retrieval is what is difficult. Information is more easily accessed from long-term memory if that information is grouped together, or "chunked" as the psycholinguists prefer to call it (Mandler, 1985). As we read, we create meaning; in fact, we bring meaning to the text, and we do so according to our own personal schemata, what Frank Smith (1988c) calls the theory of the world that we carry around in our heads. Some would call our schemata organized chunks of knowledge and feelings (Anderson, et al.,

1977) and fixed mental structures (Rumelhart, 1980). In any case, our schemata are tied to our personal system of storing information in long-term memory. We cannot help but build up mental images of how the world is organized.

For example, a friend's son, a senior in an Advanced Placement English class, was given Emily Brontë's *Wuthering Heights* to read and was expected to be able to discuss the narrative complexity of the novel. Consider what sort of schema this senior has to bring meaning to the novel. He has little experience reading Gothic romances or other Victorian novels. As an American, he has little understanding of the class differences that separate Heathcliff from the Lintons and the Earnshaws; the only class distinctions he knows in our country are based on race and wealth, so the meaning he constructed gave weight to the fact that Heathcliff is a "dark" child who must accumulate a fortune in America before returning to the Heights. This is hardly a misreading of the novel, yet it illustrates the role that schema plays in bringing meaning to literature. The meaning of *Wuthering Heights*, or any other novel for that matter, doesn't exist in the words on the page; the meaning is created by the reader. This is not to imply, however, that reading is an isolated act by a solitary reader since each reader's schema or mental image of the world is a socially created construct (Harste, Woodward, & Burke, 1984; Vygotsky, 1978.)

Although we view reading as a cognitive process, entailing both visual and nonvisual information, our model of reading is a sociopsycholinguistic one, derived from the work of researchers and linguists such as Goodman (1969, 1979), Smith (1988c), and Weaver (1988). Unlike past understandings that would have teachers believe that reading is a matter of skills and products, current reading theory takes into consideration the interactive nature of language acquisition and development. For example, schema theory in reading describes how prior knowledge of the world enables readers to construct meaning from print (Anderson, et al., 1984). When reading, comprehension occurs only when the reader interactively relates the text to existing knowledge. In other words, the text has no meaning until the reader brings meaning, through existing schema, to the text.

If one understands this definition of reading, it's easy to understand why so many students find their reading experiences in school frustrating. Because every student brings different experiences to what is being read, there can't be one single interpretation of any reading, yet traditionally, literature classes have been built around "the author's intention," a clever subterfuge for "the teacher's interpretation."

I (Kathleen) remember a favorite high school English teacher introducing me to Robert Frost's poems. I remember loving the simplicity of those lines of poetry and the images in my mind as I read "Mending Wall" and "Birches." One of my favorite's was "Stopping By Woods on a Snowy Evening." I even remember the words by heart:

> Whose woods these are I think I know
> His house is in the village though;
> He will not see me stopping here
> To watch his woods fill up with snow.
>
> My little horse must think it queer
> To stop without a farmhouse near
> Between the woods and frozen lake
> The darkest evening of the year.
>
> He gives his harness bells a shake
> To ask if there is some mistake
> The only other sound's the sweep
> Of easy wind and downy flake.
>
> The woods are lovely, dark and deep.
> But I have promises to keep,
> And miles to go before I sleep,
> And miles to go before I sleep.

I remember reading this poem days or maybe even weeks before it was assigned to the class. I pictured a peaceful journey at dusk through a lovely country landscape. The beauty and simplicity of the poem impressed me; always a lover of nature, and a romantic at heart, I felt I was on that sleigh watching the snowflakes fall on the quiet wooded scene.

Most of all, I remember how I felt when my teacher told us that the *real* theme of "Stopping By Woods on a Snowy Evening" was death. The poem, she explained, was about the end of the speaker's life, and when the poet wrote the words, "And miles to go before I sleep, / And miles to go before I sleep," he was referring to that final sleep—death. For years I carried this explanation with me; after all, my teacher said this was what the poem meant, and thus, it must be so. Years later, I read an interview conducted with the poet. When told that some people had interpreted "Stopping By Woods on a Snowy Evening" to be a poem about death, Frost said that he supposed it could be, although at the time he wrote it, he was describing a peaceful scene, one he often encountered when he did stop by his neighbor's property on snowy evenings. No hidden meanings for Frost, only the one each reader wants to bring to it.

Was my teacher wrong? No, the truth is that it could be read that way. Still, the teacher was wrong insofar as she led us to believe that her interpretation of the poem was the "real" meaning. Frost's poem could be about death, or it could be about a peaceful episode with nature, as I had originally imagined. I would guess that the interpretation my teacher shared with us was probably not even her own; it was probably the textbook interpretation, the one that she had been told was the right meaning in a teacher's manual and the one she was responsible for teaching. It wouldn't surprise me if the "'Stopping By Woods'/death interpretation" was on the year-end examination prepared by our state department of education, and my teacher had a responsibility to teach us what was "correct."

As with other aspects of language learning and teaching, there exist conflicting theories of what reading is and how it should be taught, conflicts rooted in arguments between the behaviorists and the transactionalists. These conflicting theories are often referred to as New Criticism and Reader- Response theories of reading.

New Criticism

When I described my memories of literature classes in high school and my teacher's penchant for discovering the meaning in the literary texts, such as Robert Frost's poetry, I was describing a literary theory—New Criticism—that has dominated American literary education since the 1930s. At the time, I wasn't aware that it was New Criticism or that any other approach was possible; to me, New Criticism was how educated people read literature.

New Criticism has been described as "an insistence on the text as the carrier of meaning and a corresponding insistence on limiting the reader's role to explicating this meaning, to engaging in a process of close textual analysis through which the meaning embedded in the text would be revealed" (Harker, 1987, p. 242). Teachers, therefore, who were taught to believe that explication through close reading was the purpose of teaching literature, focused their investigation on how texts were structured and how texts communicated their meaning. A text's structure depended on its form and content; its meaning was determined by how language was used. To the New Critic, the text was the only consideration; the intention of the author, including historical and biographical influences—however intriguing—and the affective response of the reader were deemed to be of no consequence to the meaning of the text. According to New Criticism, there is one correct response to every reading, and that response is embedded in the text. The role of the reader is to be able to demonstrate interpretation in terms of the text. If the reader can justify a response by giving particulars from the text, then this would verify the "correctness" of the interpretation. A teacher's responsibility was to teach procedures for correct readings so that readers might acquire the necessary skills. Carolyn Tucker (1991) who teaches at Dixon Junior High School in Kentucky, recalls a teacher who took that responsibility seriously:

> [He] always allowed one class period for us to read our story in "lit" class. If we did not finish our assignment, we read it as homework. The next day we had a ten-question quiz about the story. At the end of the week, we had a vocabulary test on words from the selection; spelling counted. Finally at the end of the chapter, we would have a major test covering all the stories and their elements: plot, character, setting, conflict, symbolism, irony. I got an A in the class; I cannot remember a single thing I read. (p. 10)

Reader Response

According to Frank Smith (1988c), reading is meaning making; any other definition fails to address the purpose of the written word. Meaning is negotiated through a variety of transactions between the words on a page and the person reading them. What the reader brings to the text—the sum of experiences, feelings, and information—is crucial in determining what meaning will be arrived upon. In other words, the reader brings his or her schema to the text. Such schemata constantly change, as new experiences and information are related to existing experiences. Because schemata are constantly changing, so meaning must too. Meaning evolves as a process rather than a product; meaning is the continuous transaction between the individual and the world, between old schemata and new (Weaver, 1988).

Louise Rosenblatt (1938) was one of the first to put forth the idea that meaning is an event, a transaction, a process. In her book, *Literature as Exploration*, Rosenblatt explains that a literary work exists as a transaction between reader and text. Later, in *The Reader, the Text, the Poem*, Rosenblatt (1978) reasons that a text is a pattern of symbols or words created by an author, but only when a reader reads the text, transacting with it by bringing him- or herself and his or her schema to the text, does it truly become a literary work; only then does it become, as Rosenblatt terms it, "a poem."

The poem, then, must be thought of as an event in time. It is not an object or an entity. It happens during a coming-together, a compenetration, of a reader and a text. The reader brings to the text his past experience and present personality. Under the magnetism of the ordered symbols of the text, he marshalls his resources and crystallizes out from the stuff of memory, thought, and feeling a new order, a new experience, which he sees as the poem. This becomes part of the ongoing stream of his life experience, to be reflected on from any angle important to him as a human being. (Rosenblatt, 1978, p. 12)

Reader-response theory—reading as an event in which meaning is constructed, elaborated by theorists such as Rosenblatt (1938; 1978), Stanley Fish (1980), Wolfgang Isher (1978), and David Bleich (1975)—takes a very different perspective from New Criticism on the role of the reader, locating meaning outside of the text. Fish (1980) says that "interpretation is not the art of construing but the art of constructing" (p.327). Isher (1978) speaks of meaning as being located somewhere between the text and the reader, actualized as a result of the transaction between the two. Bleich (1978) goes even farther when he suggests that "discussion of the work must refer to the subjective synthesis of the reader and not to the reader's interaction with the text" (p. 111). Reader-response theory posits that literature is written for readers. Such a declaration seems a simple truism, yet we need only to remember how we were taught literature. Were we taught literature as though it were written for readers, or were we taught literature as though it were written for scholars, those who study it, dissect it, and analyze it? Robert Probst (1988) points out that "literature is not the private domain of an intellectual elite. It is, instead, the reservoir of all mankind's concern. Although it may be studied in scholarly and professional ways, that is not its primary function" (p. 7). Most students in secondary school and college literature courses are not the intellectual elite. They are a cross-section of the community, from varied backgrounds, and with different life experiences. If we believe that reading is a transaction between reader and text, then we can't expect literature to be the same for different students. Instead, literature fulfills individual needs in individual lives.

As teachers, our most important responsibility is to expose our students to literature—to provide opportunities and environments where they can interact with literature. Literary history and literary scholarship are secondary concerns, and as Rosenblatt (1976) says, "All the student's knowledge about literary history, about authors and periods and literary types, will be so much useless baggage if [the student] has not been led primarily to seek in literature a vital personal experience" (p. 59).

Reader Response in the Whole Language Classroom

A Canadian high school teacher at Grand River Collegiate Institute in Kitchener, Ontario, Rick Chambers (1992) tells us that a part of the ninth-grade English course has always included a unit devoted to Greek and Roman mythology. Rick confesses that he had previously conducted this part of the course as a "read-the-stories, answer-the-questions, do-the-project" type of unit. Recently he tried a reader-response approach.

One of the first stories we did was Demeter and Persephone. The students read the story for homework. In class the next day, they worked in groups of three, and their assignment was that they had to tell each other the story from three different points of view. The first person had to tell it from Demeter's point of view (the distraught mother); the second had to tell the same story from Persephone's point of view (the helpless victim); the third had to tell it from Hades' point of view (the ogre). The students quickly decided who would be who, and then settled down to tell the stories, taking the personalities, and adding important little character details ("It wasn't my fault, Mom, honest!" and "Hey, Zeus, stay outta this, okay?"). Afterward, in the interest of academic pursuits, students wrote a short account of the story in their notebooks from a detached, third-person point of view.

We hurried through some other stories in a more traditional way—students reporting to the class on the extra-marital pursuits and birth traumas of several gods and goddesses.

Then, we came to Orpheus and Eurydice. This time, after the students had read the story for homework, the class was divided into pairs of students, one male and one female. The male student told the story from Orpheus' point of view, and the female student from Eurydice's point of view. Afterward, each student wrote a newspaper account of the incident—headline, inverted triangle organization, the journalist's 5 Ws (who, what, where, when, why) and so forth.

At the end of the unit on mythology, I administer a short quiz. In the past, the students' responses were predictable. This time, the responses were not. The weakest students in the class knew the stories of Demeter and Persephone and of Orpheus and Eurydice backwards and forwards. Their knowledge of the rest of the material was mediocre at best, but, in fact, no different than the results in previous years.

What did I learn? Students need to make the information their own. They need the time to internalize and understand it; then even students labelled as "the-less-than-gifted" can run with the rest of the crowd. I learned that reader response works. (pp. 1-2)

Reader-Response Strategies for the Classroom

Usually teachers themselves haven't had the opportunity to learn in classrooms where readers were encouraged to make meaning from texts and respond to what they read. Many agree with the philosophical stance of reader response but are unsure of how to implement it in their classrooms. Herb Thompson (1991), who teaches at Emory & Henry College in Virginia, relies on the expertise of Rosenblatt, Bleich, and Probst as he uses writing as a means of responding to literature. Herb prompts his students to write a response to what they've read according to three directions and continue their written responses after the reading has been discussed in class. His guide asks them to do the following:

1. Respond emotionally/affectively to the assigned reading. How do you feel about what you've read? Bored? Excited? Depressed? Ready to go out and change the world? Confused? In a paragraph or so, verbalize your emotional response in specific terms.

2. Make associations between what you have read and your own experience. Push until you've gotten at least three associations. You may have had a similar experience or may have felt this way before.

3. Reflect on what you have read and reexamine the text. Find a word (or words), a passage (or passages), or a feature of the selection that caught your attention. If you like a phrase or sentence, write it down. Also, write down the page number where it occurs. Try to determine why you like this particular passage. How does it relate to other experiences you have had or other things you have read? If you are confused about something, isolate it, making a note of the page number or line. Phrase a question to ask a classmate, to ask in class, or to ask me.

4. Continue your thinking after class discussion. (p. 9)

Herb often extends the response above by adding questions like: "What sort of person do you imagine the author of this text to be?" and "How did your reading of the text differ from that of your discussion partner (or the others in your group)?"
He elaborates:

Using this type of response guide, or any similar variation, not only helps students create a record of their thinking but also helps stimulate class discussion. . . . The responses, and their specific references to the text, become not only the beginning point for the discussion but also the focus, the reference point during the various levels of class discussion. Students start out with their individual response, which is expanded by small group and large group discussion, and then they are given a chance to reconsider what they originally wrote, to include ideas and concepts that have grown out of class sharing. The starting and ending point is always a reader's response to the text.

I have also found that the quality of the discussion is improved if it takes place at different levels. Quality learning in classrooms is achieved when students respond to reading assignments both individually and collaboratively in small and large groups, contend Richard and Jo Anne Vacca (1989). I have found this to be true. If students are first given the chance to claim what is of personal value to them during their reading, they are then more inclined to listen to what other students have to say. As they work in small groups, all students get not only a chance to respond and share with other group members—a chance they might not get for a variety of reasons in large group discussions—but also to expand their perceptions, to be made aware of possibilities that had not, and might not otherwise, occurred to them individually.

I ask students to review the reader responses they have written the previous night, before starting the small group discussions. Then I ask each small group (consisting of three to four students) to address the following questions, allowing students between 10 and 15 minutes to complete this part of the discussion:

> "What passages or ideas in the text did you like?" [Be specific]
>
> "What passages or ideas troubled you?" [Be specific]
>
> "What questions about the text or the ideas do you have?"

Next, as a large group, we discuss the same sequence of questions that they dealt with in their small groups. This portion of the discussion lasts anywhere from 15-30 minutes. At the end of the large class discussion, I ask students to complete their reader response by responding to questions which are essentially a summary of their thinking:

Continue your thinking after class discussion. After thinking about the questions listed below, quickly write a response to any or all of them:

> a. How do the points or issues raised in class relate to the meaning you read the assigned selections? Have you changed your interpretation of the readings? If so, in what ways?
>
> b. Has something else occurred to you that relates to your reading or to the class discussion? If so, what is it?
>
> c. What else might you want to read or do to extend your understanding of this topic? (p. 9)

Herb warns teachers that although such procedures work well for him, it's important to remember that there is no one strategy for using reader response in the classroom. Cookbook approaches should be avoided because a whole language philosophy lends itself to many strategies—dialogues, debates, rewritings and others—each providing readers with opportunities to express ideas and share responses. The important thing to remember is that the classroom must become a "forum where thought comes into being and is continually shaped through interaction with friends and partners in learning" (p. 10).

The Literature Curriculum

For years, curriculum committees, boards of education, and parent groups have tried to control the teaching of literature by establishing, along with the great scholars of our time, an acceptable canon. The canon is comprised of the literature with which one who is cultured and educated should be familiar (Hirsch, 1987). Because educators and the public still view literature as a body of information, literature courses in elementary school, high school, and college arrange the curriculum by literary history or by genre, trying to "cover" what educated students should be exposed to. One grade may study American literature and another British literature, the focus of these being on famous authors or works or historical significance. During other grades, literature is taught by genre, several weeks devoted to covering the short story, then poetry, and then, if there is time, the novel. The emphasis in such a curriculum is on technique and form. Whether the curriculum is arranged by history or by genre, the focus is the same— literature is seen as information to be learned, memorized, tested on, and more often than not, forgotten.

However, at the Dartmouth Conference of 1966, educators from the United States, Britain, and Canada spoke out in favor of encouraging students to respond to literature rather than analyze it:

> The essential talk that springs from literature is talk about the experience—as *we* know it, as *he* [the student] sees it (correcting our partiality and his; exploring the fullness of his vision and ours). Conversely, only in a classroom where talk explores experience is literature drawn into the dialogue—otherwise it has no place. The demand for interpretation—was it this or that he meant?—arises in the course of such talk; otherwise it is a dead hand. (Dixon, 1967, p. 60)

Although the Dartmouth Conference took place over twenty- five years ago, there remains a great deal of uncertainty among educators as to the purpose and focus of the literature curriculum:

> Teachers of literature have never successfully resisted the pressure to formulate their subject as a body of knowledge to be imparted. . . . The acknowledged goals of the teaching of literature are in conflict with the emphasis on specific knowledge or content. . . . There is a need to reconceptualize the "literary heritage" and its implications for patterns of teaching. (Applebee, 1974, pp. 245–247)

Even faced with imposed curricula, teachers don't have to teach literature as if it were a body of information to be acquired. Whole language teachers find ways to connect literature to students' lives so that they will have a reason and interest in reading and thinking about what they've read. Isn't this the reason we teach literature—to touch students' lives? Even the most traditional teachers, those who believe that we should teach literature because it's "good for students," would have to agree with the framers of "The Overall Plan of the Curriculum Study Center at Carnegie-Mellon University" that "literature is mankind's record, expressed in verbal art forms, of what it is like to be alive; . . . the writer of literature deals with universal concerns of every age and every culture" (Probst, 1988, p. 209).

Nevertheless, Carolyn Tucker (1991) reminds us how very difficult it is to enact change:

> When I became an English teacher, I was determined to make what I taught meaningful enough to my students that they would remember what they learned. And even though I used noted experts like Louise Rosenblatt as models, I found it easier said than done. I used quizzes and element analyses sparingly and studied plot, character, and setting only to a limited extent. We devoted much time to class interpretation, discussion, and writing in response to the literature. But, regardless of how diligent

my efforts, the literature classroom changed more in response to other elements than to my desire.

At times, the factors of time, money, materials, and curricular regulation were at odds, not only with my goals, but with each other as well. During a typical period of fifty minutes, I was expected to cover reading skills, composition, editing, vocabulary, spelling, research, grammar, and creative expression. I was expected to follow a sequence our system designed several years earlier, a document supposedly pulling various state and county guidelines together into one, all-encompassing sequence for education K–12, controlling daily lesson plans so that on any given day of the year (give or take a week) all teachers would be teaching the same thing to all county students. I hoped to provide my classes with abundant samplings from good, up-to-date, contemporary literature. But neither the school budget, nor the department budget, would cover the expense of anything other than the standard "lit" books—adopted every five years—and I had only one set of those books for four classes. I risked illegal photocopying but still fell short of what I wanted to give my students. (p. 10)

John Wilson Swope (1991), who teaches at the University of Northern Iowa, is optimistic about the effect that whole language experiences in elementary schools will have, especially the extensive range of reading experiences each student will bring to secondary classes:

When I began teaching twenty years ago, I often had eighth or ninth grade students who admitted that they had never read a whole book on their own. Students who come through a literature-based reading program with a whole language teaching philosophy will have probably read at least a hundred books as part of their elementary experience. Granted, these students will not have read all of the same books; yet, these students have already learned much about literature through their extensive reading. These whole language learners are familiar with various types of literature: poems, myths, fables, stories, novels, and nonfiction. By reading good children's and young adult literature, they have already internalized evaluative criteria for recognizing and selecting good literature. Not only do they have opinions about what good literature is, they already have favorite authors. Whole language learners are as accustomed to recommending good books to friends and teachers as they are to having teachers and peers recommend books to them. As their secondary literature teachers, we must be prepared to recommend other good books to these students when they ask. With young adults, we need to read both the literature written especially for them as well as appropriate works of adult fiction. (p. 6)

Carolyn Tucker (1991) believes a key ingredient is relevance:

Students demand that their educational experiences be relevant to their lives, asking, "What has that got to do with me?" "Why will I need to know that?" and "Why do I have to waste my time learning something that will not help me in the real world?" So I now strive to structure my literature classroom around that which relates to their world as they see it, integrating the literature study with my teaching of composition, grammar, spelling, and vocabulary.

We read biographies and autobiographies when collecting material with which they will ultimately write their own autobiographies. We read of the adventures of Heracles and the adulterous affairs of Zeus as they study ancient Greek culture in their history class. Other myths can be connected to their studies in science.

Prejudice is a major factor in our rural Kentucky society, so I have an extended unit on that issue. We read about the Nazi prejudice against the Jews in *Diary of Anne Frank*; we read about racial prejudice in *Roll of Thunder, Hear My Cry* and *Sounder*. And the literature often leads to a study of dialect, Black American English, and rap. . . .

Probably the most popular unit is entitled "Teenagers"; during this unit we read *Member of the Wedding*, *Lord of the Flies*, *Daddy-Long-Legs*, *Old Yeller*, and *Francesca, Baby*. Students also bring in pieces on teen issues from rock lyrics, scripts of docudramas, and poems and short stories from literary magazines like *Voice*.

I can say that the relevance of the topic about which my students are reading, almost without fail, generates desire in them to become involved in the literature we are studying. Admittedly, my students are not exposed to some of the classics, but until Shakespeare or Beowulf appear in rap form or as Nintendo games, I doubt they will dance their way back into my classroom. . . . As my students say, "Ain't no way those dudes have anything to say to me." (p. 11)

What Constitutes "Good" Literature?

Debate continues among educators about what constitutes "literature." Is literature found only in the novels and poetry in English classes, or is it possible that writings in science, history, and even mathematics could be regarded as literature?

Advocates of teaching cultural literacy bemoan the statistics that show students unaware of facts such as when the Civil War was fought in this country. Their solution is to teach the important facts of the war: its dates, its generals, its major battles, and its causes and implications. History textbooks contain all those facts, and history teachers dutifully cover those facts year after year. Teachers such as Amy Walker and Connie Fleeger (see Chapter 5) would suggest that when history teachers wish to cover the Civil War, they do so with literature—classics such as *The Red Badge of Courage*, non-fiction such as *The Boy's War*, autobiographies of the war's generals, diaries from the times, and journals of the pioneer photographers who documented the war. If the war were presented as literature to be read, instead of highlights to be covered, students would be culturally literate without being bored.

The discussion over what constitutes literature is made more confusing by the additional worry about what constitutes good literature—high literature, quality literature, literature with a capital L. Everyone agrees that "good" literature includes Shakespeare, but agreement breaks down after that.

In traditional elementary schools, behaviorists simplified the discussion by replacing literature with "reading" and required that students study stories from basal readers—published volumes of stories having little or no plot, stories whose sole purpose was teaching skills such as phonics and word identification. In high schools and colleges, the basal reader becomes replaced by the anthology, collections of works that are supposedly representative of the canon of authors, genres, topics of contemporary interest, thematic focus units, and the organizational focus of the course of studies.

An examination of the reading selections from a classic anthology may be instructive. The editors of the third edition of the Norton *American Tradition in Literature*, volume two, remark in their preface that their intention was,

> a freshly considered collection of great American writings representing the range and power of our literature as a whole. Our effort has been to represent major authors in the fullness of their stature and variety. Besides the titans, we have included writers of lesser stature whose works endure. . . . While we have made literary merit our final criterion for selection, we have attempted in our critical apparatus to emphasize the relations between the literary work and the general movements in American civilization and intellectual history. (Bradley, Beatty, & Long, 1967, p. xxv)

It's clear that Bradley, Beatty, and Long know full well what good literature is, who the titans are, and who the second-string players are. It's also clear that knowing good literature has much to do, in their minds, with understanding civilization—Matthew Arnold's "the best that has been thought and said."

In whole language classrooms, literature-based instruction uses a variety of literature to teach reading as well as content-area knowledge. The use of literature, however, entails tackling the controversy over what constitutes "literature" and what constitutes "good" literature. What makes *The Scarlet Letter* obvious as good literature but *Their Eyes Were Watching God* or *Kaffir Boy in America* not recognizable as such? The problem encountered by teachers in high schools and colleges is that the answer to these questions is more a political explanation than a pedagogical one. One's definition of good literature is very closely related to one's belief in the purpose of literature. If a teacher believes that the reason for studying literature is the acquisition of information, and that the only information worth remembering is that which has historical significance, then that teacher would probably favor a "great books" list of required readings.

William Williams (1991), an advocate of reader-response criticism, summarizes the conflict between defenders of the canon and advocates of multiculturalism:

> In the not too distant past, teaching literature meant teaching the traditional canons—the primarily white, male, elitist works of Western civilization—what has been referred to by some as fifteen dead white men and Emily Dickinson. However, over the last twenty years, diverse groups have argued that education should not be culturally exclusive, should not, for example, exclude the cultural productions of females, Afro–Americans, Hispanics, Native Americans, and members of lower socioeconomic classes. Culturally under-represented groups have become increasingly more vocal in their desire to be included in classrooms and textbooks, to the extent that programs of black studies and women's studies have become typical features of our curricular landscape. However, these programs neither satisfy the desires of the culturally under-represented groups to see their productions canonized nor clarify the role of the traditional literary canons in our classrooms.
>
> Over the past decade, the two strongest voices influencing curricular decisions seem to be contradictory—one insisting on multiculturalism and another insisting on cultural literacy. On the one hand, we are being asked to open our curricula, the canons if you will, to the diversity of cultures evidenced in our

country. On the other hand, we are being asked to see to it that our students are literate, not in a general sense of literacy, but literate in relation to a particular culture for the sake of efficiency and homogeneity. The problem is whether we can justify, in light of multicultural awareness, canonizing one group of cultural productions, insisting as we do so that to be considered literate, to receive a degree from one of our universities, and to hold a prestigious job requires exposure to what has been called The High Art of Western Civilization. (p. 2)

The problem of the canon and multiculturalism exists in high school literature teaching, yet it's compounded by another constraint—censorship. It's amazing what one community will label acceptable and even worthwhile to teach, and another community will label as immoral and inappropriate for young readers. There seem to be no universal criteria for what constitutes "acceptable," much less "good," literature in high school curricula. The books that are banned are often the books that deal with issues of life, issues that many people say are important for students to think about.

Since literature deals with life, in all its celebrations and failings, there will always be those who want to control the curriculum and to dictate what life situations students will learn about. Others in the community become alarmed by the "control groups" who distort for their own purposes what is being done in the classroom. Better communication between teachers and the community can help to alleviate problems caused by incomplete understandings of the educational mission of a whole language philosophy. Teachers can turn to their national professional organizations for support—The National Council of Teachers of English, The International Reading Association, and the American Library Association—and teachers should be aware that their local teacher organizations run programs dealing with the issues of academic and intellectual freedom and the strategies that have worked for others battling censorship.

Carolyn Tucker (1991) found a certain amount of irony in her censorship problems in Kentucky:

Censorship—state, local administration, and parent imposed—restricted the literature I was able to use in my classroom. A unit on mythology was challenged over religious concerns. A video of Tennessee Williams's *Streetcar Named Desire* was objected to because of its sexual overtones. Reading *A Day No Pigs Would Die* drew protest because of its references to animal mating. And *Kaffir Boy* and *To Kill a Mockingbird* met with resistance because of the racial unrest that might be generated—all this in light of the sexual, violent, and sacrilegious content that is prolific and accepted in contemporary soap operas, tabloids, commercials, movies, romance novels, news reports, and cartoons. (p. 10)

Our favorite sweatshirt slogan proclaims: "Celebrate Freedom — Read a Banned Book," followed by a small-print listing of some truly "great" books. Teachers, such as Carolyn Tucker, will always find ways to teach literature that touches the lives of their students, even though they face the constraints of censorship. Censorship won't prevent students from discovering that literature has much to say to them about life; it may, in fact, play into their sense of young adult rebellion. For this reason, many of them will become life-long readers who will read to discover, to learn, and to enjoy for the rest of their lives. Isn't that what it's all about?

For Further Exploration

1. Make a list of the books that have had a profound effect on your life. What was there about these works of literature that affected you? Where did you read them, in school or on your own? Why do you think you remember these books so well?

2. Ask several area high school and junior high schools to send you their English curriculum. What place does literature have in the curriculum of each? How is the curriculum organized—by historical significance, genre, or some other consideration?

3. Interview several college literature teachers. Ask for a copy of their syllabi. Who chooses the literature discussed in each class? By asking questions about how the teachers teach their subject matter, try to determine if the perspective of the course is New Criticism or Reader Response. Visit one or more of the classes— would your description of the interaction taking place match the teacher's own assessment of his or her teaching philosophy?

4. Visit a local library. Try to find information about censorship issues that have faced the community in recent years. What were the outcomes of some of these incidents?

5. Design a literature unit you would like to teach. How would you design the course? What works of literature would be included? Why? What would a typical day in your classroom be like?

Related Readings for Further Thought and Exploration

Bleich, D. (1975). *Readings and feelings: An introduction to subjective criticism*. Urbana, IL: National Council of Teachers of English.

*Illustrates the use of affective and associative response to litera-
ture, which forms the basis for community interpretation. Classroom teachers will find David Bleich's suggestions for response
and analysis thought-provoking and useful in classes where transactional interpretation is encouraged.*

Langer, J. (1992). *Literature instruction: A focus on student response.*
Urbana IL: National Council of Teachers of English.
*Presents a collection of essays by some of the major researchers of
the teaching of literature. Essays by Probst, Langer, Applebee,
Purves, Petrosky, and others discuss literature reform in education
today as well as offer practical strategies for student-centered literature classrooms.*

Probst, R. (1988). *Response and analysis: Teaching literature in junior and senior high school.* Portsmouth, NH: Boynton/Cook.
*Argues that students should be encouraged to make meaning as
they read, not accept the meanings imposed on them by others,
such as critics and teachers. Building on the work of Louise
Rosenblatt, Robert Probst theorizes that when reading, the meaning of what is read is not in the text itself, but rather is found in a
transaction between the reader and the text.*

Purves, A. (1990). *The scribal society: An essay on literacy and
schooling in the information age.* New York: Longman.
Looks at the term cultural literacy *and its meaning for teachers,
students, and society as a whole. The author defines literacy,
explores the psychology of reading and writing, and examines the
relationship between texts, readers, and writers. Also provoking
thought and discussion is Alan Purves's description of the current
literacy curriculum in schools in the United States and possibilities for reform.*

Rosenblatt, L. (1978). *The reader, the text, the poem: The transactional theory of the literary work.* Carbondale, IL: Southern Illinois University Press.
*Discusses the two-way process involved in the transaction
between reader and text, what is commonly called reader-
response theory. A respected authority, Louise Rosenblatt probes
the implications such a transaction has for both the reader and
the critic, and in the case of education, for teachers and students.
This is an important book for teachers of literature as well as for
teacher educators.*

Some additional resources for literature selection, as suggested by
John Wilson Swope (1991):

A. *ALAN Review*, the publication of the NCTE Adolescent Literature Assembly.
B. The "Books for Teenage Readers" column in *English Journal* (NCTE) by Elizabeth A. Belden and Judy M. Beckman.
C. *Books for You: A Booklist for Senior High Students* (11th ed.) by Shirley Wurth (ed.), (Urbana, IL: NCTE, 1992).
D. *High Interest—Easy Reading* (6th ed.) by William G. McBride, (Urbana, IL: NCTE, 1990).
E. Annotated booklists in *Literature for Today's Young Adults* (3d ed.) by Kenneth L. Donelson and Alleen Pace Nilsen, (Glenview, IL: Scott, Foresman and Company, 1989).

Chapter Four

The Place of
Oral Language
Questioning and Conferencing
in the Whole Language Classroom

*All acts of symbolization take place in a social world
framed by language; hence the importance of dialogue, ped-
agogically. We can't get under the net to reach "reality"
directly. All knowledge is mediated; all knowledge is therefore partial.*

—Ann E. Berthoff

Questions for Thought/Journal Entries

1. What is the purpose of discussion in a classroom? How is discussion initiated, and what role does the teacher play in a discussion?

2. Thinking back to your experiences in a classroom, what constitutes a "good" discussion? What are the elements that we need to hold a good discussion?

3. What part does talk play in writing? Do you ever use oral language during the writing process? In what ways—talking to yourself? To others? To whom and at what point?

4. Is talk different from conferencing? What part does conferencing play in writing? Are there any differences between peer responses to writing and teacher responses to writing? If so, what are they?

5. What problems do members of a group face when asked to discuss an issue, a piece of writing, or a response to literature? Have you ever been in a discussion group that seemed to go nowhere? What were some of the problems? What about a discussion group that seemed stimulating and interesting? What seemed to make that discussion group work?

Introduction

Whole language classrooms assume a different perspective from traditional classrooms on how language is used to negotiate learning between students and teachers. In traditional classrooms, which use an information-processing model of communication, information is transmitted from the teacher to the students, and the students confirm their reception of the information by repeating, rephrasing, or regurgitating the information back to the teacher. By way of contrast, learning in a whole language classroom is a negotiated transaction in language among students, teachers, and texts. Student response in a student-centered classroom is essential, and the teacher's role as facilitator of such response is equally important.

This chapter will look at how teachers and students use oral language in questioning and in discussion. It will also look at the role of talk in conferencing situations. While some might regard student empowerment as a relinquishing of teacher control or an abdication of classroom management, this chapter will help teachers feel organized and competent as they turn over some of the power of learning to their students.

Teacher-Talk: How Much?

Barbara King-Shaver (1991) of Monmouth Junction, NJ, relates how her students at South Brunswick High School understand the place of teacher-talk in the traditional and whole language classroom:

> At the beginning of class one day, I brought to the front of the room a lectern that had been standing in the corner, placing my notes on top of it. A student in the front of the class looked up, noticed, and said, "Oh, so you're finally going to teach today!" (p. 4)

Barbara explains that

this student was brave enough to express what many people believe—it only counts as teaching when the teacher stands in front of the room and gives information to the student. Lecterns have been a familiar sight in traditional secondary classrooms. They fit into a teaching philosophy which sees the teacher as the dispenser of knowledge, as someone whose job it is to tell the students what they need to know. Whole language teachers, on the other hand, see their job as coaches, as people who help students discover information as they interact with the material being studied and with each other. A teacher at a lectern giving notes to a class is not a frequent sight in a whole language classroom. (p. 4)

If, as whole language teachers, we are going to put our lecterns away, then we are going to have to come to grips with the problem of oral language in our classrooms—who does the talking? In what context? How will we ensure that the talk that goes on is productive? What does it mean to facilitate discussion? What do we do when students want us to give information? All these questions and more are important to whole language teachers. Most of us have spent our lives in traditional classrooms, and we know what didn't work. Even knowing what we know, it's hard to change what is familiar unless we understand the role of talk in our classrooms.

The Place of Questioning in a Whole Language Classroom

Oral language is an important part of any classroom; it's used for instruction and learning, and in the process several types of discourse communities are established. For decades, the social context of the classroom was ignored in discussions of instruction and learning due to the constraints of the model established by behaviorists.

In most behaviorist classrooms, one-third of all teacher utterances are questions (Morine-Dershimer, 1985). Known-answer questions are the most prevalent type of question asked, and questioning takes the form of what Courtney Cazden (1988) labels the IRE model—initiate, respond, and evaluate. The typical procedure is for the teacher first to ask a known-answer question, one that he or she believes has only one possible answer. Students raise their hands, and the teacher calls on one of them. Finally, the student attempts to respond with the correct answer, in the sense that it's the answer the teacher believes is correct. Many see nothing wrong with the IRE model of questioning. It is the traditional method teachers employ to find out if students are paying attention, following along, and ultimately understanding.

Thomas Good (1981) would counter that questioning often promotes passivity among students. For example, many teachers call on students perceived to be low achievers less frequently, wait less time for them to respond, and give students the answers rather than trying to help them improve their responses when they answer with anything other than that which the teacher expected. Teachers are also more likely, according to Good, to criticize such students' failures much more often than praising their successes. Soon students stop trying and become passive learners.

Gordon Wells (1986) confirms a rhetoric of the language involving the questions teachers ask. The teacher's language gives cues to students as questions are phrased and continues as the questions proceed. For example, teachers ask, "Can anyone tell me how the woods symbolize death to Robert Frost?" Such cueing is actually restrictive, an example of the teacher trying to transmit known information to the students, coaxing them to respond with the answer the teacher has in mind. "Oh, come on. What happens to your body when you die? Does it stop . . . ?" Consequently, students learn to listen carefully for these cues, trying to "read the teacher's mind," so they will be able to guess the answer the teacher feels is correct.

In a transactional whole language classroom, questioning is still used but in a very different context and for different purposes. Questioning in a whole language classroom encourages risk-taking; in such a classroom, there is more than one way to look at something and differing views are encouraged. For example, when reading the Robert Frost poem, the teacher might ask students, "Have you ever stopped an activity right in the middle of what you were doing? Try to remember a time when this happened. What were you doing? What caused you to stop? What interrupted you? Did you get back on track? What shook you up and got you back to the activity at hand?" The responses to these questions might be shared orally with the entire class or in small groups. The important thing is that whole language teachers are aware that students bring different experiences and schemata to any question, and therefore students view questions from different perspectives.

Whole language teachers must keep the student foremost in mind in regard to questioning (Wells, 1986). The teacher should:

1. Treat whatever the student answers as worthy of attention.

2. Try to understand what the student means and to look at the question from that perspective.

3. Proceed with the next comment or question based on what the student means by his or her response, not on a preconceived idea of the correct answer.

Questioning has traditionally been thought of as something a teacher does to check the level of understanding; when students ask questions, it's an admission of confusion or incomplete understanding. However, questioning in a whole language classroom is part of the meaning-making activity; it's a tool, but a nonthreatening and open-ended one. Its purpose is to stimulate thinking and response, not to elicit predetermined answers.

Whole language teachers see questions as part of an honest inquiry on the part of both teacher and students and use questioning as a tool in discussion. It's often difficult, however, to move from a teacher-directed model of questioning and discussion to one of a student-centered facilitator. Sharon Wieland (1990), a teacher in Sacramento High School, found that she had to change students' perceptions of discussion in her writing workshop, and to do so she would have to model a completely different type of discussion from what the students were used to.

Leading Classroom Discussions

Sharon had definite ideas about what she hoped would happen in her classroom when she led class discussions. She described her fantasy of the perfect class:

> I always wanted my students to become so involved in classroom discussions that they would jump into the talk passionately, stating opinions, questioning, arguing a point, providing evidence for their opinions, challenging, drawing out the ideas of others— almost as in a verbal swordfight. (1990, pp. 1–2)

Unfortunately, Sharon found, as many teachers do, that her vision of the perfect class discussion didn't always happen in her classroom. Often her students didn't care whether the class was having a discussion; they had to practically be forced to participate; and they often responded with a shrugged "I don't know."

Sharon explains,

> Frequently, students begin the school year in a whole language classroom with hesitance. As they enter the workshop classroom, they find that they are asked to behave in ways that real writers behave and to make all of their own decisions about writing. . . . Many of the students have not experienced this degree of autonomy before. The structure does not meet their expectations of what a classroom is like. [It] asks them to behave in ways that they do not usually associate with school behavior. (p. 2)

In Sharon's experience, discussion was one aspect of this workshop environment that never worked well at the beginning of the year. When she asked the students to work in peer response groups, reading their writing to a small group of peers and listening to response, she found them tentative and polite, or rowdy and rude. When she asked them to discuss writing as a whole class, she found that they expected her to take charge of the discussion. Although the discussions began to function the way she had hoped by November or December, she was still bothered that it took so long. "Why couldn't my students hold good discussions at the beginning of the year?" she wondered (p. 2).

Sharon decided to try to find out just what was shaping students' notions of what a discussion is. She hoped to be able to describe a model of classroom discussion that students had when they entered her high school, hoping that information would help her plan for better discussions in her classes. Sharon questioned forty-nine summer school and summer sports program participants at a nearby college, who ranged in age from seven to fourteen. After obtaining their teachers' permission, Sharon conducted an informal survey seeking to describe students' perceptions of class discussions. Sharon said that this was the quickest, least obtrusive way that she could think of to get information from students without disrupting their programs. The questions and informal assessment method were based on two informal studies: one, done by W. Page and G. S. Pinnell (1979), tried to describe students' models of reading, and the other, done by Pat Hartwell (1981), tried to describe students' models of writing. Sharon asked the students to write their answers to three questions:

1. What are the rules for having a discussion in a classroom?
2. What are the rules for asking a question in a classroom?
3. What are the rules for answering a question in a classroom?

Sharon said,

The students' answers to the questions dismayed me. They described classroom discussion that called for student passivity, that was elicitative in nature, and that saw the teacher as authority. In other words, they *expected* the teacher to initiate, direct, and restrict the talk in the classroom. From the first through the seventh grades, this model was well established among the students.

To my question asking about the rules for having a discussion in the classroom, the students responded similarly:

- wait until the teacher is finished;
- the teacher has to tell you something;
- don't talk, listen; be quiet, listen to the teacher;
- listen to the teacher, no fooling around;
- raise your hand and wait.

In fact, of the 49 students polled, 90 percent of the responses were of the wait, listen to the teacher, and do not talk variety, and only 10 percent of the responses included the possibilities of asking questions or giving opinions. A full 100 percent believed the teacher directs the discussion. (p. 2)

Sharon said that when she inquired about the rules for asking a question in a classroom, these students responded in ways that, again, didn't fit her ideal model of a discussion.

The students responded:

- raise hand and wait [patiently];
- raise your hand, and in the proper voice, ask the question;
- ask something the teacher would like to hear.

In responding, 94 percent perceived the procedure as raise your hand and wait, while 6 percent felt empowered enough to ask proper and appropriate questions. (p. 2)

When Sharon asked them her final question about the rules for answering a question in the classroom, the students continued in the same vein.

The rules for answering for 83 percent of the students depended more on procedure than on the appropriateness of the answers:

- you must know exactly what you are talking about;
- wait for the teacher to call on you;
- raise your hand, make sure it is appropriate to the discussion;
- no smart remarks—raise your hand.

How strange that no students suggested that discussions might take place among a group of students without the teacher present, that questions might be used for finding out information, or that answers are ways of explaining one's point in an argument. Of course, I knew that the very phrasing of my questions contributed to much of the way the questions were answered, but, still, I found it curious that the students seemed so much in agreement on their definition of class discussion. (p. 2)

It was clear to Sharon that the students viewed their role in the classroom as passive—quite different from the behavior she wanted in her writing workshop class. "No wonder my students have difficulty accepting my model of classroom discussions," she continued. "These secondary students come to class with years of experience in what is considered 'acceptable' school behavior. I had been battling against a perception of what is proper behavior that had been learned in the first grade, one that became more ingrained with every passing year" (p. 2).

Sharon's research shows that students learn what teachers want in their classrooms, and unfortunately, their learned behaviors are part of a model based on the transmission of knowledge and student passivity rather than on transactional learning and student involvement. Because of the environment that is often typical in teacher-centered classrooms, students learn not only what their teachers want but that teachers expect a rigid, controlled environment in their classrooms. What Sharon found is the IRE model of teacher questioning and student response described by Courtney Cazden (1988).

As a whole language teacher, Sharon asks, "If students feel they must speak 'properly' and 'appropriately' and say 'something the teacher would like to hear,' then to what extent are they able to make discussion a tool which works for them in improving their writing?" (p. 3).

As a result of her study, Sharon found that it takes time for students to be able to actively write and discuss. Still, she tried to devise ways to help them begin to use discussion effectively a little sooner in the year, particularly peer response and classroom discussion of writing. As a result, Sharon devised five of her own rules to use in her writing workshop classroom:

1. Become a listener. In order to become a listener in my classroom, I listen to students rather than "direct" the discussion. I want to learn from students and find out how they can direct their own learning in discussions.

2. Check nonverbal behaviors. I watch that my nonverbal behaviors help all students to participate in discussions and that my nonverbal behaviors value the contribution that each student makes to the discussion. I hope to encourage students from all ethnic and cultural backgrounds to participate more effectively in discussions.

3. Help students become their own interpreters. Helping students become their own interpreters of meanings and situations rather than having me interpret for them demands that I consider each student's differences as uniqueness, not deficits. The writing workshop helps me to do this as I view myself as a collaborative writer, learning to write with my students. This collaborative stance necessitates diminishing the role of "teacher as authority."

4. Make "talk" a chief content item of the curriculum; I try to structure discussion into the daily writing workshop in ways that are most helpful to writers. I look for natural times that writers need to talk during the composing process and help my students use these discussion times to improve their writing.

5. Finally, a simple rule: eliminate the words "tell me" and "I want you to . . ." from the classroom. . . . If I ask them to "tell me," I take away all chances for them to lead the discussion. If they merely "tell me," they are always acting only because I decided that they should. I want my students to be active in a discussion group, not passive listeners. (p. 3)

Sharon knows it won't be easy for students to become passionately involved in leading discussions, especially since by the time they are in high school, they have learned a very different model of discussion. Whole language teachers have to establish trust, a sense of community and purpose, and then they must model a type of discussion that encourages students to think and to take risks. This type of discussion not only gives students opportunities but it also requires that students become more responsible and involved. Yet, like many other changes in whole language classrooms, discussion must be modeled and new rules of behavior must be established.

Small-Group Discussion

The fact that we often think of discussion as a give-and-take situation among as many as thirty participants—the whole class and the teacher—is another problem. The numbers alone in a typical classroom preclude what is needed for active discussion—attention, participation, and interaction. In discussions involving a whole class, the teacher almost always talks too much as a consequence of assuming the role of moderator or discussion leader, the one whose role it is to keep the discussion moving forward. A more sensible way for teachers to include all students is to try small-group discussion within the class. Unfortunately, this can't happen immediately in the beginning of the semester because most secondary students are still uncomfortable with risk-taking.

Before any type of real discussion can take place, the teacher must establish a sense of community, a relaxed but focused climate for conversation. The tone of the response from the teacher must be sincerely warm and friendly; students know when their teacher is faking it or pretending to be interested when he or she has another agenda. Conversation, whether at a dinner party or in a classroom, is a profound social activity that is based on genuine respect—respect for other's ideas, feelings, and reactions and humility in understanding that each speaker is only one person in the conversation, someone with opinions but willing and eager to learn from others, including students.

Before students will be comfortable joining in a discussion or responding to others, their teachers must refrain from dominating the discussion. Yet, as difficult as it is for teachers to let go of the leader role, it's equally difficult for students to become active participants in a discussion. When students are put in groups and simply asked to discuss something, the results are predictable. They initially sit and look at each other, and then one or two will try to guess what it is that they are supposed to say. Obviously, the climate is often strained and uncomfortable. Students need to be shown *how* to discuss matters in such a way that these groups will be productive, stimulating, and enjoyable. Providing students with a discussion model often helps them discover how to begin while giving them the opportunity and responsibility of facilitating discussion.

There are many such models, but in any discussion the participants must understand what the purpose is and that all members of the group have a role to play. Assigning a role to each member will help students all take part, especially early in the year when they're unfamiliar with the class and community has not yet been established. In our classes, we often assign the following roles: leader, note-taker, time-keeper, questioner, and reporter. The role of the leader is to restate the question for discussion and keep the participants on track. Since it's this person's responsibility to be looking for those who tend to dominate, the leader has the job of drawing people who have not said very much into the discussion. The time-keeper sets up a schedule before discussion begins. After the establishment of the items to be discussed, the group decides how long they'll spend on each part of the discussion, and the time-keeper's responsibility is to keep them on task and to move them along so they don't belabor any one point. Often groups will leave a few minutes at the end to go back and sum up or return to an issue they did not fully cover. The note-taker functions as a scribe and jots down important facts as the discussion progresses. We've found that if this person is called a secretary, females are usually assigned the role, so we prefer the term *note-taker*. The questioner's responsibility is to devise questions from the discussion that will be posed later to either the small group or the whole class. The reporter's role is to work with the note-taker and the questioner, usually for a couple of minutes at the end of the discussion time and report back to the class.

At first such models may seem somewhat stiff and formal, and students may pay more attention to format than to the quality of discussion; but after awhile, the format becomes routine, and students have a forum in which to share ideas and respond to one another. They take turns assuming different roles and do so matter-of-factly as they go about their discussions.

Helping All Students Become "Intelligently Verbal"

Students discuss many things in whole language classrooms, but much of the discussion revolves around reading and writing. Some teachers mistakenly believe that not all students are capable of discussion—that is, they are not capable of learning by thinking and responding. This is often true with students who are labeled "at risk"—those in lower tracks, those labeled learning disabled, and those in what are euphemistically called "basic" classes. Whole language teachers believe that all students can learn from discussion, and when given the opportunity to orally respond to what they have read or to what has been written, many at-risk students are capable of sharing exciting ideas or opinions with their class. Again, the importance of modeling and environment cannot be stressed enough. At-risk students, as much as any other student, must believe that what they have to say is important and that their ideas will be respected.

Students placed in the lower track or in basic classes often find themselves on an institutional path that is theoretically parallel to the other tracks, with its own content requirements and "approved" lists of texts, but headed nowhere nevertheless. These students are given a curriculum whose very nature insures that they will be kept busy in meaningless tasks, completing a series of drill-for-skill sequences. Suzanne Miller (1991) from the State University of New York at Albany says that "remediation such as this signals low expectations and promotes passivity . . . because students are treated as objects to be filled rather than subjects who must create their own knowledge" (p. 11). Suzanne observed firsthand one at-risk program cited for excellence by the National Council of Teacher of English, one challenging the self-fulfilling prophecies of traditional tracking. Suzanne watched students learn "to enter [productive] conversations, students who had failed in regular classes. This at-risk program focused on the whole student—intellectually, socially, emotionally, and physically—through behavior and attendance contracts, peer counseling, and extra program activities, and, in English class, by engaging them in discussions of what they read" (p. 11).

Suzanne observed that Laura, the teacher of the at-risk senior English class, "consistently made space for real conversations so that her students could think, make connections and feel important. Before, during, and after reading, Laura asked for her students' spontaneous responses . . ." (p. 11). At first Laura's students were reluctant to enter the conversation, but Suzanne says that "when these students saw that Laura was willing to listen to whatever they had to say, they became increasingly willing to think about things" (p. 11), expressing their thoughts first in their journals and then in class discussions. The difference in Laura's classroom was that she not only acknowledged each response and encouraged others, she refrained from evaluating them, dismissing the notion of the one correct answer or interpretation. Discussions in informal, everyday language gave students an opportunity to share exciting ideas or opinions, thereby provoking further discussion and thought. Laura used a variety of sources—"songs and movies, adolescent, modern, and multi-cultural novels and, sometimes, the classic texts of the senior curriculum" (p. 11)—to engage her students in discussion.

When students believe that what they have to say is important and that their ideas will be respected, they can't help but be engaged in learning. Sometimes during a shared reading in Laura's student-centered classroom, "she would stop reading aloud and ask questions about possible implications, meanings, and problems. This collaborative reading and pausing externalized the internal dialogue that readers carry on with the text, a conversation concerning its possibilities" (p. 11). The students told Suzanne in interviews that they were beginning to "ask questions to ourselves" as they read, and beginning to wonder if there were "enough clues to give us a reason to think a certain way." In classroom discussions,

> Laura saw her students developing what she called "literate thinking," as they considered alternative views and multiple connections. For instance, when these at-risk students raised the issue of why Holden Caufield "doesn't want to try" in school, Laura asked them if they knew anyone like that. Her students offered possible explanations:

- "he wants to be noticed";
- "his parents don't 'really' care";
- "he's 'putting on a big act'—he's already labelled, so he figures he'll live up to that."

Together they examined whether Holden was "normal," and found problematic contradictions between what he did and what he seemed to feel. The pull of genuine conversation and the spark of their puzzlements spurred student response and thinking.

Laura made sure her students learned how to take their part in such conversations using a reader-response approach— responding, questioning, connecting literature to their experiences, to their feelings, and to the world. As she focused on what students had to say about what they read, she learned "how exciting it is to see their understanding develop from themselves."

Drawn into dialogues of meaning-making and problem-posing, Laura's students began to create new images of themselves as learners. One student, Kate, who had previously failed ninth- and tenth-grade English, told Suzanne that she used to sit in the back of the room and "didn't exist to anyone." Kate, the only girl to graduate from her auto repair class at Vo Tech, also explained how in Laura's class, she and her classmates talked in "open-minded" ways about books: "We usually get ideas going . . . we always discuss, figure out what's going on, and why it's happening, and what we think will happen." Another student, Bret, who [had previously failed but who] later graduated and joined the Navy, told Suzanne that discussions in Laura's class "always had meaning": "We learn from everybody else's experience as well as our own when we take part." Before heading off to community college, another student, Mark, thanked Laura for transforming him from being illiterate to being "intelligently verbal," as he himself put it. Kate, summing up the benefits, said that learning and thinking in discussion "help[ed] me academically and as a person." (Miller, 1991, p. 11)

Learning to Be a Listener

Language arts is generally thought of as reading, writing, listening, and speaking—listening being a receptive activity dependent on speaking, parallel to reading as the receptive activity dependent on writing. Although teachers expend a great deal of energy trying to teach three of the language arts—reading, writing, and even speaking, little is done in classrooms to help students learn to listen. When teachers complain that students "don't listen," all too often they mean that students don't seem to listen to teachers, as if listening was something involuntary, like breathing, and choosing not to listen was a willful act, one resulting from being lazy, rude, or inattentive.

How many of us remember the conundrum of philosophy class, "If a tree falls in the forest, and there is no one around, does it make a sound"? The answer to the puzzle is that there is no "sound" if there is no ear to hear, since the sound is created in the ear of a hearer. We all remember being falling trees in the classrooms—no one heard us.

Teachers and students need to develop good listening habits, ones in which the object of a discussion is more than everyone saying something. Consider a discussion in an American Literature class, one in which a student offers, "Poe's *Raven* poem reminded me of a time when I was left alone in the house, and I was up late at night because I kept hearing all these sounds." The teacher might respond, "Good," and move on to other responses, this time a classmate's tale of a "really large bird" she saw at camp last summer. The first student's response is another tree in the forest. The teacher or another classmate with active listening skills could draw out the discussion from several points in the first student's statement:

- "How did you feel being left alone?"
- "What sounds did you hear?"
- "What in the poem reminded you; what exactly brought this back to you?"
- "How does Poe's narrator feel about being alone?"
- "What would have made you feel better about being alone?"
- "Why were you alone?"
- "Why was Poe's narrator alone? What would make him feel better?"

At the point in the discussion when the first student offered the original response, it was unlikely that the student had fully considered the memory of being alone or drawn comparisons between personal experience and the poem. If the class discussion had moved on to the story of the "big bird at camp," the first student's "compenetration" with the text, as Louise Rosenblatt (1978) says, falls silently in the forest of thought.

And the benefits, although many, don't accrue exclusively for the student being listened to. The active listener who draws the story out of the first student, guiding and prompting the recall of circumstances and emotions, as well as all of those present to the discussion, will enjoy the classmate's story and the poem, support the classmate's development of critical thinking, be able to respond with a similar tale to the classmate's story, and, moreover, learn something about the classmate and the poem in the bargain. Active listening in class can take place when discussing writing, literature, and content knowledge in subjects such as history or biology. The feature that distinguishes a discussion in a whole language classroom from the IRE sequence is that the discussion resembles a real conversation, one in which participants contribute something they truly wish to share, and the others listen because they care about the person and the topic.

Conferences: Teacher Response in Writing Workshop

Discussion in a whole language classroom can be an intimate conversation; that is, it can take place between one student and one teacher during a conference. Conferences with students should be seen as opportunities to *discuss* writing, helping students verbalize their purpose for writing, their plan for the piece, and their feelings about what they are writing. The role of the teacher is to listen to what the student has to say about the writing and to respond to what the student perceives as his or her needs as a writer. Steven Zemelman and Harvey Daniels (1988) propose that "by suggesting thought processes the writer can use, rather than prescriptions for words on the page, the teacher can give help and yet still leave it to the student to solve the problem" (p. 167).

Teachers of writing need to do two things for writers—get them to write and provide response to their writing. Elsewhere we speak of how to find prompts, cues, and assignments that bring contextually natural writing to traditional academic writing and the processes of writing and revising. The challenge is responding to writing. Authors agree that feedback from concerned and helpful audiences— questioning, suggesting, collaborating—is crucial, and the caveat for helping student writers is the same as that which we apply when responding to each other's writing (journal articles, letters to parents or administrators, poems): provide direction to revision without taking over control of the writing. When talking about writing, both about the process and the product, the conversation must be supportive rather than directive. There's no one ideal time to conference, but the way the teacher handles these conferences and the role of talk is an essential element in the success of conferencing in a whole language workshop. Nancie Atwell (1987) cautions that if teachers wait too long to talk with students about pieces they're writing, the intervention will seem punitive; in other words, such a conference will be perceived as a discussion in which the teacher will "correct" what is wrong with a piece of writing. If the individual writing conference is the best way to deliver this feedback, then the best time is during the writing process.

Donald Graves (1983), in his book, *Writing: Teachers and Children at Work*, suggests some specific ways teachers can use "process conferences" to help students make decisions about their writing rather than directing them how to proceed or how to "fix" their writing. In a writing conference, much is said without words. A teacher who sits across a table or desk from a student engages the same dynamic in effect when the teacher sits at the big desk in front of the room. It says to the student, "I am the authority, and I will tell you what you should do." Furthermore, inexperienced teachers tend to look at the paper but rarely at the student. Truly, our body language and the sitting arrangement say a great deal to the student about our perceived roles.

To discuss writing—to listen to what a student has to say and interact—requires being near the student. This means sitting together on the same side of a table or desk. When the student must hand the paper across the table in order for the teacher to read it, the student gives up the paper, in a very real sense. A side-by-side arrangement avoids the necessity of taking the paper away from the student and presents several options: the student may read the paper aloud to the teacher, may place the paper on the desk between them, or may actually hold the paper while the teacher reads it. If the conference is held in a computer lab, the teacher is able to sit next to the student at the keyboard and read the text on-screen. Either way, maintaining control of the paper sends a signal to the student that he or she is also in control of the discussion; the teacher is sitting in as an advocate, not as an adversary.

It's equally important to remember that a conference involves talking, not merely reading over a paper and giving verbal red-marks. To help start the conference, teachers should ask questions that give students a chance to talk about the process and their paper. For example, asking Melissa, "What's your paper about?" gives Melissa a chance to verbalize the purpose of her writing and gives the teacher the opportunity to respond as someone interested in the premise of the paper, not someone making judgments. If Melissa explains that she is writing about her desire to attend an out-of-state college and her discussion of this situation with her parents, her teacher might respond by saying, "I see that attending this school is very important to you. I don't know much about that school. How did you find out about it?" Questions like this signal to the student that her teacher is interested first in what she has to say, rather than worried about how she will go about saying it. When students realize that teachers are interested in their ideas, they are more likely to be open about their needs as writers. Melissa might just say in the course of the conference, "It's not enough for me to write about how great this school is and how much I want to go; I have to find a way to convince my mom and dad to send me."

As a conference proceeds, process questions help students see where they are in their writing and help them decide how they might want to proceed. A teacher might reflect the thoughts Melissa has expressed: "Okay, Melissa. You say that you don't think you are being convincing enough. Explain to me first, what you are trying to say." Giving students a chance to explain what they see as the purpose of their writing allows the teacher to ask questions that help to focus, such as, "Of all the things you'd like to tell your parents, what's the most convincing point you're making?" When students answer questions like this, they often make their own discoveries about what is needed to improve what they have written.

When asking questions in a conference, teachers should ask questions which students can answer, rather than ones that put students on the spot. (Remember, the teacher's responsibility is to facilitate, not to show who is smarter.) The point of conferencing is to encourage a writer by what is said—to direct and guide as well as support. If the student thinks a paper is finished, the teacher might ask questions about what the student likes best or how the student thinks a reader will respond to certain parts. At this point, a teacher helps the writer read the paper as a reader would.

One of the most difficult listening skills for a teacher to practice is being quiet. Teachers know the importance of "wait time" when asking questions in whole-class discussions, but sometimes they forget that wait time is valuable during conferences. Students need a chance to think about what they're trying to say. When a student is silent, teachers must resist the impulse to jump in and manage the situation. Thoughtful reflection should be respected.

Teachers in a whole language class are constantly challenged about the appropriateness of marking errors in standard edited English and lapses in stylistic etiquette. Writing involves conforming to convention; however, the traditional overemphasis on usage and correctness would hold adherence to convention as an end in itself. Regardless of how fixed, sacrosanct, and socially desirable adherence to convention is, there is more to writing than conforming. There is a time for teaching editing conventions, and that time happens to be late in the process. If teachers first respond as someone interested in the writer's ideas, then they can help the writer discover how best to communicate those ideas in an editing conference that focuses on form. Even then, what the student learns about form should be what he or she is ready to learn. In a conference, teachers should limit their focus to one skill at a time, something the student sees a need to learn. It hardly makes sense to use the conference time to explain the varieties of *their/there/they're* if the student has simply mis-spelled the word or to teach the subtleties of the semicolon if the student has no need to use one. There's not enough time to try to do everything in one piece of writing.

Even if there were enough time to do everything, conferences should still be kept relatively short. It's unnecessary to listen to the student read every word written. If a teacher does that, it's another way of taking control of the writing. It's more important to talk about the writing and concentrate on a part that the student self-identifies as one in need of attention. Students have been trained to wait for their teacher to solve all their problems and work on the entire piece. Donald Graves calls this "writer's welfare"—students sit back and let someone take care of the writing, instead of taking responsibility for the writing themselves. This dependence on the teacher is slow to disappear, but the whole language teacher trusts that as students write more, make more choices, and understand that risk-taking is encouraged, independence will surface in the classroom.

What to Ask and How to Ask It

Having said so much about the importance of speaking and listening to students, we realize teachers may feel tongue-tied when holding one-to-one conferences. We would like to offer some strategies adapted from Nancie Atwell (1987). As mentioned earlier, the teacher might ask some opening questions at the beginning of the conference: "What's your paper about?" or "How is the writing going?" The teacher might ask the student to read the paper, if it's short enough, or to read a section that seems to work particularly well or is particularly troublesome. At this point, the teacher must comment, saying something that the student will regard as helpful rather than critical.

If the piece seems to have too many ideas, trying to cover them all in a scattergun approach, the teacher might respond, "I can see that you are interested in many different ideas," naming some of them to be more specific. Then the teacher could ask, "Which idea strikes you as the most important?" or "What's your favorite part?"

Most likely, by suggesting that the student concentrate on one part or idea, the next draft will suffer from a narrowness of focus. At this point, the teacher might respond simply by saying, "I don't understand" or "Could you tell me more about this?" Another approach would be to say, "I get the feeling that you've had to leave out other things you know about your topic, but I'm interested in hearing all of it." If the student counters that he or she is out of ammunition, the teacher could ask, "Where could you go to find out more about your topic?" or "Who could you ask so that you can build on what you have?"

Sometimes students overwrite; that is, they put too much information in a piece of writing, perhaps overgeneralizing a rule from an earlier conference—tell the reader more, more, more. A teacher might ask, "What point are you trying to get across to your reader? What parts of this are most important to what you're trying to say?" The teacher might then ask the student to consider what parts could be trimmed without loss to the piece as a whole.

Most pieces of writing begin as narratives. This is only reasonable, inasmuch as we organize our literate lives around stories. However, students sometimes make their writing little more than a list of events—and then, and then, and then. Often, a sense of reflection is missing. A teacher might simply ask the student to consider, "What do you think this means?" or "How did you feel when this happened?" The teacher might respond, "I can tell that this event is significant to you. Why do you think this is? Have you changed in any way because of it?"

Sometimes writers take forever beginning a piece, taking time to set the scene, introducing the major characters or elements, going on about contextual details rather than introducing their thesis. A teacher might feel that the piece really begins on the second page but avoids explicitly pointing this out. Instead the teacher might ask, "Does this introduction bring your reader right into the piece?" or "What is the purpose of your introduction?" If the students seems unsure where to begin, the teacher might even suggest that students use their hands or a piece of paper to cover up paragraphs or sentences to see how the piece would sound without them.

Endings are difficult; some people have trouble saying goodbye. In timed situations, from classrooms to live television shows, endings are sometimes rushed, "Well, that's all we have time for today"; other times they're padded because we've ended too soon—television producers give the sign to stretch out the ending, resulting in the "happy talk" at the end of shows such as the eleven o'clock news, and teachers fill the time with personal anecdotes or a review of what was just discussed. Writers have the same problem—sometimes the conclusion to a piece feels either too rushed or else it seems to repeat itself over and over. During a conference, the teacher might ask some or all of these questions, "How do you want your reader to feel at the end of your piece? What would you like the reader to walk away knowing after finishing? Does your conclusion do it?" In the case of an overly wordy conclusion, the teacher might ask, "Are there any other places where your piece could end?" and encourage students to use their hands or a piece of paper, as they did with the introduction, to get a visual sense of alternative endings.

Ending the conference may be as difficult as ending a piece of writing. Instead of shouting "next!" or reviewing what was discussed, a teacher might better see what the student gained from the conference by asking, "What do you think you'll do next?" This approach reinforces the notion that writing is continuous, recursive, and directed. If students leave with a plan for revision or for a new project, they will leave with a sense of themselves as writers rather than as students who have been examined.

The phrasing of questions is as important in individual conferences as it is in group discussions, and the way teachers conduct conferences can influence how much responsibility students assume as writers.

Peer Response in Writing Conferences

As productive as teacher-student conferences are, a whole language teacher's goal is also to help students learn to respond to each other as readers and as writers, accomplished first by modeling effective conferencing and later by teaching them how to work with each other in peer conferences.

We have heard many teachers, frustrated by unproductive peer conferencing, say that students don't know how to give advice in conferencing situations. We would counter that conferencing is not about giving "advice." The purpose of a conference between students is not to "fix up" a classmate's paper; it is a chance for writer and reader to share ideas and reactions, an opportunity to share a piece of writing with a real audience, who reacts as any reader does, by asking questions, sharing perceptions, and offering suggestions when asked.

As with any new activity, peer conferencing must be learned. By the time students are in secondary school, many are uncomfortable sharing ideas in peer groups. This is not to say that students are shy or reticent. Much of the discomfort felt working in groups can be traced to the competitive pressure for grades, compounded by a belief that sharing is cheating, a form of "not doing one's own work." Whole language teachers must reassure students through their own actions and attitudes that ideas rarely belong to any one person and that real writers are not graded by teachers but evaluated by readers reacting to what they say and how they say it. Conferencing depends on students working together collaboratively and noncompetitively.

Thus, members of a class need time to get to know one another. Groups can be established according to interest (students sharing concerns or curiosities), personality (students simply enjoying working with each other), convenience (students working on the same piece of literature or at similar places in their writing), and need (students whom their teacher feels may learn from each other). Working together necessitates moving desks around or using a table, but more importantly, group work necessitates knowing what each person's role is in the peer conference.

Each person in a group conference is primarily a listener, constituting an audience of one. As the writer reads aloud, students need to learn to listen in order to discuss the subject of the piece, focus on its ideas, ask real questions about what they're interested in knowing, indicate what parts of the piece "work" and what parts are vague or confusing, and let writers know what they, as listeners, want to know more about. By listening to the writer rather than reading the piece, peer responders avoid assuming the role of proofreader. (A listener can't hear comma faults and misspelled words.) Editing can be dealt with later at conferences set aside specifically for that purpose.

In the beginning, and often long into the semester, students will tend to give shallow and unhelpful responses. Frequently the responses go in either of two directions: "This is wonderful, great; I can't think of a thing to tell you to make it any better" and "This piece is lousy; It's not what the teacher wants, but I don't know what to tell you to make it any better." Obviously neither response is of much help, but the second is definitely the more demoralizing. A rule in conferencing, then, is to be constructive and supportive. Students should be encouraged to look for what is good and then to continue beyond merely congratulating the writer, "This is great . . . "

In the beginning, students appreciate some helpful hints from the teacher for peer conferences. They might be simply presented as a formula at first. For instance, "Retell what the writer is saying, so that the writer can determine if the piece of writing says what the writer thinks it does." A procedure technique might be suggested: "Identify for the writer what you consider to be the strongest part of the piece, explaining why you feel this way, and then ask one question of the writer that you feel would clarify for you any part that seemed vague or unclear." Some teachers and students find guidesheets useful. We add one caution here: guidesheets can easily become extensions of teacher control. Guidesheets in a whole language classroom are not prescriptive; instead, they are open-ended enough to allow for genuine response and questioning. Even teachers who understand this distinction must make clear to their students, who have had years of experience with worksheets and dittoed directions, that guidesheets are meant to help them structure their conferences, and if at any point they feel other concerns are more important or they enter into a productive discussion of any one area, it is not necessary to address all the questions on the guidesheet. A peer conference guidesheet can be constructed to suit the class and the topic and modeled after one used by Steven Zemelman and Harvey Daniels (1988) (see Figure 4–1) or another used by Thomas Reigstad and Donald McAndrew (1984) (see Figure 4–2).

Because techniques for peer conferences must be learned, many teachers abandon them before giving students adequate time to feel comfortable with them. Since teachers often have little patience and want everything to work immediately, when a group has difficulties and seems to be floundering, teachers need to give students the chance to solve their problems themselves. Peer conferences need teachers to support them rather than to solve all their problems. If the time comes when it's to the students' advantage for the teacher to intervene, it should be done strategically. For example, there are times when re-grouping intervention is needed—one student is dominating, personalities are in conflict or simply not meshing, or the students do not seem interested in each other's topics. Teachers will only know these things, however, if they are acting as facilitators, careful observers of

Figure 4–1
Peer Critique Sheet: Personal Narrative

Be as specific as you can in answering these questions. Your comments will help the writer improve his or her paper. Share your responses orally with the writer after he or she has read the piece through at least once.

1. What event did the writer focus on?
2. Why do you think the writer chose this topic?
3. How did the writer feel about the incident when it happened? How do you know?
4. How does the writer feel about the incident now? How do you know?
5. What part of the paper did you like best? What part impressed you the most?Why?
6. What, if anything, confuses you about the narrative as written?
7. What would you like to know more about?
8. What would you change about the content or arrangement of this paper?

Figure 4–2
Tutor Critique Sheet

---

1. Make a positive, rapport-creating statement to the writer.
2. Make two positive comments about the paper. What are its strengths?
3. Describe any weakness you find in the areas listed below. Suggest a strategy to eliminate each weakness.
   a. thesis or focus
   b. voice or tone
   c. organization
   d. development

4. List any weaknesses you see in sentence structure, punctuation, usage, and spelling. Suggest a strategy to eliminate each weakness.

---

the conferences. Changing partners can be done positively, letting students see that their teacher is supporting the process, by suggesting, "Darren, I see that you wrote a paper about the news media. Would you please change partners with Sally, so that you can respond to Eric's paper about reporting in the presidential campaign." The students involved will see the intervention as helpful and none will feel singled out as failures in the conferencing process.

Peer conferences depend on the climate in the classroom and the expectations for writing and responding set up in the class. If students are given opportunities for responsibility and feel that the purpose of writing is to communicate their thoughts and feelings about a topic to a real audience, they will react accordingly in a peer conference. If students get the impression that the purpose of writing is to receive a good grade, to write in a way that their teacher feels is best, or to exhibit a knowledge of form and structure, then the conferences will proceed accordingly. It's really up to the teacher to decide such goals.

Suzanne Miller (1991) concludes, "When students . . . discuss . . . with the support of an encouraging teacher, they can examine what they know, and learn to actively shape, question, elaborate and remake knowledge. . . . When students transform . . . their discussion of texts, they also move toward a personal sense of intellectual self-worth in their new images of themselves as readers, writers, and thinkers. If we want to open students to possibilities in texts and in their lives, we need to encourage teachers to talk with their students, who . . . sadly remind us, have very likely never heard their own voices in school (p. 11.)."

For Further Exploration

1. Observe several classes where teacher-led discussion takes place. What model of questioning did the teacher use (IRE, open-ended, etc.)? What evidence did you observe to support your assessment? What were the reactions of the students to questions that were being asked? What follow-up was given by the teacher to students' answers?

2. Become an observer in a class where small-group discussion is being used. How were students prepared for the discussion? What roles did they assume in the discussion? What did you learn from your observations or what suggestions would you make to enable these groups to be more productive?

3. As a teacher, student teacher, or class participant, assume the role of teacher in leading a classroom discussion. How would you facilitate the discussion? How would you phrase questions? Respond to students? What was the most difficult part of being the facilitator? What will you have to work on as you try to improve your abilities to lead discussion in your classroom?

4. Tape record a writing conference you conduct with a student. As a teacher, what are some of the techniques you employed? Why? How would you change the conference if you had a chance to do it over again? What will you do when you conference with this student again?

5. Observe a class where the teacher prepares students for peer conferencing. How was this accomplished? Observe several pairs of students as they conference with each other. What did you observe? Could these conferences have been more productive? In what way? What would you do as a teacher to help your students learn to conference with one another?

Related Readings for Further Thought and Exploration

Cazden, C. (1988). *Classroom discourse: The language of teaching and learning.* Portsmouth, NH: Heinemann.
Looks at the way language is used in the classroom, often unconsciously, and how such interactions can affect student learning.

Heath, S. B. (1983). *Ways with words: Language, life, and work in communities and classrooms.* New York: Cambridge University Press.
Reports how misunderstandings between teachers and students can be traced to differences in dialect and language. More

importantly, Shirley Brice Heath's Trackton study shows how these differences can even cause misinterpretation of students' ability.

Mehan, H. (1984). Language and Schooling. *Sociology of education*, *57*, 174–183.
Examines the use of language in schools and how such language results in social stratification among students.

Reigstad, T. & McAndrew, D. (1984). *Training Tutors for Writing Conferences*. Urbana, IL: National Council of Teachers of English.
Offers teachers and students concrete advice on conferencing. A best-selling, practical book originally written as a support for peer tutors in writing centers.

Zemelman, S. & Daniels, H. (1988). *A Community of Writers: Teaching Writing in the Junior and Senior High School*. Portsmouth, NH: Heinemann.
Shows teachers of writing in all subject areas how to support students' growth in writing. A good source for ideas on conferencing.

Chapter Five

Reading and Writing to Learn
An Integrated Language Approach

Understandings about language are increased and intensi-fied when [students] use language . . . across the curricu-lum. They speak, listen, read, and write as they conduct a science experiment, as they consider problems and discover patterns in math, as they engage in an inquiry in social studies, as they reflect on an art project. Because the con-tent of these disciplines or curricular domains is different, [students] discover that different registers of language both oral and written must be employed in their projects.
—Christine Pappas, Barbara Keifer, & Linda Levstik

Questions for Thought/Journal Entries

1. In secondary schools and colleges, how is language used in sub-jects other than in English class?

2. From your experience as a student, in which classes did you learn to read and write?

3. What do you think is meant by the phrase, "writing to learn"?

4. Have you ever kept a journal or learning log? How did this expe-rience affect you as a writer? As a learner?

5. What do you think of the observation, "Every teacher is a teacher of language"? How do you think other teachers feel about this concept? Why?

Introduction

An integral part of the change to whole language is the integration of language across the curriculum. Teachers, regardless of their subject areas (Science, Social Sciences, Math, the Arts, as well as English), must realize the importance of literacy in learning and the use of writing as a mode of thinking. This chapter will help teachers understand the theory as well as specific strategies of literacy learning across the curriculum and the effects of reading and writing on the learning of content knowledge.

The Use of Literacy as a Tool to Learning

It seems that much of what's taught in history classes is the exchange of political power, the expression of which is traced by the campaigns of war. Students learn dates, generals, contributing causes, and decisive battles, yet beyond memories of yellow ribbons and coverage of the Gulf War on Channel One, they know very little of the realities of war. Connie Fleeger, a substitute teacher in Erie, Pennsylvania, decided to have her twelfth-grade students learn about war through writing. She asked them to complete a journal entry on the topic of "innocence." The next day in class the students shared their thoughts about innocence: "innocence is ignorance"; "innocence is purity," and so forth. In class, she read a poem dealing with World War II, a textbook war in the sense that neither she nor her students lived through the war. The poem is "Innocence," by Thom Gunn:

> He ran the course and as he ran he grew,
> And smelt his fragrance in the field. Already,
> Running he knew the most he ever knew,
> The egotism of a healthy body.
>
> Ran into manhood, ignorant of the past:
> Culture of guilt and guilt's vague heritage,
> Self-pity and the soul; what he possessed
> Was rich, potential, like the bud's tipped rage.
>
> The Corps developed, it was plain to see,
> Courage, endurance, loyalty, and skill
> To a morale firm as morality,
> Hardening him to an instrument, until
>
> The finitude of virtues that were there
> Bodied within the swarthy uniform
> A compact innocence, childlike and clear,
> No doubt could penetrate, no act could harm.

When he stood near the Russian partisan
Being burned alive, he therefore could behold
The ribs wear gently through the darkening skin
And sicken only at the Northern cold,

Could watch the fat burn with a violet flame
And feel disgusted only at the smell,
And judge that all pain finishes the same
As melting quietly by his boots it fell.

After reading the poem, Connie asked the students to respond to a checklist of statements about the poem and about war. The checklist elicits opinions rather than testing reading comprehension. Its directions ask the students to place a check beside the statements they agree with:

1. Because of the positive traits of the young soldier—"courage, endurance, loyalty, and skill," most people would consider him to be a good person.
2. After witnessing the torture of the Russian, the young soldier is still innocent.
3. War is simply legalized murder.
4. Nothing is worth dying for.
5. The difference between right and wrong is largely a matter of one's point of view.
6. The end justifies the means.
7. There is no more dangerous kind of a person than an unthinking "tool" who obeys orders innocently and without question.
8. Man is basically evil.

Connie formed the students into groups of three or four, allowing them time to compare their responses, and before long saw heated discussions begin concerning the poem and the responses. Her students followed the activity by reporting to the class as a whole what their group found worthy of discussion and by writing a brief summary of response in their journals. The students talked about the nature of war, the bravery of soldiers, and the need to defend one's homeland. Connie's students never worried about the rhyme scheme of the poem, its meter, or poetic figures of speech; they were too busy experiencing the power of the language in the poem. The next day, Connie gave them a follow-up question for the journal, "If you were on a jury trying this soldier for a war crime—burning the Russian prisoner of war alive, would you place the blame on him, his officers, the training system, or his government?" Some of her students wished to read more war poems, and Connie satisfied their appetites by suggesting poems featuring people much like themselves, for example, Wilfred Owen's "Anthem to Doomed Youth" and Randall Jarrell's "The Death of the Ball Turret Gunner." The students in Connie's class approached the study of war and battles with a different sensitivity because of her writing-to-learn activities.

The Importance of Schema in Building Knowledge

Everything we learn, both in and out of the classroom, is based on something we already know. The traditional paradigm, one still operating in many classrooms today, assumes that teachers must give students knowledge, or transmit knowledge through lecture and reading. Whole language teachers believe that learning happens in a different way, as discussed in Chapter 1. Knowledge is actively constructed by each learner, drawing upon both the learner's lifetime of experiences and the learner's theory of the world (Smith, 1988c).

If knowledge is constructed, then it's important for teachers to understand how to facilitate such construction, using what students bring to the learning situation. In a social studies class or a science class, for instance, students have individual theories of the world of history or chemistry based on their experience. For example, when students begin to study the history of the Civil War, they are not a roomful of blank tablets upon which teachers write the important facts about that conflict. Each student arrives in class with varying conceptions about war, civil conflict, the military, racial injustice, and democratic government. Just as Connie Fleeger found with her students, few traditional college-age students and even fewer secondary students will have actually experienced war; however, many of them will have seen movies about it (varying in quality from *Rambo* to *Glory*) and television news reports of military around the globe. One student's schema may be colored by family vacations to historic sites such as Gettysburg and Antioch. Another student's schema may be informed by a parent's tales of serving in the military, including perhaps details of duty in Vietnam. Another student may have no schema of war and instead draw heavily on a schema of opposing sides, much as might be found in the Superbowl conflict. Still another student might draw upon a personal-conflict schema, built up by living in a family where every member seems in conflict—parents against children, brother against brother, spouse against spouse—and where every day seems to bring another battle. All of these conceptions go into forming the individual's schema, the theory of the world that students each carry around in their heads, as Frank Smith (1988c) puts it so poetically. Students' schemata permit them to form hypotheses; from these hypotheses, genuine questions arise. Learning, then, is the result of discovering answers to these questions, testing, and rejecting or confirming individual hypotheses, broadening and making schemata more complex as knowledge about a topic is acquired. Teachers labor to broaden their students' world, building upon what they know or at least what they theorize about the subject.

This approach to teaching, affirming that students create and construct knowledge, means that they must be responsible for their own learning. They must be given opportunities to think and discover; they must be encouraged to take risks and test their ideas and hypotheses. It's the responsibility of the whole language teacher to facilitate this learning, to build on students' schemata and help learning become meaningful and authentic. If they are to truly learn about the Civil War for instance, not just memorize names and dates, then that war has to become real or meaningful to them. In other words, real learning is long-term and broadens a student's concept of the world.

Using Language to Facilitate Learning

How, then, do teachers facilitate such learning? The use of language, whether oral or written text, is central in learning. Whole language teachers insist upon the importance of oral language in secondary classrooms as students listen and speak to construct meaning. They also insist upon the importance of reading and writing—both the written text of the "experts" and that of the students—in the construction of meaning.

The Connection of Thought and Writing

When discussing writing, whole language teachers employ a comprehensive definition: when the mind is engaged, putting thoughts into words, words onto paper, writing occurs. Thus, writing may include note-taking, list-making, memos, letter writing, essay answers, artistic or narrative writing, and any other type of activity that involves putting thoughts into written words. What it *does not* include are activities that require little thought and are actually passive activities, such as copying and fill-in-the-blank exercises.

Lev Vygotsky (1978), an early twentieth-century Russian theorist, proposed that we hold various types of conversations with ourselves by which we think things through. Vygotsky calls these nonverbal conversations "inner speech," and through this inner speech, we rationalize, debate, connect and begin to formulate our thoughts. Drawing on the work of Vygotsky, Britton (1975) claims that speech symbolizes reality. To give some type of shape to experiences, we use what he calls "expressive speech." Through words, we take such experiences and make them real and concrete. Ann Berthoff (1979) believes that writing is the essence of thinking: "The work of the mind is in seeing relationships, finding forms, and making meaning. When we write, we do, in a particular sense, what we do when we make sense of the world. We compose by virtue of being human" (p. 12).

Donald Murray (1978) echoes Berthoff, explaining that language is used to discover what we are going to say. When we write, it is to find and create meaning. In fact, Peter Elbow (1973) holds that we don't start with meaning when we write; it is what we end up with. Writing is more than just personal thoughts and ideas in written form. It is not a transcript of brain waves; it is a way of constructing pathways, making connections, seeing new relationships, imagining what is not yet—writing is a way of learning.

Toby Fulwiler (1987) builds upon Vygotsky's notion that thought is born through words, pointing out that the key to knowing and understanding is the taking of bits and pieces of information and experiences that confront us and manipulating them until we can give them some type of verbal shape. We learn by this processing; talking with ourselves and with others is an important part of learning.

Janet Emig (1977) in her research with student writers says that writing represents a unique mode of learning. When we write, we manipulate our thoughts and in the process of writing we make our thoughts visible, allowing us to see them, interact with them, and change them as we so choose. Unlike speech, writing is an act of discovery where we can see our thoughts and ideas; as Vygotsky put it, the deliberate structure that writing provides produces a "web of meaning." Emig (1978) says that writing is the perfect self-regulating learning activity since writing connects the hand, the eye, and the brain. Thoughts are given form in writing by the hand; in the very act of creation, the eye perceives the written shapes and passes the information back to the brain to be interpreted. In the act of writing we become our own readers. Speech has similar cycle (mouth-ear-brain), yet its production is transitory and ephemeral. While a speaker may rehearse what will be said, there is rarely a postproduction record of what is said to be reviewed. A writer, however, may rehearse what will be written and always has the artifact of writing to review at the moment of creation as well as at a later time, if desired. Writing is the perfect feedback loop for learning.

The Use of Writing in Schools

Writing as a means of thinking or learning is not always a recognized aspect of school curricula. Although research has told educators that writing is a way of learning, James Britton (1975) and his colleagues who conducted a research study involving eleven- to eighteen-year-olds in British schools, found that very little of the writing done by secondary students was expressive writing, writing done in order to develop ideas. In other words, students did not use writing as a way to think. Most of the writing produced in these schools, over 60 percent, was communicative writing—students writing to communicate information that had been given to them by teachers or by texts. A little more than 20 percent of the writing was creative or poetic writing, and less than 10 percent was expressive writing. The rest of the writing actually consisted of exercises, such as fill-in-the-blank worksheets.

Arthur Applebee (1981) conducted similar research in American schools and produced parallel results: very little time is spent in expressive writing or using writing to learn. In fact, Applebee added another category of writing to his research—mechanical writing. This category, which included copying and fill-in-the-blank exercises, accounted for up to 24 percent of all writing done in the American schools studied.

Donald Graves (1983), trying to explain the lack of writing in general in American schools, pointed to a reliance upon transmission models of literacy instruction. When the model of learning changes to a transactional model, writing moves forward to take its proper place of importance in a whole language curriculum. Reading and writing in whole language classrooms are active learning processes; when students read they process information to arrive at meaning, and when they write they produce language to make meaning.

Writing is important to learning because it places learners at the center of their learning. It can be used to generate thought, to manipulate thought, and to refine thought. In order for any type of writing to be a tool to facilitate learning, however, the learner must view the writing as purposeful. Regurgitation of what the teacher or the textbook says is not using writing as a means of thinking and learning. Restating transmitted information is passive and requires no personal thought or connection to schema. However, if the writer is allowed and encouraged to write what is observed, to use writing to question, or to begin to make connections, then such writing is used to promote thinking and discovery.

Richard Grinstead, an art teacher at California University of Pennsylvania, was approached by a colleague in the English department,

William Murdick (1992), who suggested the idea of using writing in his Introduction to Drawing class. Bill Murdick convinced Richard that students in a drawing class, though often already independent learners, could profit from using writing to analyze and evaluate their own work and their own growth as artists, instead of relying solely on their teacher's evaluation. He tells us that Richard's students write briefly in journals every day at the end of the class, just before leaving the studio.

> At the beginning of the course, his students are given several prompts and told that they may write to any of them, or on any subject that struck their fancy:
>
> - What did you learn today and how did you learn it?
> - What kinds of problems are you having?
> - Describe your successes.
> - What have you seen other students or professional artists do that interests you?
> - How are your attitudes toward art, or yourself as an artist, changing? (Murdick, 1992, p. 4).

The purpose of these prompts is to encourage students to think deeply about what they are doing as they learn how to draw. Richard collects the journals daily, writing responses in them, returning them the next class. The writing done by the students and their professor allows both to monitor their learning, and in some cases, their failure to learn.

When Richard began to use journal writing, he received guidance in theory and practice from Bill, who acted as his mentor. Bill recorded Richard's observations and reflections:

> Richard believes, because of the writing, his students are thinking more about their art. The articulation of their drawing problems in the journals causes the students to look harder and retain the insight. Otherwise when examining their product at the end of the day, they might experience a moment's frustration, and then forget about it. These students, by contrast, intellectualize their problems and work them out, monitoring their learning instead of having their teacher do it for them. Their self-evaluation increases their learning. (p. 5)

In later notebook entries, Bill marked other observations by his colleague: "These students ask what they think of as 'stupid' questions in the privacy of their journals; this helps their teacher know what concepts to repeat or clarify in class. In their journals, you can see the changes in attitude toward art, from scared to confident" (p. 5).

It was not only the teacher who noticed the changes that writing brought to the art class. One student wrote in her final journal entry,

> Writing these journals made me realize how much I really did enjoy [the course]. It showed me things I really didn't know consciously until I wrote the journals. It made me realize my strengths and weaknesses. But most of all writing journal entries every day gave me confidence in myself. Because I am very modest, I never give myself much credit. But writing the entries forced [me] into taking the credit along with the criticism of my work. (p. 8)

Another student concluded, "I thought this journal idea was a good move. You get to express yourself when otherwise you wouldn't say anything" (p. 8). The significance of that closing remark was not lost upon Bill, an English teacher who believes in the role writing plays in getting students actively involved in their education—"You get to express yourself when otherwise you wouldn't say anything" (p. 8).

Why Aren't All Teachers Using Writing-to-Learn?

Many, including James Britton and his team of researchers, have questioned why writing-to-learn is not encouraged in public schools. Critical thinking, one of the outcome-based goals in school curriculums today, is what separates those who think, discover, and create from passive learners, and the vehicle to such creative thought is expressive writing, or writing-to-learn. Why then is so little of it being done? Perhaps the reason is political. If students are allowed to question and to think, to participate in "liberating education"—to use the expression of Paulo Freire (1970)—the result could be dangerous to the social, economic, and political structure of the existing society. Such reasoning leads us to suspect that the aim of education is not the creation of an informed citizenry but a country of mindless automatons. Another explanation is simpler but just as disturbing in another way. If the reason is not political, then the reason must be that teachers simply have a limited understanding of the power that written language has on thinking. Since writing in schools has traditionally been minimal, many teachers are themselves products of an educational system that used writing in very restricted ways. If students are to be afforded the opportunity of using writing-to-learn and are to be given opportunities to use writing as a mode of thinking, then teachers must understand the role and power of language in the classroom and be willing to open their classrooms to questioning and risk-taking. Whole language teachers are doing just that.

Classroom Strategies for Writing-to-Learn

All too often secondary students go through their schooling with few opportunities to use writing-to-learn and are understandably fearful of writing. Students become accustomed to writing for the teacher or writing for evaluation; they rarely see writing as a way to discover or writing-to-learn as a vehicle to thinking. Teachers must first help students feel comfortable with techniques that encourage students to put their thoughts down on paper in some form.

The Use of Freewriting

Over the last two decades, theorists such as Peter Elbow (1973) and Ken Macrorie (1984) have provided strategies to get students writing. One simple yet effective strategy, discussed by both Elbow and Macrorie, is freewriting. The purpose of this activity is simply to generate thought, and the directions are equally straightforward: write without stopping—without concern for punctuation, spelling, or even coherence—for a limited amount of time. For example, after a class discussion or after the reading of a text or piece of literature, the teacher can ask students to write for five or ten minutes about their thoughts about and reactions to the subject. Freewriting gives students an opportunity to write just as they think, simply to generate text, and although it has been used primarily in English classes, freewriting works well in most content-area classes.

For many writers, one of the most difficult tasks is to begin; however, freewriting relieves that anxiety because there is no beginning in the traditional sense of that word. Writers simply write, and when writing to learn, meaning is discovered as thoughts spill out on paper. When using such a strategy in the classroom, students should be attuned to the idea that they're writing to discover. One way to convey this message is to make certain that such writing is free of any evaluation on the teacher's part, placing the emphasis on thinking, on generating thoughts through writing. Even when asking a question as a prompt for the writing, as in a focused freewriting, the teacher should not give the impression of looking for a "correct" answer to the question. The purpose is not to organize or to write for anyone else but to generate thought—to use writing as a way to think. In a literature class, for example, the teacher might ask students to freewrite their reactions to a character in a novel or a situation they've been reading or talking about. Terrie St. Michel (1992), of South Mountain High School in Phoenix, Arizona, uses freewriting at the beginning of each class. She turns off the lights, projects a writing prompt on the wall with an overhead, starts a cassette tape of soothing music, and once the tardy bell has rung, sets a kitchen timer for six minutes. Many of her students begin writing as soon as they enter the classroom, and all of her students have learned to begin writing quietly once the timer has been set. Terrie doesn't answer questions, give directions, or write out-of-class passes during this time. Although the writing prompts range from "Summarize yesterday's discussion about *Macbeth*" and "Write down everything you know about mythology" to "Define the key components of the writing process" and "Describe what color you feel like today," her students know they are always free to choose their own topics.

Terrie says,

My primary purpose for having students write each day is to get them thinking. However, I have found there are other benefits. Year after year my students report that they look forward to the daily writing. Their reasons include having an opportunity to express their feelings, to relax, to focus on the subject (English), and to stimulate their thinking. . . . I respond to my students' writings as an interested reader. I make positive comments, ask questions, relate my own parallel experiences, and highlight the best of what is presented. In this way I foster trust and establish an open dialogue which carries over into other class interactions. (pp. 1–2)

Using freewriting to begin class is also a classroom management tool, as Terrie St. Michel employs it. The six minutes of writing provide a transition from the social nature of the hallways to the educational nature of the classroom; it "enables my students to come in and tune in," she explains. And her students are typical of any large urban high school with a mixed student population—56 percent Hispanic, 26 percent African–American, and 18 percent Anglo—a school making a commitment to reducing the dropout and absentee rate and increasing the number of students who continue through graduation. Terrie credits writing with playing a key role in improving the students' academic achievements. "Writing," she says, "has many merits and, ultimately, can be implemented by all teachers in all content areas with all students regardless of age, diversity, and ability. We can use writing to help define the parameters of our classrooms in meaningful ways" (p. 3). The use of freewriting at the beginning of class contributes to creating an entrance; everything that follows, for the most part, is direction, adjustment, and response. "I work with seniors, students who are often set in their ways with inflexible expectations about their learning and who are not easily persuaded to acquire new behaviors," says Terrie. "The first six minutes are crucial, and in a short period of time, my students begin to see the value of this activity; and, as they embrace its worth, their behavior changes. This transformation requires only an openness to their expressions and a few minutes to respond to them, through writing. In short, it's the only magic I know how to do" (p. 4).

Teachers in other disciplines can use freewriting for the same purpose—to help students think. James Moffett (1981) points out that writing can be used in all content areas to teach all subjects. When writing, the writer is actually making knowledge. In an introductory drawing class taught by Ray Dunlevy at California University of Pennsylvania, students used freewriting at the end of the class period to reflect upon, among other things, what they had learned that day. One student, early in the semester, wrote about his vague dissatisfaction with a drawing project, "I know for sure now that if I had to make a living from my artwork, in this particular part of drawing, I would starve to death. I am still trying to do my best, but it doesn't seem to be coming to me. I am having trouble blending light and dark areas together" (Murdick, 1992, p. 16). The feeling this student expresses is a common one, a dissatisfaction quickly shrugged off before quitting for the day. What is remarkable is that this student, who must write an entry at the end of the class, finally gets down to figuring out what *it* means in his statement, "it doesn't seem to be coming to me" (p. 16). The act of writing helps him to name his trouble—blending light and dark. Writing brought knowledge, the identification of his difficulty, and such a realization is a step toward solving the problem.

Critics of writing-to-learn charge that the approach only works in small classes that enjoy the luxury of not having an extraordinary amount of content material to cover for an exam or curriculum requirements. Colleagues at California University of Pennsylvania, Phil Schaltenbrand and Richard Miecznikowski—art teachers who are traditional in their method of slide-show lectures, classes in which their students sit in a darkened room taking notes while listening to their teacher discuss a masterpiece reproduced by a slide projected on a screen—were also approached by William Murdick (1992) and asked to make a commitment to employ writing-to-learn strategies in their art appreciation and art history courses. Throughout a semester they asked their students to write in class, attempting to imitate the teacher's sophisticated responses to various pieces of art.

Students began with a personal, expressionistic kind of written response in which they took note of the holistic effect of what they saw in the artwork. The in-class writing didn't constitute direct exam preparation, and the exams didn't ask questions on artworks that were written about during the writing-to-learn sessions. The in-class writing wasn't done as an aid to memorization. Instead, the writing emphasized aesthetic evaluation—a kind of procedural knowledge—rather than factual recall of content. From the results they saw on their final examinations, Phil and Richard are convinced that, whatever other benefits students may derive, by writing about art in a manner similar to the way the teacher talks about art, students develop a keener interest in the subject, become more engaged by the course, become more involved in their own education, and show up to class more alert and better able to follow the teacher's lectures. The difference in learning that these two art teachers witnessed came from the student's increased engagement with the subject, an engagement supported by writing (Murdick, 1992).

The Use of Journals and Logs

Another vehicle for using writing-to-learn is the classroom journal or log. Used in composition and literature classrooms for several decades, journals in subjects other than English have begun to see more common use. The purposes for using journals or logs are varied, but they all have one thing in common—they are a vehicle for students to think, a medium of discovery and thought.

There are many definitions of *journals* and *logs*. Some teachers use the terms interchangeably, while others think of journals in English composition classes as accumulations of freewriting that might later be used as topics for developed pieces of writing and logs as accumulations of writing about content knowledge in other areas such as science and social studies. Still others distinguish between reader-response logs in English classes and journals kept in history class. Either term is meant to describe an accumulation of writing generated for the purpose of thinking; so, for the sake of consistency, we will use the term *journal* throughout this chapter to refer to all types of journals and logs.

Journals exhibit their own language features. For example, the language used in journals will be much like written-down speech (Britton, 1975), and writers will use informal word choice and short, simple expressions. Language shortcuts such as abbreviations and contractions will be common as will the frequent use of the pronoun *I*, indicating that what is being written is personal reflection. Lapses in conventional punctuation will be found, as well as experimentation with forms and styles not used in more formal types of writing.

Toby Fulwiler (1987) believes that teachers will find some or all of the following in their students' journals, as students become more adept at thinking critically through their writing:

- *Observations.* Student writers often write in journals about what they see, trying to make sense of the world through these observations, much the way researchers in sociology and anthropology would.

- *Questions.* Learning often is the result of questioning and the searching for answers or possibilities. Journal writers will often use questioning in their writing to generate thought or work through uncertainties.

- *Speculation.* Writers will use journals as a vehicle for wondering, writing equivalents to "let's suppose" and "I wonder if." In journals, answers are not important, the thinking process is.

- *Self-Awareness.* While writing in journals, students often discover how they feel about things, how they are like and different from others, and what they have feelings about.

- *Digression.* Thinking rarely happens in an organized way. Journal writers often digress in order to tie in or connect what they are thinking about to how they already understand their world.

- *Synthesis.* There are times when journal writers are able to pull ideas together while in the process of writing.

- *Revision.* As writers work through ideas and as they learn more about the world, their schemata enlarge. Journal writers often look back on earlier writings and write, "but now I know this, because. . . ."

- *Information.* Often novice journal writers use journals to record information they've been given because they don't trust their own thoughts. As students become more comfortable with writing as a mode of thinking, information is found in journal entries as support for original thought or understanding.

Terry Wansor, who teaches English at Hempfield High School in Pennsylvania, uses response journals in a class called The Psychology of Language. Although this is not a writing course per se, Terry recognizes the power of writing as a mode of thinking. The purpose of these daily journals is to observe and record observations that apply to the course content and its concepts or to refute such concepts according to observations from the students' lives. Basically,

Terry explains, the students see these writings as "a search for truth. The entries basically tell what, when, where, who, and most importantly why or why not. The purpose is to take learning out of the classroom and into the real world."

One student, Stacey, writes the following entry:

"Tonight when I was talking on the phone, I noticed something I do that I've never noticed before. I am a very big user of crutch words. The one in particular that I use most (Well, its actually two put together to make one word) is 'like, um.' I swear, I must use it in every sentence!" Stacey did not simply learn a definition of crutch words in class; she was able to recognize it as a part of her own speech, thus making the definition meaningful and authentic. She used writing for observation as well as self-awareness. Stacey continues:

"After I actually thought about it, I tried to go without saying it. I could not do it! When I say 'like um' it seems to make me feel secure and safe in some way. . . . When I'm nervous it is something I can rely on." In this passage, Stacey seems to be synthesizing, pulling things together and discovering a reason for her use of the crutch word.

"Like um," Stacey continues, "does seem to be a crutch word for most teenage girls, though. I think it possibly started back in those valley girl days when all the girls used to say, 'like, you know' all the time." At this point, Stacey is speculating about the origin of this phrase, something that she thought of while she was writing, not something she was taught in class.

Journals are used for many reasons: to help students make connections, to provide a way for them to think and question, to serve as a place to record observations, or to give writers an opportunity to generate topics and ideas for future formal pieces of writing. However, journal writing does not occur spontaneously. Teachers must provide time and opportunity for it, allowing students to write in class and writing along with them when possible. Modeling will illustrate for students a teacher's commitment and belief in journals, especially when the activity is shared and experienced as a member of a learning community. Students should share entries with each other and their teacher, always without fear of criticism or evaluation. If students are going to think on paper, ideas must be respected and risk-taking must be encouraged. Teachers would do well to avoid grading journals, in the sense of evaluating them for content; however, because students have been conditioned through years of schooling to believe that anything worthwhile must "count," teachers may wish to assign points for completion or for number of pages written. Kate Kessler (1992), a teacher at Chambersburg High School in central Pennsylvania, sets a minimum number of pages for her students to write during a unit in order to receive full credit. What she found is that her students often write double the minimum number of pages, and in fact, her students seem to forget that there is a minimum. Kate's students know that she values the journal by having the activity count in her grade book, the traditional signal by which students know what each particular teacher considers as important. More importantly, her students soon understand that the purpose of journal writing is to help them think, and they tacitly understand that writing is a vehicle for achieving this.

Reader-Response Journals

Whole language teachers, who believe in a definition of literature and literary response as discussed in Chapter 3, find reader-response journals a way for readers to think using writing, reacting as readers do to any piece of literature or text. The success of reader-response journals rests almost entirely on the attitude of the teacher. If a teacher views reading as the decoding of information, then response to reading can only be a predetermined exercise, the location of otherwise hidden meaning. However, if the teacher views reading as the creation of meaning and believes that each reader brings to the reading a unique perspective, based on who he or she is, then response journals become a way to communicate and share those thoughts, ideas, questions, and perceptions. As stated by Alan Purves and Richard Beach (1972), "At the center of the curriculum are not the works of literature . . . but rather the mind as it meets the book" (p.27). Again, whether or not response journals are used successfully comes down to a question of one's philosophy.

Reader-response journals are a way for readers to genuinely respond to what they are reading. In English class, such response is usually about literature read in or out of class. In other subject areas, students have opportunities to respond as readers—questioning an essay they read in history class; connecting a science reading about ecology to an environmental problem in their neighborhood; or reacting to the psychology of politics while reading about the presidential campaign in world government class. Reader-response journals give students a chance to "discuss" their reading through writing, much the way readers will talk about a book or article they have read. Sometimes response journals are meant only for the writer, serving as a way to sort out ideas and questions, not so much looking for answers as taking the opportunity to think in the very act of expression, much the way we think aloud in conversation.

Reader-response journals can take a variety of forms; there is no one right way to approach them. Students can write in spiral notebooks, loose-leaf notebooks, or whatever suits their purpose best.

They can write daily, weekly, following a major assignment, or whenever they see a need. The theory behind using response journals is important, not the external form it takes. Nancie Atwell (1988) crystallizes this perspective: "When we invite readers' minds to meet books in our classrooms, we invite the messiness of human response—personal prejudices, personal tastes, personal habits, personal experience" (p. 154). Through the use of response journals, we invite students to make a reading their own, and happily there is no single and correct way to do this.

Because readers often like to share responses with other readers, the response journal may serve as a vehicle for readers to share perceptions with each other and with their teacher, who responds not as an evaluator, but as a fellow reader, respecting the interpretations of others, yet having interpretations of his or her own. Students must be reassured that all responses will be treated as correct, in the sense of honest and personal, and that thinking on paper is a viable way to create meaning. In other words, teachers must foster risk-taking as students respond, assuring them that they need not fear having to think like everyone else or like their teacher. This is not to say that journals and writing-to-learn encourage weirdness for the sake of difference or egocentrism. Meaning will be negotiated as students read the interpretations and ideas of others and begin to look at the topic or text from a perspective that was, prior to reading another's journal, beyond their experience. Sharing response journals can open up worlds that a single reader could not envision alone. An excellent way to share responses is through the use of dialogue journals.

Dialogue Journals

Logistically, it is nearly impossible for teachers to respond to every journal entry. Not only would teachers burn out quickly but the journals would become yet another exercise or activity completed only because teachers will read and evaluate them. If journals are written solely for the teacher—regardless of whether they are called response journals or learning logs—they become a performance rather than a response. One type of journal, however, uses the power of conversation to promote response—the dialogue journal. Whether used in English class or any content area, dialogue journals provide students and teachers with the opportunity to use writing in much the same way as we use conversation—to negotiate thoughts and ideas through the use of language. Instead of oral conversation, the dialogue takes place in writing.

As with other types of journals, there is no one method for setting up dialogue journals, but students are usually asked to purchase a spiral notebook with a double margin or to draw in margins, dividing the page in half lengthwise before writing. Typically after reading or discussion, students respond by writing on one side of the pages in their journals, expressing their ideas, concerns, reactions, and connections as they would in other journal experiences. Then students share their dialogue journals with each other and with their teacher. The teacher provides time for the students to read each other's entries and to respond, using the other side of the double-margin page. The responder, be it teacher or student, must actually listen to what the writer has to say. After listening (in this case, reading), the responder writes back in the journal, sharing a bit of self—opinions and ideas, building on what the writer has said—intent upon carrying on a conversation. The journal's owner is then free to write a further reply. The purpose is to carry on a conversation, not to make a judgment about the thought or idea.

The possibilities for such journals are very powerful, as we can see by the experiences of Kate Kessler (1992) and her students at Chambersburg High School. Kate's students wrote dialogue journals in response to two works dealing with the Holocaust, Anne Frank's *Diary of a Young Girl* and Elie Wiesel's *Night*, sharing their reactions with self-chosen partners. The dialogue journals gave students opportunities to respond as real readers. Kate found herself impressed by a pair of boys who dialogued about Wiesel's preface for *Night*, analyzing why Francois Mauriac wrote the preface and questioning whether beginning the book with a certain character was effective:

> I think this is a great book so far. I wonder why that special journalist captured Elie's sympathy. What do you think?
>
> *I think the reason is because he was a young Jew, and he had seen many other young Jews killed. Also he wanted to publish his book, but no one wanted to publish it. I wonder how old this reporter is.*
>
> Elie calls him a child. Do you think they started off the book right? I mean they start it with Moshe the Beadle when he is not really a main character. Also, the beginning is the only time that Moshe is in the book. Even if this is weird, I really do like how they start this book off. (p. 234)

Kate was also impressed by a pair of girls who used their dialogue journal to make personal connections with the characters:

> . . . That boy Juliek must have really loved his violin. To risk trying to bring it with him—could you imagine the pain and suffering? At least Juliek got to play one last song on his violin before

he died. How sad. This book is too emotional! The next thing you know someone will be jumping off a bridge because they can't handle it.

Some people always have that one special thing that they love. Just like I have a porcelain [clown] that my mom got me about four years ago for Christmas. I got it, and I'm so protective of it. My mom thinks I'm crazy, and she says it's just a stupid old clown. I'm really not sure why it means so much to me. I'm sure you have something like that too. I would probably risk trying to take my clown, too. . . . I think it's good that Juliek got to play the violin one more time. I would want to hold my clown one more time before I died. (pp. 195–196)

Kate also found that her students "wrote themselves into dialectic discovery just by the process of writing to someone." She says that one student "answers herself before her partner even responds":

If I was in a camp and the leader was homosexual I think I'd be staying away from her. Now—the poor kids who were molested by the camp leader were (if you think about it) probably "selected" to be killed. If the leaders couldn't trust them to keep their mouths shut, they could probably kill them once they had the power. . . . I was also thinking about the guy in the very beginning of the book who told Elie to say he was eighteen and told his father to say he was fifty. I think he knew what would go on with children under eighteen. That was really nice of him. Now that I think about it—I see why he did it to Elie. I still haven't figured out why he told Elie's dad to say he was ten years older than he actually is. Maybe so he would look younger than his age and the Germans would think he was stronger than the average fifty year old and then keep him longer. That's a real idea. I think I've figured it out! FINALLY! (p. 197)

Kate was most impressed by the inquiring, dialectic dialogue exchanged by two extremely shy, quiet girls who had not volunteered one spoken word all year:

Sounds like he's pretty angry at God. That is wrong.

I don't think it's wrong to be mad at God, just that you think hard on why you feel that way. . . . I agree with Anne that crying can bring a lot of relief. . . .

I know that crying helps bring out a lot of my relief too. Some people are afraid to cry. I don't know why though because crying is natural. (pp. 200–201)

Kate said that real, dynamic dialogue was found embedded in the more cautious summarizing and analyzing typical of beginning dialogue journal entries; the two girls wrote about what were, for them, vital social issues:

> I kind of felt the same way Anne did when her father started paying more attention to her sister than to her. I thought my dad did the same thing with my brother—spent more time with him. I told him so, but he never believed it. . . .
>
> . . . *I know what you mean when your father pays more attention to others instead of you. It feels really bad.*
>
> . . . I think Anne's family is too hard on her. They seem to criticize everything she does. Some of the things they blame on her could be turned and pointed at them if they would think. . . .
>
> . . . *I know how she feels when she's being blamed for things. It hurts. Words hurt. . . . (p. 206)*

These dialogue exchanges "might not have been created in a classroom where social dynamics were controlled by the teacher," Kate concludes (p. 206).

Reading and Writing Across the Curriculum

Writing across the curriculum has been advocated in high schools and colleges for the last several decades, but implementation is often met with frustration and misinformation. Some of this can be attributed to a misunderstanding, or perhaps a lack of understanding of the philosophy that informs the writing-across-the-curriculum movement, or WAC, as it is commonly referred to. High schools and colleges are almost always compartmentalized with departmental subject areas taught in limited time segments (forty to seventy-five minutes) and in isolation from all other disciplines. Little communication exists between departments, and students rarely see connections between courses, even the most obvious ones such as American Literature and American History. For example, English teachers when teaching Walt Whitman might traditionally assume that their students have a working knowledge of the American Civil War, and history teachers when teaching the Civil War might traditionally argue that they don't have the time or the interest to teach Walt Whitman or *The Red Badge of Courage*. Writing across the curriculum embraces cross-curricular learning, not merely the creation of a written product; WAC provides opportunities for writers to express thought, thereby enabling them to use writing as a mode of learning.

C. H. Knoblauch and Lil Brannon (1983) point out that many of the pitfalls that face WAC programs exist, not because writing shouldn't be used for learning in all subject areas, but because many WAC programs have been imposed on teachers who misunderstand the transactional philosophy behind such programs and the concept of writing-to-learn. Too often students are expected to write what the teacher thinks, instead of what they themselves think, and their writings are even corrected for mechanics and surface features, concerns that should not be addressed in this type of writing. What teachers using WAC should be looking for is an understanding of what their students are or are not learning. Such an approach to writing is a wonderful way for teachers to assess not only their students' understandings but the strengths of their own teaching as well.

As with any strategy that is based on a philosophy of teaching and learning, WAC cannot be imposed; it must be accepted and implemented by teachers who understand its purpose. WAC is more than its application in many high schools and universities—the purpose of WAC is not simply giving essay tests instead of multiple-choice exams and assigning a final paper or even using journals. The purpose of WAC is to provide an opportunity for students to bridge the gap between their language and the discourse community of a specific discipline. The purpose of such courses is neither to make all teachers into English teachers nor to make students better writers, although this is often a secondary result for some students, due to the simple fact that they are writing more. A teacher who believes that writing is a mode of thinking empowers students to use their own language to think about a particular idea, concept, or discipline. For example, students interested in biology must first write about biology in their own language while they read and learn about biology. Students who write in content courses use technical vocabulary in context as they are writing, as it becomes necessary, instead of memorizing technical vocabulary in lists. Gradually some will enter the discourse world of the biologist, with vocabulary and purposes specific to that discipline.

Students in courses where teachers use WAC begin to think on a much higher level than when they're sitting in a class taking notes from a teacher's lecture. When students are allowed to question, connect, and apply what they're reading about or observing or discussing, they often discover that writing to think through concepts brings a deeper understanding of context.

Integrated Learning

Secondary and postsecondary schools are not set up for collabora-tion; they are compartmentalized with each department responsible for teaching in its own content area. We know that students don't learn this way. John Kent and Thomas Trevisani, Jr. (1989), chairs of the Social Studies and the English Departments of the Arlington Public Schools in Massachusetts, began a writing-across-the-curriculum project with the belief in writing as a means to learn content in any discipline. Their project expanded to one of interde-partmental cooperation—much as they had accomplished with English and Social Studies—for planning and responding to curric-ular issues from a school-wide perspective, rather than from a discipline-based one.

Teachers in many secondary schools and colleges, aware of the fact that learning is cross-curricular, have devised what are called thematic or integrated units of instruction to teach in two or more courses. These units reflect thinking, goals, and concepts that are common to different subject areas, and the topics chosen for the-matic units are often broadly required by the district or the depart-ment. For example, the history department may be told that they must cover the Second World War, and the English department must cover the novel with emphasis on characterization, theme, plot, and conflict. Based on the broad theme, "World War II," history and English teachers have an opportunity to integrate learning across both content areas, working as a team, using literature and writing to build knowledge in social studies.

Thematic units also provide students with many choices about how to pursue their learning, engaging them in learning what is meaningful and interesting. Although one novel may be required reading during class time, students may be given time and opportu-nity to read novels or nonfiction works of their own choice, reading in a more specialized area of interest relating to the broad theme. The classroom, both in social studies and in English, becomes a commu-nity of learners who read, write, discuss, research, and share.

Whole language teachers, knowing that learning must be pur-poseful, look to student interest as a way of identifying thematic units. Although units may often need to be chosen based on curric-ular requirements, themes can emerge from student interest. Once such themes emerge, a teacher might contact fellow teachers in other disciplines to test whether there is an area of interest across the cur-riculum. When choosing a theme, however, teachers would do well to choose one broad enough to incorporate many subtopics, books, articles, resources, and activities, so that even within the theme, the students still have personal choice.

Planning a Thematic Unit

Before beginning a cross-discipline unit, teachers and students must plan together. A good way to begin to conceptualize the unit is to use webbing, a brainstorming of free-associated words that defines the topic by identifying categories and subcategories. Brainstorming helps teachers and students identify resources that will be needed, set up time schedules, and generate student groups to conduct research in areas of common interest. For example, using the curricular requirement to study World War II, the brainstormed ideas might look like this on the chalkboard:

World War II

Hitler	Pearl Harbor	German concentration camps	
American concentration camps		army	generals
Eisenhower	draft	patriotism	campaigns
Holocaust	Japan	death	hate	Roosevelt

After generating such a list, the students and teachers use the ideas to construct a web, a pictorial representation of relationships. The web might end up looking something like that shown in Figure 5–1.

The teachers, along with school librarians, can suggest readings like the ones mentioned on the web, and students will often find fiction and nonfiction books related to the overall theme on their own. As the web illustrates, some students might research a subtopic like the bombing of Japanese cities and read books such as *Looking the Tiger in the Eye: Confronting the Nuclear Threat* and *Barefoot Gen: The Day After*. Others might research American concentration camps by reading books like *Manzanar*. Students share information through discussion, projects, presentations, and they become experts on their subtopics. While students work on their chosen topics, teachers facilitate by providing mini-lessons, speakers, movies, and readings about World War II in general.

Of course, teachers could come to class with a prepared web by simply consulting the school curriculum guide or a teacher's manual for a listing of topic headings. However, this violates the philosophy of writing-to-learn: to create meaning, not to cover material. The web will and should vary from class to class, even across classes taught by the same teachers during the same year. As the unit progresses, learning social studies and language will happen in both classes, and the notion of considering some projects English Class Activities and others as Social Studies Activities will be seen as artificial and unnecessary.

As with everything about whole language, there is no one right way to set up integrated units, and teachers must often work within

Figure 5–1
Web of World War II Unit

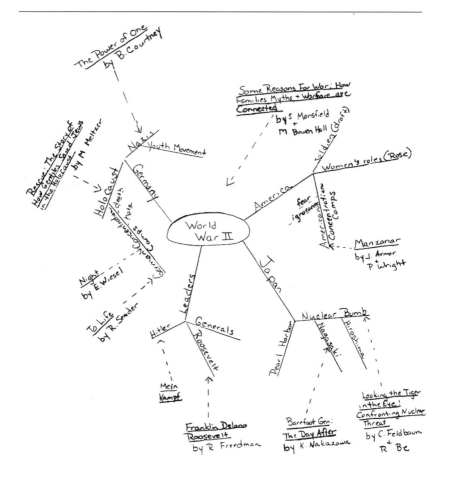

a structure that has been imposed on them by others. Nevertheless, we offer a few guidelines:

1. When using a novel as the core of a unit, talk to the students first to make sure the majority of them have not read it previously and be prepared to suggest novels or nonfiction that might be appropriate and interesting to students.

2. Use the school's required curriculum as well as student-interest surveys to help choose an appropriate topic of study. The theme should have many possible connections and be appropriate for conceptual learning, working independently and in groups. It

should naturally and meaningfully tie in with several areas of the curriculum. Remember themes emerge from student interest.

3. Compile a web or semantic map according to academic subjects or topics and begin to brainstorm how each subject could appropriately relate to the theme.

4. Compile goals and objectives for the integrated unit. The overall goal should be broad, and the objectives will develop from both teacher and students.

5. Plan possible activities that would be appropriate to meet each objective. Remember, a whole language class is student-centered and the teacher's responsibility is to facilitate learning; therefore these planned activities are *possibilities*. Planning for any unit should be flexible and open to change according to the needs presented as the students become engaged and involved in the topic.

6. Gather resources (books, maps, audio-visual material, software, speakers, etc.) and create centers or resource areas. Although units will begin with materials anticipated for each content area, the resources will grow as the students add others that they come across during the unit.

7. Engage students in various activities throughout the class and the unit. Be flexible in scheduling. While students participate in individual and group projects, plan to assess their needs, evaluate the strengths and weaknesses of activities, and adjust the teaching plans to meet the needs of the students.

8. Design a daily schedule to help plan ways to teach language across the curriculum, providing opportunities for students to experiment, research, think, discuss, and question as they read, write, and learn. Remember that learning is a process, and these activities are not isolated lessons. Let philosophy guide planning.

9. Assessment is an ongoing part of teaching. Think about how to assess the progress of the students so that assessment "drives" daily teaching plans. Evaluation is an end product of ongoing assessment, and the best evaluation involves both the students and the teacher. Include assessment and evaluation strategies for each content area in the unit, and when doing so, refer back to the objectives.

10. Integrated units involve a great deal of work on everyone's part, but they are exciting nevertheless. Consider a culminating activity that would be a celebration of what was learned and that could be shared with parents and/or others in the building.

For Further Exploration

1. Begin keeping a response journal to a reading you are engaged in. Periodically add an entry addressing how keeping the log is affecting you as a reader; as a writer; as a learner.

2. Visit a school that professes to be engaged in writing-across-the-curriculum. How is WAC defined by administrators in this school? How do the teachers define it? (Ask several teachers across disciplines.) How do the students define it?

3. Visit a classroom that uses journals as a part of the curriculum. How are the journals used? Interview students. How do they view this experience? How do they feel about keeping journals? What do they think they're learning from the experience? Interview the teacher. How is he or she involved in student journaling? Are journals evaluated? If so, how?

4. Visit a middle school or high school that has team teaching. How is the school organized? Does team teaching in this school facilitate teaching across the curriculum? If so, how? If not, why not?

5. As a group or a class, try to organize an integrated unit that crosses content areas. It would be best to actually experience this, but if that is not possible, simulate a unit for secondary students. Remember, student input is essential.

Related Readings for Further Thought and Exploration

Elbow, P. (1973). *Writing without teachers*. New York: Oxford University Press.
Shows the value and relative ease of using writing as a mode of thinking. A landmark book although it is twenty years old.

Fulwiler, T. (1988). *The journal book*. Portsmouth, NH: Boynton/Cook.
Collects ideas and examples of how journaling can be used across the curriculum. A valuable book for teachers in every content area.

Gere, A. R. (Ed.). (1985). *Roots in the sawdust: Writing to learn across the disciplines*. Urbana, IL: National Council of Teachers of English.
Presents a collection of essays aimed at using writing to learn strategies across the various content areas—for example, mathematics, history, art, foreign language, science, and philosophy.

Pappas, C., Kiefer, B., & Levstik, L. (1990). *An integrated language perspective in the elementary school*. White Plains, NY: Longman.

Provides practical ideas for teachers to use when implementing an integrated approach to teaching. For any grade level, even though the examples given are for elementary grades.

Routman, R. (1991). *Invitations: Changing as teachers and learners K–12*. Portsmouth, NH: Heinemann.
Offers practical suggestions to help teachers who are trying to put theory concerning language learning and teaching across the disciplines into practice.

Chapter Six

What About Grading?
Assessment and Evaluation in Whole Language Classrooms

The range of possibilities for evaluating and grading is limited only by our imaginations. I think it's entirely possible to back away from all formal testing and still meet institutional record-keeping requirements. And certainly there must be room for student input into the process.

— Judith M. Newman

Questions for Thought/Journal Entries

1. Think back to your experiences as a high school student. What do you remember about report-card time? How did you feel about the grades you received? Did you understand what they meant? Were grades important to you? Why or why not?

2. Name some of the standardized tests you have taken in your life as a student (SAT, GRE, NTE). How do you feel about such exams? Why did you take them? What did these exams tell about you as a learner? As a person? As a teacher?

3. Why do teachers give grades? What are the political reasons for grading? As a teacher, what is your responsibility when grading a student? What are some different ways teachers approach grading?

4. Is there a difference between evaluation and grading? Between assessment and evaluation? Between assessment and grading? If so, how would you explain the differences?

5. Do grades help or harm students? In what ways? What is the purpose of grading? Has that purpose changed over the years? Is that purpose different for different people? If so, how?

Introduction

Even teachers who are convinced about the worth of whole language are concerned about how they will be able to carry out the rigid methods of evaluation imposed by their districts, schools, and departments. This chapter will help teachers understand the place of evaluation and assessment in whole language classrooms. More importantly, it will help teachers use both assessment and evaluation effectively and realistically to become better teachers as they help their students to grow as learners.

The Report Card: Evaluation or Torture?

The report card is considered by many to be an instrument of torture. Issued periodically, normally four times a year, report cards document student performance with numerical or letter grades, usually arrived at by averaging a series of tests, quizzes, essays, and other assigned work administered throughout the marking period. These grades are taken seriously by school boards, supervisors, parents, institutions of higher learning, prospective employers, and the students themselves.

Report cards give students a mirror by which to see themselves. During her senior year in high school, our daughter Laura, although proud of the grades she received, covered herself for each coming marking period by saying as she handed us the card, "Now, don't expect this next time." Her friend, Leah—not as proud of her grades—retrieved the card from the mailbox each time, hiding it from her mother for weeks, knowing that the marks would sentence her to dishonor and imprisonment—being grounded. They both graduated and continued on to college, but both still live in terror, frightened that each semester's grades will brand them with a numerical statement of their worth, and that their cumulative grade-point average may haunt them throughout their entire eight semesters.

Report cards present an image of the student to parents as well. Beth, another friend of Laura's, always got 90s, but on her report card for the third marking period during her junior year, she got an 87 average. Her parents became upset about the report card, though we wondered about how they were interpreting it. Is a report card like a stock-market report—Beth's stock previously sold at 93 but at the closing bell, sold at 87, a drop of 6 points? Does a report card give them information like a pie chart—she knew 87 percent of what she should, but she somehow failed to learn 13 percent of it? And if so, was there something very important to know included in the missing 13 percent? It turns out the report card told them that she was spending too much time on what she loved most, her music lessons, and not enough time on her homework. Beth's younger sister, Louise, probably breathed a sigh of relief, having been compared unfavorably all her life to her older sister. Louise, who had to wait until fourth grade before seeing an A on a report card, would probably be happy with her sister's 87.

Report cards also present the teachers with an image of who they are as they fill them out each marking period. If teachers regard their students as little experiments to be kept track of, calculating their success rate in percentages, then perhaps the traditional assessment and evaluation marking system makes sense, in much the same way that giving a report card to a race horse, a baseball player, a skier makes sense—listing averages and performance scores. Yet, if teachers regard their students as learners who study under their guiding eyes, growing in maturity and ability, it no longer makes sense to evaluate them with objective tests and measurements. Students deserve praise and constructive criticism, especially in terms of their language abilities.

Report cards and grades are the product of a system of assessment and evaluation that has changed little since our grandparents went to school. Grades, in effect, become who we are as learners. Everyone has heard teachers, parents, and even students themselves say something to the effect that "he's a C student," or "she's a B student," as if this were enought to define who someone is. Yet ask any teacher, parent, or student what these definitions are, and they will answer with vague explanations such as "average" or "above-average" and even sweeping generalizations such as "superior" or "failure." Even allowing for such broad definitions, few teachers, parents, or students truly understand what the grades actually stand for. They may be based on notions such as the ones mentioned above (C equals average), or they may even be more "scientifically" based, determined by percentage scores, as Beth's were. But, realistically, they mean little, whether they are letter grades or percentages. To one social studies teacher, a B grade means one thing; to another teacher of the same subject in the same department in the same school, a B grade means something entirely different. The biggest problem with a subjective system of evaluation is that grades end up meaning nothing yet carrying an incredible amount of weight in determining how a student is perceived and what his or her future holds.

"Furthermore, . . . the tacit assumption [is] that the most important outcomes of schooling are measurable," says Elliot Eisner (1992), professor of Art and Education at Stanford University, "and that a common test or array of assessment tasks will lend themselves to a procedurally objective way to make meaningful measured comparisons" (p. 3). Eisner continues to say that such an assumption fails to recognize the limits of quantification in revealing what one has observed. "To describe a human being in numbers alone is to say *some* important things about that person's features. It is also to neglect those features that do not lend themselves to quantitative description, and the features neglected may be precisely those considered most important for particular purposes. If I want to purchase a pair of shoes for a friend, knowing my friend's shoe size is important, but it is also important to understand what kind of shoes my friend is likely to desire" (p. 3). Whole language teachers demand accountability; they know that numbers and percentages are abstract and stand for little; real assessment and evaluation require knowing students as people, being aware of their strengths and needs, and knowing how best to support their learning.

The History of Testing

Testing, usually thought to be an objective measurement of knowledge, has traditionally been used in both assessment and evaluation. Historically, testing has been accepted in public education in the United States since Colonial times (Hodges, 1977). That is to say, it has been generally agreed that learning in schools needs to be tested and that it's the responsibility of teachers to periodically check the academic performance of their students. However, there has been little agreement concerning the types of tests to be used to assess student learning. Since research studies have shown that grading on teacher-constructed tests is very subjective, most people would think that the tests that are preferable are those that ask a large number of questions whose answers can be standardized. In fact, for over 100 years, standardized tests have been used in elementary schools, high schools, colleges, and graduate schools for a variety of purposes

ranging from tracking to determining such things as a school's eligi-
bility for federal and state funding and a student's admission to university and graduate programs. However, almost since their incep-
tion, standardized tests have been met with criticism. Many feel that
such tests not only are used incorrectly but also are unfair to certain
groups, since the tests are designed for a "general" population and
usually ignore minority or underrepresented groups.

Despite the criticism, standardized tests are still being widely
used across the country. Although they vary in scope and purpose,
standardized tests fall into two categories—norm-referenced and
criterion-referenced tests. The purpose of norm-referenced tests is to
measure the standing of the test-taker within some known group,
such as all twelfth graders in the United States (Gronlund, 1985).
Norms for the test—set standards of achievement—have been
derived from the average scores of a large sample of people who represent the group being measured. Consequently, scores are reported
in percentiles placing the test-taker in relation to the larger sample
group. For example, after taking a norm-referenced test for mathematics in tenth grade, a student might receive a score of 69, which
would indicate that he or she did better than 68 percent of all students taking that test, and that 30 percent scored higher than he or
she did, based on norms determined by the representative group.

Criterion-referenced tests try to provide a measure of performance based on much narrower, more clearly defined criteria. The
tests are intended to indicate areas of strength and weakness, measured against a predetermined level of acceptable performance.
Scores are reported in percentages correct as opposed to percentiles.
Criterion-referenced tests indicate the test-taker's mastery of the subject area as defined by the test items rather than the test-taker's performance as compared to others taking the test. For example, students in tenth grade might be expected to answer twenty out of thirty
questions on a tenth-grade mathematics exam, and if they do, a level
of acceptable performance would have been reached for that grade.
Both norm-referenced and criterion-referenced tests use the same
types of questions, and both use inferential statistical interpretation.
They are also both judged by the same standards of validity and reli-
ability.

A major problem with standardized testing is how the test results
are used. Education majors are often required to take a course in
"Tests and Measurements," in which they examine clinically the
virtues and drawbacks of various test designs. Yet, test results are
not simply a matter of approximating bell curves. Test results affect
each student's academic life, sometimes to such a great extent that
test results operationally prevent a student from being admitted to

college, or they place a student within a group or track that limits the options of study and the levels of academic challenge. Because of the significance of test results and the immense pressure they exert, teachers too often find themselves teaching to the test, in order that their students do well and the teachers appear to be doing their jobs.

And yet standardized tests are frequently found to be poor indicators of higher level thinking skills and sometimes undemocratic and even racist in their bias. Many in education are calling for changes in testing. Bernard Gifford, chairman of the National Commission on Testing and Public Policy, quoted in the report, "From Gatekeeper to Gateway: Transforming Testing in America," holds that,

> There is ample evidence that the testing enterprise has in many instances gone haywire and is driving our educational system in the wrong direction. . . . Current testing, predominantly multiple choice in format, is over-relied on, lacks adequate public accountability, sometimes leads to unfairness in the allocation of opportunities, and too often undermines social policies. (Evangelauf, 1990, p. A1)

Elliot Eisner concurs:

> . . . As a profession we are currently unable to give the public an assessment of our own schools in ways that reflect what we really care about. Our ability as a profession to assess what matters and to provide a telling picture of the strengths and weaknesses of our institution and the capabilities of our students on dimensions that have educational, not simply statistical significance, is quite short of what we need. This shortfall has been a function, in part, of our history in testing. We have looked toward specialized agencies to provide precise, discrete, measured indicators of student performance on tests that reflect more the technical aspirations of psychometricians than the educational values of teachers. We have been part of a tradition that has not served us well, and we have not, as a profession, created alternatives.
>
> Furthermore, there is more than a little ambivalence in our own behavior concerning test scores. We have a strong tendency to proclaim the educational poverty of test scores and then turn around and use them as indices of our own success, thus legitimating the validity of the public's concerns about the quality of education. If test scores in their conventional form do not reveal what really matters in schools, we should not use them to judge our "success." At the same time, until we have something that is better than what we have been using, I fear we will be obliged to continue to use what we believe does not matter from an educational perspective. (p. 4)

As schools and educators look at the ways they teach and how students learn, a different view of assessment and evaluation is now being called for, one that reflects a transactional philosophy. Meaningful assessment and useful evaluation methods are being employed in many classrooms and schools, and many state departments of education are recognizing the need for more appropriate measures of student performance.

Rationale for Whole Language Assessment and Evaluation

Evaluation and assessment may be the most political of all issues connected to a whole language philosophy. Therefore, it is important that teachers understand what assessment and evaluation are and their roles in teaching and learning. Although many people use the terms *assessment* and *evaluation* interchangeably, they are actually two distinct matters. Assessment refers to the collection of data that allows evaluation to take place. Good teachers assess constantly; they observe what is happening in the classroom, how their students are responding, and they adjust their teaching based on such assessments. At the end of each class, some teachers think to themselves, "That went well today," while others think, "That was a disappointment"; on good days and bad, both wonder what could be done to have made things better. In much the same way that good teachers constantly assess their own performance, they constantly look for indicators of information about their students, as a group and as individuals. Although this type of student assessment takes many forms and is managed in a variety of ways, two features are important: assessment is ongoing, and it is a process of collection of information, data, and facts to help teachers put the pieces together, as researchers do when looking for an answer to a problem. Teachers investigate learning, gathering evidence to illustrate what their students are learning.

Evaluation is the product of assessment. After gathering data—information and evidence—teachers must put these pieces together to evaluate students' progress and the products of their efforts. This evaluation should not be an opinion the teacher has about the students' work, but rather a detailed and thoughtful look at the students' work and progress, based on all the information that has been gathered on a daily basis over a long period of time. Such an evaluation will be understandable, helpful, and no surprise or mystery to students who have been informed about what has been assessed and who have themselves participated in many areas of the assessment.

Our evaluation practices operationally define what really matters for students and teachers. If our evaluation practices do not reflect our most cherished values, they will undermine the values we cherish. We need, in other words, to approach educational evaluation not simply as a way of scoring students, but as a way in which to find out how well we and our students are doing in order to do better what we do. Evaluation should be regarded as an educational medium, an important source for school improvement. And what it addresses should reflect the educational values we believe important. (Eisner, 1992, p. 5)

A Rationale for Assessment and Evaluation

Philosophically, assessment and evaluation in whole language classrooms must reflect the tenets of the whole language philosophy—that is, such evaluation must be student-centered and carried out for the sake of the students, encouraging their growth as learners (Harp, 1991). Obviously, teachers need to evaluate student performance, but whole language teachers assert that more honest, worthwhile, and humane ways exist to assess than have been employed in traditional classrooms.

The rationale for assessment and evaluation must be based on the philosophical principles of whole language, according to Bill Harp (1991), editor of *Assessment and evaluation in whole language programs*. Teachers should be cognizant of the fact that assessment and evaluation must:

1. *Be based on a transactional philosophy of learning and teaching.* Like whole language itself, effective assessment and evaluation must grow out of a belief in student and teacher empowerment and must have as its goals student support and growth. Many times school districts, and even state departments of education, try to impose an evaluation system on teachers, one that they may even call "holistic"; however, unless the teachers understand and accept the philosophical underpinnings out of which such "holistic" evaluation systems grow, imposed systems can't work.

2. *Regard reading and writing as processes.* The reading process is not an accumulation of skills, but a meaning-making process. Likewise, writing is not grammar exercises, spelling, five-paragraph essays, and assigned research papers on teacher-generated topics. Rather, writing, like reading, is a meaning-making process, a way to think and a way to communicate thoughts, ideas, and feelings. In many classrooms across the

country, students are reading for real purposes and using their interpretations of what they read to think, to question, to research, and to write. When language learning is viewed this way, assessment and evaluation must go far beyond weekly tests on the parts of language. Assessment and evaluation that has language growth as its purpose must first recognize that students' reading and writing behaviors must be assessed and evaluated along with their written products if students are to grow as readers and writers.

3. *Keep observation at its heart.* If teachers believe philosophically in the importance of recognizing the behaviors of readers and writers in order to support them and further facilitate their learning, then teachers must step back from their lecterns and observe as their students participate in genuine reading and writing activities. Yetta Goodman (1978) calls this observation "kid watching," emphasizing its importance in assessment and evaluation. As teachers observe their students using language, they're able to assess what is happening, recording their observations in a variety of ways.

4. *Use student needs to drive instruction rather than depending on a set curriculum or program.* Teachers often find this requirement difficult, especially those in high schools who are handed a predetermined curriculum and told that the content must be covered. The temptation is to let this predetermined curriculum drive teaching, hoping that students will score highly on school-constructed or state-administered exams. Whole language teachers resist the temptation and develop ways to cover the curriculum but still meet student needs and interests.

A colleague of Rick Chambers (1992) at the Grand River Collegiate Institute had just finished covering *The Great Gatsby* with a senior English class, having taught the material in a very traditional, socratic, chapter-by-chapter method. The teacher decided to take a risk and teach the next novel, *The Stone Angel* by Canadian author Margaret Laurence, in a more student-centered fashion, asking the students to periodically record in their journals their thoughts about events, characters, style, settings, moods, or anything else that occurred to them in the course of their reading the novel. Class and group discussions were also held concerning ideas that arose from the novel. Completed journals were eventually submitted to the teacher, and the students highlighted the four or five entries that they were particularly interested in having their teacher read for evaluation.

Given a choice of novels to write about on their examination, more than 90 percent of the students chose to write about *The Stone Angel*, responding to the traditional essay question with authority, carefully developed organization, and a mature understanding and appreciation of the novel. This teacher not only covered the material but found that, instead of simply telling students teacher-known information, the student-centered approach let students learn the material, expressing insights that they saw perhaps for the first time and sharing them with others by writing them down.

5. *Keep standardized tests in perspective.* We hear repeated calls for a national curricula and national testing in order to make our students competitive in the international marketplace, calls carried in popular magazines and issued in statements by government officials. We know that such claims are ridiculous, but we also know the power of educational politics. Although the tests are changing—a reflection of the dissatisfaction of teachers who are aware of the limitations of testing—an end to standardized testing is nowhere in sight.

As much as we would like to advise teachers to put aside any consideration of standard tests because these instruments help neither our teaching nor our students' learning, we are also realists. Tests will still be used for grouping, tracking, funding, and entrance to colleges and universities. Teachers, however, can put the importance of such testing in perspective: Students who are readers score highest on standardized tests (the use of language in context helps students' vocabulary grow, not the word lists memorized and regurgitated on weekly tests), and grammar drills, spelling tests, and diagramming sentences do not help students become better writers—writing does. Knowing this, teachers should be confident that when they allow students to read and react and to write and communicate, teachers are doing what they are paid to do—help their students learn. In the process, not only will their students do as well or better on the tests given but also will receive much more than if they had been in a classroom that only prepared them for a standardized test, an exam that has little to do with real learning.

6. *Use a variety of instruments employed in a variety of contexts.* Evaluation does not necessarily mean testing. Authentic evaluation is based on information accumulated to indicate growth, information gathered with a variety of instruments, many of them teacher-constructed. Testing is simply one of these instruments, and if teachers are interested in growth, then the tests chosen will be open-ended instruments demonstrating what students have

learned, instead of multiple-choice, one-answer tests demonstrating how much students have memorized of teacher-told material. Whole language teachers use instruments that record how students use knowledge and where they are in the developmental process. They also use instruments and techniques that are understandable and valued by the students, the ones who ultimately must be able to use the information in order to set goals for further learning.

7. *Be developmentally appropriate and culturally sensitive.* Unfortunately, many of the instruments that are commonly used in education are biased in regard to gender, ethnicity, and socioeconomic factors. Students come to school as proficient language users; however, their language is not always the language of the academy or the language of privilege. Standards have a place, but that place should not be to make students feel excluded from the ranks of the academic elite, those who have determined the standards in the first place. Many standardized tests have been determined to be culturally biased, yet they're still given and used to control students' destinies. For example, the residents of western Pennsylvania, where we now live, have a "to be" deletion rule for certain grammatical constructions, a rule that they're unaware of for the most part. A native western Pennsylvanian would say (and write, unless made aware of the distinction through hyper-literate schooling), "My car needs washed," instead of "My car needs to be washed." We have traced the origins of this construction to a rule derived from the Scots who settled the area, a construction considered quite proper in formal Scottish grammar. The point is that an assessment instrument, perhaps a "spot-the-error-in-the-sentence" grammar test, which is unaware of the regionalism might have any number of sentences using "to be" constructions conflicting with regional usage. How many other variations must be accounted for if standardized tests were to begin to consider regional dialects, racial/ethnic dialects, class dialects, and gender differences?

Students in secondary and postsecondary classrooms must be afforded opportunities to make choices about their language and about their learning. Whole language teachers realize that their task is not to make all students speak or write according to artificial predetermined standards; their task is to help students develop as learners, affording them opportunities to make choices about matters such as dialect or language, choices that develop as students perceive the need. Therefore, it is up to classroom teachers to use assessment and evaluation techniques that value who students are and what they bring to the learning situation.

Being developmentally and culturally appropriate means looking at assessment and evaluation from the learner's viewpoint. Terrie St. Michel of South Mountain High School in Phoenix, Arizona, says that she spent her first three years of teaching English in an inner-city high school trying to do all the things she thought she should or must according to the policies and procedures set by the school and district. Her approach to teaching was as traditional as "read these pages; answer these questions; and complete this assignment by this date. . . ." But Terrie confesses that she began to discover that her students had opinions, desires, questions, and abilities that they wanted to explore and expand upon, but they didn't know how to. Her recognition of who her students were, "urban" or not, freed them to ask their questions and to take risks, freed them to *want* to try new things and to accept that "failure" at a task is simply a statement of not having enough information to complete the task as required, rather than a statement about their intelligence. By emphasizing genuine caring for each student and assuring each student that he or she was valued and accepted where he or she was at the moment of development, Terrie convinced her students that it was okay to "not know." When Terrie's assignments and assessment tools allowed her students to demonstrate an awareness of the resources and potentials they themselves possessed as learners, then the threat of evaluation—being exposed as "not knowing"—diminished. In short, Terrie aligned the shoulds and musts imposed by the school and district with the wants and needs of her students, using techniques that afforded her students the opportunity to grow in directions that they felt were important for their lives.

8. *Occur continuously.* Evaluation is not three tests given throughout a semester. If assessment and evaluation are to drive instruction, then they must be a part of the daily life of a teacher, determining what will be taught the next day, the next week, and the next semester. Teachers who use assessment and evaluation on a daily basis are always searching for patterns, supporting students as they take risks and move forward, and watching in order to better facilitate further learning. They listen to students, talk with students, and try to understand how each student is progressing. When the purpose for assessment and evaluation is to support students, observation occurs continuously as the students learn and grow.

9. *Focus on students' strengths rather than on deficiencies.* For years, educators have let students know what was wrong with them. Their papers have been red-penned and the number wrong marked at the top, and what little written comment appeared always conveyed a message about how to "fix" what was wrong with their work. In life, people learn and grow based on what they know, what they are good at, and what their strengths are. Whole language teachers are sensitive to this distinction; they genuinely believe in students' abilities and strive to help students see the possibilities of future learning.

10. *Be primarily for the students to recognize strengths and to set goals for themselves.* If teachers believe in their students' right to be all that they are capable of being, then teachers have a responsibility to communicate this belief to their students. They must communicate a respect and an interest in what students are able to accomplish. They must help students recognize what they can do and help them set attainable goals for themselves. Then, teachers support students as each works toward these goals.

Assessment and Evaluation Strategies

Understanding the principles informing whole language assessment and evaluation is an important beginning for instituting such techniques into a classroom, but it is only a beginning. Teachers must understand *how* to effectively assess, how to manage such assessment, and then how to use such data to effectively evaluate student progress and performance.

Observation

We have briefly touched upon the importance of observation in whole language classrooms, but we have yet to discuss what the teacher observes, how the teacher observes, and for what purposes.

We have discussed the importance of a student-centered classroom and the inappropriateness of teachers lecturing at students. In a whole language classroom in secondary or postsecondary schools, students will be found actively engaged in learning. The very atmosphere of a student-centered classroom lends itself to the teacher acting as an observer. If teachers turn over some of the responsibility for learning to the students, then teachers are able to work as part of a community, observing, supporting, conferencing, and recording what they see for assessment.

It would be simple if there were only one or two "correct" ways for teachers to keep track of observations, but the truth is, each teacher devises instruments that best meet the needs of both the teacher and the students. Because most secondary teachers are responsible for over 100 students, any management system for assessment must be efficient as well as effective. The teacher must also be able to record data over extended periods of time, and the instruments must be helpful in organizing a great deal of information clearly. Two common methods of recording such data are checklists and anecdotal records.

Checklists. These usually contain a list of traits that the teacher, students, and curriculum have established as desirable for a certain subject or task. The teacher, acting as observer, looks for evidence of such traits while working with students in the community of the classroom. The purpose of these assessment instruments is to keep the teacher focused on what is important and to keep a record of student growth. Checklists need to be to-the-point and require a minimum of writing on the teacher's part. Checklists are only helpful if the teacher can quickly record observations while working with students. Often teachers keep checklists on a clipboard, easily carried from group to group or from student to student. For example, a teacher in an English classroom may want to keep track of writing behaviors that are important for development in composition. As students are working on drafts, conferencing, revising, or editing,the teacher may be watching for evidence of the students' understanding of the writing process. If so, a checklist like that found in Figure 6–1 may be helpful.

As seen in Figure 6–1, the checklist will make it easy for teacher and student at the next conference to pick up where they left off. For example, after the conference on 3/21, Susan knows that she needs to work on the conclusion of her piece and to check for ways to make transitions and sentence structure clearer. At the next conference, her teacher will be able to immediately identify the areas on which Susan was working.

Checklists may be cumulative or summative—that is, they may be used for assessment or for evaluative purposes. The checklist in Figure 6–1 would be used for assessment purposes, but teachers also use checklists, along with other assessment instruments, in order to evaluate student progress based on the data. An example of a summative checklist is found in Figure 6–2. This type of checklist can be rather formal, as in the case of one that is used in place of or along with report cards, or it can be informal and even filled out by the student and teacher together in order for self-evaluation.

Figure 6-1
Writing Conference Checklist (Cumulative)

STUDENT'S NAME (Title of Work)	DATE	FOCUS/ THESIS	ORGANIZATION	TRANSITIONS	SENTENCE STRUCTURE	CONCLUSION	MECHANICS	COMMENTS
Susan B. (Questions)	3/21	+	+	✓	✓	—	+	work with Mark on conclusion
Mark R. (A Quiet Thought)	3/21	+	+	—	—	+	✓	good idea—help with structure
Laura M. (Through My Eyes)	3/23	✓	✓	✓	✓	NA	—	early stages still very rough
Jason P. (Justice)	3/19	+	+	—	✓	✓	—	
Nathan M. (Walk to The Beat)	3/20	+	+	+	+	✓	✓	working on conclusion
Kelly D. (Animal Protection)	3/21	✓	✓	—	✓	—	—	feels strongly about this topic
Greg W. (Untitled)	3/23	+	✓	—	✓	✓	✓	

Symbol explanations:
+ well developed
✓ satisfactory
− needs attention
NA not applicable

Figure 6–2
Research Methods Checklist (Summative)

STUDENT'S NAME	DOES NOT APPEAR	1 OKAY	2 ADEQUATE	3 IN DETAIL
A. *Discusses the Issue/Topic* defines terms makes connections				
B. *States The Overall Question Being Studied* a thesis				
C. *Timely Explanation of Reason for Constructing Questions* why give a survey				
D. *States Method for Gathering the Data* who was asked how they were chosen				
E. *Discusses the Responses* significance of the statistical information analysis of the responses				
F. *Draws conclusions* summarizes the findings implications for further thought				
G. *Appendix Presentation* the questionnaire interview questions number of responses table of responses				
H. *Overall Writing Quality* well organized mature sentence structure free of mechanical errors interesting				

(One copy to be completed by the student and one copy by the instructor for discussion during a conference.)

Teachers can share ideas and formats with one another about the numerous uses for checklists, but whatever the format, checklists used to record observations should be efficient and clear in their interpretation and evaluation of student growth.

Anecdotal Records. These may be used by teachers for a variety of assessment activities—recording observations of students as they work in class, recording student comments about process or product, recording student responses to situations or tasks, recording how students synthesize what they are learning, and recording their own questions about what they are seeing.

Anecdotal records need not be as laborious a task as case study research; they are meant to be quick notes of observations, items that teachers think they are going to remember but, unless written down, are often forgotten. When teachers look over their notes, they are able to put together pieces and draw conclusions that would have been more difficult if the observations weren't recorded.

Amy Walker, a special education teacher in Mars, Pennsylvania, keeps anecdotal records in her teacher's journal. She jots down notes about what she is observing in her class of middle school students, reporting that such short notes help her to piece together a larger picture. For instance, the following entries are typical of Amy's anecdotes:

9/11—Loretta is bored and wants textbooks; Tanya has the same problem. Maybe I can work out of the old science texts when we talk about the senses. Tanya's becoming vocal about her displeasure. I'll have to try to "wean" them away from these gradually.

9/16—Tim is so improved. What wonders a year of maturation can make. He really seems to be enjoying independent reading. He's only reading about sports heros, but at least he's reading! It doesn't seem to be just to please adults either. I think I'll try the dialogue journal with him. It may make him feel special, and he needs that attention right now.

9/17—David is a puzzle—very angry! Directing that anger to other kids—acting superior and condescending. He is reading more though. I'm not sure how he feels about what he reads, just as I'm not sure what he feels about anything.

10/9—Robb wrote a fairly decent story today—see lesson notes—I was pleased and so was he! Finally, a bright spot!

10/16—Shannon *still* has great difficulty putting ideas down. There's some improvement but I have to work on her prewriting strategies. Maybe if I get her to talk more before writing it will help.

These entries are short and quickly written; time is as precious to Amy as it is to any busy teacher. Still, Amy begins to see threads throughout her observations; she has learned to let her students' needs drive her instruction. The anecdotes reveal Amy's reporting, questioning, and projecting. They show Amy trying to figure out what her students know and how she can help them move forward in their learning. Her musings about her students are much the same as those that cross the minds of every good teacher throughout a day, except that they are written out. Amy says that writing in her anecdotal log helps her to sort things out; it's a type of writing for discovery. Amy used observation to help her evaluate and support Gary, a student who had met with failure for years in schools and was practically a nonreader. As Amy wrote the following entry, she was reporting her observations and thinking about where to begin:

> Gary is *really* preying on my mind. He's having so much trouble with language, but I'm not sure if it's neurologically-based or due to years of failure and frustration. I think I'll try having him talk into a tape recorder for some of his writing. That may not be much better though, because he rambles so much. He decodes on about a third grade level I'd guess, but I don't think he has more than surface comprehension. His handwriting is illegible, and he is unhappy with it—I'll have him try word processing.

As she reports and questions in her log, she often comes up with a teaching strategy she hopes to try, much as was the case with Gary. Words like *try* and *maybe* indicate that she didn't believe there would be an easy answer. Her actions show she is a risk-taker, working with her students, talking to them, and discovering their strengths and weaknesses. She doesn't blame students for what they don't know; she tries to identify strategies that might support them as learners. She doesn't try to make them fit into the system; instead, she assumes responsibility for finding a way to support them and meet their needs at the time.

Teachers discover that keeping anecdotal records also requires some kind of management system. Some teachers, like Amy, keep a notebook or log, writing in it at different times of the day. Other teachers, those responsible for large numbers of students, jot down quick observations during the day on a sheet of peel-off blank address labels carried on a clipboard, notes that can be removed at the end of the day and stored in a notebook divided according to classes. No matter how teachers decide to manage it, this information helps them become reflective decision makers and makes later evaluation more concrete as they have specific incidents to reflect on and analyze.

Journals and Logs

Journals have been advocated as learning tools; however, they can also be used as evaluative instruments, reflecting growth over a period of time. Teachers and students are able to evaluate growth in areas such as self-expression, depth of thinking, and understanding of the subject area as they look at journals over the course of a semester, a grading period, or a year.

For example, students in my (Kathleen's) methods courses keep logs of their reactions to the assigned readings. As I read and react throughout the semester, I'm able to assess not only an individual student's understanding of each particular reading but their growth—how well each individual student is connecting those readings to class discussions and developing an understanding of the concepts central to the teaching of language. An example can be seen in Figure 6–3, a sample journal entry by Kim McCann, one of my students in a Secondary English Methods class. The entry reveals that as Kim is reading, she is questioning, projecting, connecting with her own experiences and drawing conclusions. (I have written my assessments in the left column.) Kim's journal shows that she knows it is permissible to say when she doesn't understand or doesn't agree. As I read journal entries such as Kim's, I'm able to assess Kim's understanding of the readings and of what is being discussed in class, adjusting my teaching to meet my students' needs.

Portfolios

For years teachers have been requiring students to keep portfolios, collections in manila folders of works-in-progress and graded pieces. What is different about today's increasingly popular portfolios is the concept of using such collections as an artist does, as a showcase for presenting his or her best work to prospective employers or clients.

One of the major differences between portfolio assessment and other collections of student work is the fact that what is contained in portfolios is negotiated. Portfolio assessment can grow out of collections in which students keep everything, including notes, drafts, and student and teacher reactions. These are often called working portfolios. Portfolios should be growing accounts of students' work over a long period of time rather than collections of a week's worth of work. Students make decisions concerning what will be put into their showcase portfolios—the collection of what each student considers to be his or her best work, pivotal pieces, and examples of growth. Portfolio assessment gives students an opportunity to learn how to self-assess their work, enabling them to recognize their strengths—what they can do—and to set reasonable, attainable, and personal goals for growth—what they hope to do.

Portfolio assessment gives teachers and students an opportunity for long-term assessment that is authentic and collaborative. Portfolios, examining students' effort, achievement, improvement,

Figure 6–3
Sample Journal Entry

My Comments	Kim's Journal Entry
Connecting with own experience	This chapter [of the textbook] helped me with a question I've been wondering about—revision. I think revising your own work is really difficult (at least it is for me.) I like the idea of peer reading. Sometimes suggestions (criticism) from another student is easier to take than from a teacher.
Technique	I think reading aloud is the best method of revision. I know myself that I can catch more errors if I read my papers aloud. It also helps with mechanics because it lets the reader hear where the pauses and stops go.
Questioning— "I want to learn more!"	I'm not sure if I understand the divisions and steps in editing. I'm not sure if editing can really be divided into steps. Maybe we can discuss this in class (?)
Projecting	I'm also not sure if I agree that a student can revise a piece of work easier if it means something to them. I know if I write something I really like, I get more sensitive when people try changing it. If I don't like it as much, I can revise it easier.
Searching for answers— Needs clarification	I can't believe how much Kirby and Liner [authors of the textbook] stress revision and rewriting. I never went through all this in high school. Even now I don't revise with all these steps. Can we talk more about this in class?

and processes, provide the accountability that schools have tried to establish in the past using testing programs. Sheila Valencia (1990) notes that "no single test, single observation, or single piece of student work could possibly capture the authentic, multi-dimensional, interactive requirement of sound [portfolio] assessment" (p. 339).

Every school district and every teacher must decide how to use portfolios—for assessment and/or evaluation, throughout a student's schooling and/or for shorter periods such as each school year. Whatever is decided, there are commonalities that apply to most portfolio assessment systems. Portfolio assessment is more experimental than structured in the beginning; Donald Graves (1990) warns against planning a rigid system that can't be adjusted to meet the needs of the teacher and the class.

When teachers begin to use portfolio assessment, they may find the following guidelines helpful, suggestions based on those offered by Robert Tierney, Mark Carter, and Laura Desai (1991). Teachers should:

1. Remember that the work in the portfolio belongs to the student and respect that ownership.

2. Collect samples of students' work in a classroom where students have choices and make decisions, are able to pursue their interests, and are allowed to collaborate.

3. Regard parental involvement as helpful in secondary schools. Parents begin to understand the value of a transactional approach to teaching and learning when their children share their work with them. Parents will feel assured that their children are learning everything prescribed in the curriculum and learning in an atmosphere that encourages responsibility and goal setting.

4. Discuss with students how and why portfolios will be established, what criteria could be used to select pieces for their portfolio, and that such choices should demonstrate their strengths, interests, effort, and development in the content area.

5. Explain to students what the teacher's role will be in selecting work for student portfolios. Give them opportunities to analyze and compare their pieces and to conference with peers and the teacher about their decisions.

6. Require students to articulate their reasons for including each piece in their portfolio. All pieces of work should be dated, and on a separate cover sheet, students should write the strengths the piece shows and why it was selected. Encourage students to be explicit in stating *why* they feel certain pieces should be included and how they reached their decision. Suggest that peer responses to work also be included. Portfolios should include a table of contents, whether arranged chronologically, by sections, or by themes.

7. Evaluate their own teaching. As teachers review portfolios, in addition to evaluating student work, the collections provide answers to whether the objectives of the course have been met, how well, and what can be done in the future to further support students. When appropriate, checklists can be created to help with this self-evaluation.

8. Update portfolios. Since constant updates should help students to document progress, earlier pieces should not be removed. How frequently portfolios are updated and the number of pieces

they contain depends upon the length of the course and the purpose for the portfolios.

9. Share portfolios with other students, with parents, other teachers, and administrators. Students should be given opportunities to appreciate each other's best work by sharing some pieces orally or through some other type of forum.

10. Evaluate portfolios based on criteria set up at the beginning of the process and mutually decided upon by the students and the teacher. Portfolios are a useful tool for goal setting. Peer evaluations should be supportive but helpful and be based on criteria that has been discussed.

Many school districts are using portfolio assessment to replace more traditional means of assessment such as testing. Anne Picone, a teacher at North Hills High School in Pittsburgh, uses portfolios in her classroom as an assessment tool based on the Pittsburgh City Schools' district-wide model called the Propel Writing Portfolio Project.

Anne's goals for using portfolios, which are shared with the students, are to provide an alternative to the final exam as a form of evaluation, one integrating reading, writing, speaking, and listening in the classroom more effectively than a two-day written final exam, and to allow the learner a choice in the assessment.

Anne's students generate a substantial amount of writing during the school year. From this collection, the students choose six pieces to be included in the portfolio and add a final reflection. The portfolio, titled "A Portrait of Myself as a Writer," includes:

1. An important piece and a cover sheet.

2. A satisfying piece and a cover sheet.

3. An unsatisfying piece and a cover sheet.

4. Two other selections and cover sheets.

5. A journal entry.

6. A final reflective essay.

By choosing the pieces that will be included in their portfolios, Anne's students are afforded an opportunity to evaluate their own work, an important component of evaluation usually ignored by traditional evaluation techniques. The cover sheets are explanations by the students as to *why* each piece was chosen, supported by specific reasons, and what they learned from the experience. For example, as part of her cover sheet for her most important piece of writing, Carla Braun, a twelfth-grade student in Anne's AP English class, wrote the following:

> When I thought of the word "important," I wanted to select a piece of my writing that marked a turning point in my writing. Therefore, I felt that a poem that I wrote this year would be most important. I had a difficult time deciding whether to choose the *Beowulf* poem or my personal poem, "Questions?", but I finally chose my *Beowulf* poem, despite the fact that it is less powerful [than the other poem]. I decided that my *Beowulf* poem is very important to me because it is the first time (since fifth grade) that I had written a poem. I had a fifth grade teacher who forced our class to write conventional, rhyming poetry, which I was not good at, and from that point until this year, I was convinced I could not write poetry. Therefore, this assignment caused me great stress until I really jumped in and started to write. It was then I came upon the revelation that I actually can write poetry. . . . I feel the special strengths of the poem are the line form (not only does it look good, but the form really helps to emphasize important words and ideas) and the clear movement and progression of the attitude and feelings of the speaker (from skepticism, to rejection of Beowulf, to hopelessness). . . .

Carla continues in her assessment by explaining what she learned from this particular writing and what she would do if she were to continue to work on this piece.

A student's ability to express why a piece of work is unsatisfying is as important as recognizing strengths and successes. By identifying areas of weakness, goals for future writing can be established. Carla selected an essay she wrote concerning *Rosencrantz and Guildenstern Are Dead* as her most "unsatisfying work" and wrote on her cover sheet:

> This piece is unsatisfying to me for many reasons. First of all, I used terms in the introduction that I did not identify. This though, was the least of the evils in my paper.
>
> Although I really enjoyed reading *Rosencrantz and Guildenstern Are Dead*, I had trouble getting a firm grasp on its meaning and purpose. For this reason I was very general in my essay and made very few points pertaining to the essay question, and therefore had little evidence from the play.

After assembling their portfolios, Anne's students prepare a short oral presentation for others in the class, their teacher, and an administrator who is invited to attend. During these presentations, students reflect on their own learning and describe their development as readers and writers in this class with the use of examples from their portfolios. Anne reported that the students in Carla's class sat in a circle during these presentations and for three days listened to one another describe their portfolios. During the presentations, Anne scripted each talk. These notes helped her provide data for convincing those who have doubts about the use of portfolios. The students also benefitted from the oral presentations of their classmates' portfolios, as is evident in Carla's final reflection essay:

> This final portfolio assessment is one project I have really enjoyed. In listening to the other students in the class give their reports, I feel that I have been able to learn a lot about study habits [and] writing styles, and other people's strengths have given me some things to strive for.
>
> This project has also enabled me to learn about myself. Had we taken the traditional test at the end of the year, I never would have gone back and reread all my papers. In this way, I was able to really note my improvements and also things I could improve (conclusion paragraphs for example). I was forced to really examine my abilities as a writer, and I realized that I'm not as bad as I had thought. I'm looking forward to English next year because I feel that with some work, I can really develop my writing skills.

No other form of evaluation could claim to reveal more about what Carla had learned than Carla's portfolio.

Grading

Although impossible to justify in a whole language philosophy, grading is still required of many teachers by district policy. Whenever possible, whole language teachers avoid grading, a practice that compromises their belief in individual learning and in trying to promote evaluation that encourages rather than points out deficiencies. Yet sometimes letter or number grades must be given because of political pressures. When forced to assign traditional letter or number grades, whole language teachers must devise systems that do the least harm. In such situations, it's important that grades are not a mystery, evaluations based on criteria that seem understandable to only the teacher. Some teachers employ a contract type of grading system, which takes into account effort and accomplishment. Other teachers use checklists of traits, which are discussed and made clear early in the course, that can be checked off by students as they provide evidence of accomplishment. If reasonable expectations are agreed upon by students and teachers, then students will, at least, be aware of what an A means and how such a grade is attained. No matter what type of assessment and evaluation system is used, whole language teachers encourage students, support them, help them to set personal goals, and provide opportunities for all to grow.

For Further Exploration

1. Grades are sometimes defended as necessary rewards in recognition of hard work. Consider whether this system of rewards and punishments was fair in your schooling. Ask students whether they were ever motivated to work for a grade. How satisfying did they find the grade, if they achieved it? How did they feel if they didn't get the grade they worked for?

2. Tests are defended as methods of comparing the performance of students across school districts, across the state, across the country. Why do we feel compelled to compare our performances? Interview a school administrator about his or her school's relative performance. Challenge the assumptions that underlie the school's beliefs in its ranking. Notice the similarities between the school's academic standing and other variables, such as their sports program's standing.

3. Collect report cards from your own previous years of schooling. Ask parents, grandparents, neighbors, and teachers for their report cards. What changes do you notice between report cards of your day and those of yesteryear? What items have not changed? What items should change?

4. Interview the teacher with the reputation as the "hardest grader." Ask about how that teacher sees his or her role in the classroom (listen for characteristics of the transmission model of learning). Interview the teacher with the reputation as being "an easy A." Ask the same questions, noticing the similarities and differences. Finally, interview the teacher with the reputation as being "the greatest." Is attitude about grading a predictor of whether the teacher will be "whole language"?

Related Readings for Further Thought and Exploration

Goodman, K. S., Bird, L. B., & Goodman, Y. M. (1992). *The whole language catalog: Supplement of authentic assessment.* New York: Macmillan/McGraw-Hill.

Offers a collection of explanations, ideas, stories, and tools for assessment and evaluation. A follow-up to their wonderful Whole Language Catalog, *this book contains many practical and inspiring examples.*

Graves, D., & Sunstein, B. (1992). *Portfolio portraits*. Portsmouth, NH: Heinemann.
Addresses the use of portfolios from elementary school to graduate school. This book tells stories of how portfolios are used in the classroom and offers ideas on the use of portfolios as a means of instruction and evaluation.

Harp, B. (Ed.). (1991). *Assessment and evaluation in whole language programs*. Norwood, MA: Christopher-Gordon.
Presents assessment and evaluation in a manner in keeping with the philosophy behind whole language. An excellent book for teachers and administrators, it also contains a chapter for Special Education teachers interested in learning how to write whole language IEPs.

Rief, L. (1991). *Seeking diversity: Language arts with adolescents*. Portsmouth, NH: Heinemann.
Discusses evaluation beliefs and techniques, written from the perspective of a classroom teacher. A complete chapter deals with portfolio evaluation.

Tierney, R., Carter, M., & Desai, L. (1991). *Portfolio assessment in the reading-writing classroom*. Norwood, MA: Christopher-Gordon.
Gives practical advice to teachers who are considering using portfolios in their classrooms: how to begin, what to include, and how to manage portfolios analysis and record keeping.

Chapter Seven

Whole Language for "At-Risk" Students

*If you set up the right conditions, try as best you can to cross
class and cultural boundaries, figure out what's needed to
encourage performance, . . . if you watch and listen, again
and again will emerge evidence of ability that escapes those
who dwell on differences.*

—Mike Rose

Questions for Thought/Journal Entries

1. During your life in school you were probably placed in ability
groups for certain classes or subjects. What were your experiences in a "track" or "level" that placed you with other students
who were supposedly on your level?

2. How have you been grouped in the past? By testing? By grades?
By parental request? How did you feel about the accuracy of the
grouping? What makes you feel this way?

3. Some teachers say that it's not possible to teach students of varying abilities in the same class. Based on what you have read in
the preceding chapters, why do you think these teachers feel this
way?

4. Have you ever known anyone who had severe difficulty learning
in school? How did that person feel about school? Why do you
think he or she had these difficulties? Did the person have a label

such as "dyslexic," "learning disabled," or "remedial"? How did the person feel about him- or herself as a learner?

5. If you are not trained in special education, should you be expected to teach students who are labeled "learning disabled"? What is your responsibility for teaching such students? How do you feel about mainstreaming?

Introduction

Whole Language, as a philosophy of teaching and learning, is appropriate for all students, not just those in academic or college-bound classes. This chapter will help teachers understand how to reach out to all students, regardless of their "levels," using the same materials and strategies.

The Danger of Labels

We don't believe in labels. They may be fine for laundering instructions on new clothes, but labels on students tend to obscure more than they reveal. Take dyslexia for example.

We don't believe in the explanation that dyslexia is a perceptual or visual problem. We know that thousands of people do. We know that people we work with claim to be dyslexic. We know that a very prestigious organization exists to promote treatments for the illness, an organization whose very existence therefore requires a belief that dyslexia exists. By way of analogy, we don't believe in UFOs, although thousands of people do, although people on television claim to have been aboard them, and although prestigious organizations are dedicated to establishing communication with them. The trouble with belief systems is that the thousands who already believe in mysterious things will not believe our contradiction or that of notable authorities such as Frank Smith (on dyslexia) or Carl Sagan (on UFOs).

We do believe that those who have been labeled (and the actual label doesn't matter) have real and serious problems, but to say that they can't learn because they have a learning disability is not really saying anything at all. Labels, unfortunately, are at the heart of our traditional educational system. As educators, we live with sets of labels to describe just about everyone, from the gifted to the minimally brain damaged. Labels allow some in education to do things to those so labeled that they wouldn't do to the normal population (such as prescribing drills-for-skills programs, which we know don't work). Labels allow some in education to treat those so labeled in ways that are different from the rest of the population (such as placing them in less challenging situations and expecting less of them) and hiring someone else to be responsible for those students with labels. Nevertheless, labels tell teachers very little. Once the label is attached, it then becomes the cause for their difficulties, and efforts are made to cure the patient of the illness. To believe that labels actually define someone or someone's abilities is to believe a biological and neurological explanation for how that person does in school. "To accept, for instance, that a student is 'learning disabled' is to accept a legally-sanctioned explanation that a 'perceptual handicap' or 'brain injury' or 'minimal brain dysfunction' is interfering with 'one or more of the basic psychological processes involved in using language' (Franklin, 1987, p. 1)," explains Neil Cosgrove (1991), director of the Writing Center at Slippery Rock University. It is difficult enough for clinical researchers to prove that someone is minimally brain damaged; even when there is evidence of neurological damage, it is even harder for researchers to demonstrate the part that such a dysfunction plays in a person's academic difficulties (Coles, 1978). After daily contact with students who have been given various psycho/biological labels, Neil argues that the difficulty with employing clinical and psychological explanations for learning problems is that they ignore other possibilities for academic troubles. "We must remember," Neil cautions, "that to accept such labels is to accept a neurological, biological explanation for a child's difficulties in school. Depending upon the individual, such an explanation may be the right 'diagnostic' path to follow. Nevertheless, the further one proceeds along that path, the more difficult it becomes to . . . explore other possible explanations" (p. 2). For example, how might environmental factors have affected a student's learning; how might emotional factors, cultural factors, or economic factors have influenced how a student has learned or failed to learn in a system that expects all students to behave and progress in the same way and at the same time? The psycho/biological label "implies that emotional, environmental, cultural, and economic circumstances have been ruled out as the possible causes of academic failure. In other words, according to this explanation, it is no longer necessary to consider those factors because a student's difficulty has been clearly established; appropriate remediation can begin" (p. 3).

Fortunately, even teachers unfamiliar with a transactional whole language philosophy of learning will agree that numerous factors, such as home and school environment, cultural aspects, and emotional considerations, play a role in how students learn both in and out of the classroom. However, such numerous factors in learning can't be easily given a label because they can't be quantified. And since these factors can't be tested and measured in numbers, they aren't considered in the diagnosis and treatment.

The political implications for such labeling is even more problematic. Federal law mandates that students with "learning disabilities" are entitled to certain "rights" in public schools. The difficulty with the regulation is that the definition for this label is vague, broad, and extremely general, not surprising since no one is sure what such a label means. In fact, the label is so broad that it might refer to any child having problems in school (Franklin, 1987). Some school districts report as many as 20 percent of their students are "learning disabled" and require special federal assistance in the form of remedial teachers, aides, etc. Labels have become a political instrument to generate monies for school districts but have done little to help those students who are being led to believe that they have something neurologically wrong with them. We have had successful college students tell us that they are learning disabled, yet they are very uncertain what that label means, other than knowing that learning has been difficult for them, that they were placed in special programs in school, and that they often do not remember how they acquired the label.

Labels imposed on children in elementary grades usually follow them for the rest of their lives. In *Learning Denied*, an eye-opening book exposing how children are labeled in public schools, Denny Taylor (1991) warns educators of the dangers of such labeling. In this report, Taylor recounts the story of Claudia and Pat, two parents who only want what is best for their son, Patrick, but who find themselves caught up in a battle with the bureaucracy of the special-education division of their public school. At first they had turned to the school for advice and guidance, as concerned parents, but in the end, they were forced to try desperately to protect their son from this same system, even resorting to legal means to do so.

Taylor outlines Patrick's early life in school, from the beginning of kindergarten through the next two grades. Patrick's parents were informed of an early diagnosis of perceptual difficulties on a preschool screening test. A few months later, his kindergarten teacher pointed to motor-skill difficulties, evidenced in not cutting straight with scissors. Taylor documents the extent to which the school went to confirm their diagnosis of a suspected disability, as over the course of the next two years Patrick was subjected to a battery of tests that did little more than prove to a six-year-old that something was wrong with him. These tests discouraged Patrick to the point where he stopped trying to read in school. In sharp contrast to his school life, Patrick continued reading and writing at home during this same time, and in private tutoring lessons, he was able to compose stories, to choose increasingly difficult stories to read, and to discuss what he was reading and writing in ways that real readers and writers do. Patrick's abilities were assessed only by test scores and by reports from "experts," each of whom had met Patrick only once and only in clinical situations. None of Patrick's out-of-school evidence was even considered in the school's diagnosis.

Teachers seem to believe in biological labels because those labels come with "scientific" evidence to back them up—in other words, test results. Such tests and their resultant labels are the leftover remains of an educational system based on a behavioral philosophy, one that quantifies and categorizes in order to explain, one that embraces a reductionist view of learning in order to quantify and categorize. Neil Cosgrove (1991) warns that easy acceptance of these explanations absolves teachers of looking at other possible reasons for difficulty in school. Sociologists have criticized labels based on testing, such as "learning disabled," because such labeling often "masks" possible environmental causes for failure in school, such as poor teaching, disruptive social conditions in the student's life, and inadequate opportunities in home and school (Carrier, 1983).

Taylor (1991) reveals the amazing and at the same time horrifying power that standardized testing has over the educational fate of young children, despite the research of the past twenty years proving the limitations of such tests. As teachers, we recognize that Patrick's fate is not unusual. Throughout our daughter's schooling, her teachers frequently remarked how surprised they were by Laura—her work often exceeding what the tests predicted she was capable of accomplishing. Even in college, her SAT scores predicted borderline success, yet her work surpassed what others with much higher scores achieved.

There are far too many Patricks in our schools, students who have been convinced by the time they are eight or nine years old that they are unable to learn, students who will undoubtedly struggle in frustration until they reach their sixteenth birthday, the age at which they can legally escape a system that has in effect denied them the right to learn. How often have teachers witnessed students caught in the system and felt powerless to change the inevitable outcome?

Though we don't believe in labels, we know that no one learns in the same way, at the same time, or as easily as everyone else; however, their differences, their uniqueness as learners, need not separate them. Some educators and too many school districts mistakenly react to the differences in learning abilities by believing that the best way to satisfy everyone is to group students so that they learn at their own rate with others who are at the same level. Such grouping of students, called "tracking," is common in secondary schools.

The practice of tracking, "a system of placing students by achievement scores, learning styles, behavior patterns, or career intentions" is a system for "inevitably labeling students," explains Carole Bencich (1991, p. 7), a teacher- educator at Indiana University of Pennsylvania.

Carole believes that "a gap between theory and practice fuels the debate over tracking, a practice which is widespread and deeply engrained in American curriculum," a practice created "to accommodate differences in emotional, intellectual, and academic development among groups of children" (p. 7). Carole says that the

> proponents of tracking argue that such a system reduces the risk of frustration for some students and the danger of boredom for others. In theory, tracked students learn at a pace that allows them to succeed. In practice, however, ability grouping consigns some students to a repetitive and reductive sidetrack curriculum, and channels others into a more challenging fast track of conceptual knowledge and inquiry.
>
> John Goodlad (1984), in *A Place Called School*, describes a significantly divided curriculum in American schools, citing the disproportionate numbers of black and Hispanic students in basic level programs. Goodlad questions the educational benefits claimed for tracking and warns of the negative side effects which in effect deny many students access to knowledge. (p. 7)

Carole finds it telling that

> when the *English Journal* asked its March 1990 Round Table respondents for commentary on tracking, not one teacher wrote in support of ability grouping. Instead, the replies from six teachers spoke of the enrichment of classrooms through diversity; the humanizing effect of mixing social classes, races, and ethnic backgrounds; and the gains in self-confidence, skills, and cooperative behaviors which accrued to students in heterogeneous classrooms.
>
> By December, however, three teachers had written to *English Journal* defending the other side of the tracking issue. The December writers offered convincing proof that tracking could be made to serve all students well, while admitting that tracking might indeed favor some advanced students and stigmatize basic students. A tracked program works with "proper placement, small classes, teacher training and support, a well designed curriculum,

and healthy goals," argued Ellen Jo Ljung (1990, p. 70). Class size figured prominently in these discussions. "To eliminate tracking without addressing class size is like pulling off the top of a weed and leaving the root to flourish," said Vicky Greenbaum (1990, p. 68). (p. 7)

The Myth of Homogeneity

Carole Bencich (1991) argues that the use of tracking only perpetuates a myth of homogeneity, a belief that it is possible to group students according to ability.

> In an effort to achieve group similarity, the tracked curriculum establishes an academic/vocational polarity, with options based upon the projected career choices of students, as well as their abilities. Further refinement of the tracked curriculum creates three tracks, adding one in the middle to serve the large group of "average" youngsters who either cannot or will not master advanced academic challenges, but who nevertheless wish to retain the option of postsecondary education. When three tracks fail to provide adequate homogeneity, classes for gifted and learning disabled children must be added. Yet even when I taught in a five-track-plus-exceptional-education system, some spoke of the need for additional subdivisions to eliminate the wide range of abilities in the middle track. (p. 7)

Carole challenges the myth of homogeneity, pointing to the reoccurance of "students who are 'misplaced,' and therefore either not working up to their potential or going through the minimum learning behaviors in an advanced class" and the reality of parental or societal pressures, which compromise academic criteria as the basis of placement. She says,

> the truth is, every class has as many tracks as there are students. Every student is a track unto himself or herself. Test scores and other external criteria which suggest that some children are similar to one another merely mask other differentiating factors.
>
> Worst of all, the myth of homogeneity leads some teachers to believe they can rely on whole class instruction. If individualization has been accomplished by ability grouping, they reason, then one specially-tailored curriculum, one textbook at an appropriate reading level, and one set of expectations will suffice for the entire class. Such a myth assumes that students of similar abilities will respond in a similar way to appropriate methods

and materials, will arrive easily at similar solutions to problems, and will reinforce one another in their mastery of new learning.

The myth of homogeneity ignores the rich possibilities of divergent thought and the shared construction of meaning which can result from multiple interpretations, varied backgrounds, and expanded linguistic codes. James Moffett (1983) points out the limiting effects upon language when students are grouped. Disadvantaged children "can learn standard English only by speaking with people who use it," Moffett notes (p. 94). On the other hand, advantaged children can benefit from learning the "emotive and communal uses of language as well as the mythic and metaphoric qualities of lower class speech" (p. 94). Thus, while tracking keeps some students out of "the literacy club" (Smith, 1988b) by preventing their exposure to academic discourse and behaviors, it bars other students from involvement with the multicultural language and attitudes of a rapidly changing world.

Goodlad calls tracking a "self-fulfilling prophecy" because "the work of upper and lower groups becomes more sharply differentiated with each passing day" (p. 141). By fourth grade, he points out, the spread in scholastic achievement, as measured by test scores, is four to six grade levels. Self-esteem varies correspondingly: students understand very early in life that if they do not want to go to college, they will not be held accountable for demanding academic performance. As Paula Hatfield (1990) put it, they become "in-school dropouts" (p. 75).

Labels such as "basic" and "advanced" become as familiar to students as old T-shirts. They form a kind of identity, with "basic" carrying as much cachet in some circles as "advanced" does in others. A top-down decision to end tracking would accomplish little. Evolutionary change of American curriculum—using collaborative methods, team teaching, and voluntary programs—would let students merge their own individual tracks into a collective pathway of learning. (pp. 7–8)

Meeting Students' Needs

If students are not tracked, then how do teachers meet their needs? This question is repeatedly asked at professional conferences, in graduate classes, at district meetings, and in teachers' meeting rooms. For many years teachers were conditioned to believe that it was the responsibility of the remedial teacher to meet the needs of students who were having academic difficulty (or the responsibility of the resource-room teacher or someone else who was trained and equipped to work with students having difficulty). Many secondary teachers and college professors actually operate from the "sink-or-swim" position—in other words, in their classes, where high standards are maintained, students either accomplish the work that is expected (what the teacher determines as acceptable), or else the student fails; it's as simple as that. In fact, such thinking has actually preserved the notion that tracking is a viable way to teach the students who many teachers feel ill-equipped to teach; "After all," they capitulate, "we were never trained in special education." And teacher training is precisely where this thinking originates, a training grounded in behavioral philosophy. Teachers trained in this way feel that they were called to teach "normal" students and that all others became the responsibility of trained clinicians, those whose calling was to "fix" remedial students.

In reality, all students have individual needs, and some find learning more difficult than others. Teachers, regardless of their training or misperceptions, have a responsibility to teach *all* students and to help them reach their full potential. In this paradigm, teachers must believe in the students and help the students believe in themselves while setting goals for future learning. Teachers are responsible for looking for ways to support all students as each one moves forward at his or her own pace.

Realizing Potential and Offering Support

Martha Dolly (1992), an English teacher at Frostburg State University in Maryland, tells of how she met the needs of one of her students enrolled in a required junior-level advanced composition course. Greg had been diagnosed as dyslexic by a school psychologist at his high school, and regardless of the accuracy of the label, he had real problems with written language. Since struggling to pass his first-year college composition course almost three years earlier, Greg admitted to Martha that he had avoided writing completely, behavior that was neither hard to understand, nor unusual, as many people avoid that which is difficult and unpleasant. At the beginning of the semester, in answer to a question about writing strategies, he wrote, "It hasn't worked well for me bacaus I don't write enough. It depend on what I'm writting about if I'm interested I'll work qwickly, if I'm uninterested I tend to be easly distracted" (p. 1).

An indication of how Greg's problems had been diagnosed and handled throughout his schooling can be glimpsed in the following excerpts from the records of Greg's tutor:

1/31—Greg has a distinct problem with pulling out central themes and ideas from a reading.

2/3[—Greg] seemed in a hurry so we looked at lower-order concerns. . . . He didn't realize that his sentences did not have subjects.

2/5—He didn't really let me explain the various errors. . . (comma splice, subject-verb agreement, fragments, just to name a few) and he wanted me to tell him what's wrong. I don't know if this is a result of his disability or laziness.

2/13—I was particularly concerned with his lack of initiative, although this could stem from his discouragement about writing.

2/25—I gave Greg a transition help sheet because he had *no* transitions in his paper.

2/26—Aaargh! Sometimes I wonder whether or not Greg is a brick wall!! Greg constantly wants to use my thoughts and words in his paper and, in my heretical opinion, has no desire to think for himself, 98.2% of his errors. . . could be avoided if he would take the time. (p. 2)

"Upon receiving the 2/26 report," Martha says, "I took up the proofreading issue with the learning disabilities specialist and then with the writing center director, who discussed it with the tutors. After that, the tutors reported working more on strategies and document-level matters than on explanation of errors accompanied by exhortations to proofread" (p. 3).

Martha worried that he wouldn't be able to pass advanced composition in one semester, but Greg managed to earn a C by spending twenty-five conference hours in the writing center (in addition to regular conferences with Martha) and by keeping an extra-credit journal to help him become more comfortable with the act of putting words on paper.

Greg had a long way to go over the course of that semester. "Rather than focusing on his problems, which might have made him all the more fearful of writing, we emphasized developing an appropriate amount of confidence, balanced by awareness of the value of certain kinds of input from others. During the semester, Greg also became more confident about word processing, overcoming his initial fear that, 'If [I] screw something up it erases all of your [sic] work' " (pp. 4–5).

"One of Greg's main problems was reluctance to develop his points, for which he seemed to have two reasons: (1) the more words he wrote, the more he had to (painfully) edit, and (2) merely putting any words on paper was a struggle for him" (p. 1). "Around midterm

I suggested journal writing," Martha tells us, "as a way of overcoming his fear of putting words on paper or screen. Considering that in the journal Greg was not attempting to correct sentence-level matters, his last entry suggests increasing ability at that level as well as a certain fluency":

> I really do feel thaat I have learned a lot in this class. I am no longer powerdnoid about writting. I know my writting is not the best and my spelling is horible. I do feel I can write a letter or a note and not have to worry about it. I have learned how to read over my papers and to pick out minor details that are wrong. I do realize thaat I need someone to look over my papers. Now after this course, I can pick out what is wrong and mark it for someone to go over it. I have become a lot more confident toward writting my papers. In the past I would have someone toltally help me write a paper and have someone else type it. Now I use a word processor and I type my own paper and I have some look over my paper after it's written it. I do realize that my spelling is horrible, but with a spell checker, it covers most of my errors. (p. 4)

Martha continues, "By the end of the term, Greg was familiar with a variety of strategies, such as reading his drafts aloud to spot problems, and Greg created his own checklist to assist other students who had similar problems, passing on the tips he learned about writing to others who shared his difficulties" (p. 3).

Greg's "Writing Checklist" contains good advice for all students, regardless of ability:

> 1. Just start writing.
> 2. Don't worry about commas and spelling until later.
> 3. It doesn't matter where you start writing the paper: Example, intro, body, or any point.
> 4. Go to the writing center tutors to help revise or just to make sure you're going in the right direction.
> 5. Continue going to tutor until you're done with your paper.
> 6. Type [your] paper on word processor. Do not forget to use the spell checker.
> 7. Make sure you have someone to look over your paper after you type it.
> 8. Ask the tutor to look for homonyms like to/too.
> 9. Make sure you make any other corrections needed.
> 10. If you do not continue to use the writing skills you learn, you may forget. (pp. 3–4)

Martha confesses that "some would say that no one deserves to pass advanced composition without being able to independently handle sentence-level matters such as distinguishing between *do* and *due*, but I felt that what Greg most needed to develop were coping strategies to help him produce reasonably solid documents in the future" (p. 2).

"Requiring another semester of advanced composition might help Greg improve his writing further but perhaps at the cost of his newly-acquired confidence. Even if he does not follow the last piece of advice he gives other 'learning disabled' students, he now knows how to regain fluency and confidence and how to cope with some of the rhetorical and sentence-level problems that will no doubt always plague him. Most of the evidence suggests that improved confidence and writing strategies should help Greg 'get through' future writing projects" (p. 5).

Meeting Individual Needs in a Community of Learners

Teachers often search for a technique or strategy that they can use that will make a difference in the life of a learner. Amy Walker, the special-education teacher introduced in earlier chapters, is continually looking for ways to meet the needs of her students whose ages range from eleven to sixteen years and whose abilities are even more diverse. Her students carry with them almost all the labels that educators know how to use—learning disabled, emotionally disturbed, educable mentally retarded, remedial, at-risk, and even gifted. What is even more amazing is that Amy teaches all these students in a self-contained classroom on the grounds of an institution, and as a whole language teacher, she has created a community of learners who support each other but who are respected by their teacher and their classmates as individuals with their own strengths and individual needs.

Amy's class has common goals, units of study, classroom procedures, and even state/district-mandated grading, and yet she is able to provide students with what each needs to grow individually. One student, David, came to Amy's class with academic potential complicated by a myriad of both social and academic problems. As Amy does for all her students, Amy searched for ways to provide David with the means to develop his interests and strengths while still functioning as a part of the larger community.

David—Growing as a Reader and Writer

When I (Kathleen) observed David while in Amy's class, he reminded me of so many students I had seen in other classrooms in public schools. He had such potential; he was bright and capable, yet his school career had been less than stellar. Although placed in regular classes in public school, he had always had problems, both academic and social, and he seemed to have developed a type of aloofness and distrust of adults, especially those he met in the classroom.

David was sullen and withdrawn when I first met him. He always seemed to have a scowl on his face, talked only when addressed directly, and even then answered with as few words as possible. David came to Amy's class in the middle of the school year, having been placed at this school for reasons other than academic ones. He had never been in a special-education setting, and it was apparent to me and to others who saw him that he was very unhappy about his placement in the classroom and at the school. He told his staff guardian that he "hated this place. . . . It was for dummies." Knowing that David had a normal IQ and had always been in regular classes, I assumed he was entering with somewhat different experiences from those of the other students, all of whom had experiences with special remedial programs or resource rooms. Even the classroom itself was different from what David had known previously—no desks in rows, no teacher's desk, and only ten students in a very small room.

David was very quiet those first few weeks. He kept mostly to himself, and although he participated when expected, he didn't seem to want to become part of the community. He rarely smiled, talked only when asked a direct question, kept his chair on the outskirts of any discussion circle, and moved slowly and half-heartedly. Amy sensed that David acted the way he did hoping everyone would realize he was bored with what was going on; she felt challenged to find ways to interest him and help him feel a part of the community.

David seemed to be capable reader, but he told me he had done very little reading before coming to Amy's class. A few weeks after David's arrival, Amy began the book, *The Outsiders*, as a class novel. From the day she introduced it, David seemed to perk up. He seemed intrigued as Amy talked about the teenage author, a sixteen-year-old girl who called herself S.E. Hinton. The first day Amy talked about the novel, David sat up in his chair and looked at Amy as she spoke. It was noteworthy because he had previously spent most of his time with his head on the desk or staring out the window. Amy read the first couple of chapters aloud to the class, and David seemed totally engrossed in the book. When Amy suggested that the students put the books away for the day, David, along with the others in the class, pleaded for her to keep reading. Amy noticed this new interest of David's, so she read one more chapter with the class.

As the days went on, David became more and more involved with the novel and the characters. Because this seemed to be the first time he ever shared literature with other readers through response and discussion, he began to become a part of the community. It was gradual but the change was obvious: When discussing favorite characters, David shared his thoughts and feelings about Darry, the oldest brother, his favorite character. This novel also gave the students a chance to hear how the characters learned to deal honestly with feelings and emotions, characters that they identified with and respected. When the character of Johnny explained, "nothing gold can stay," the students, David included, responded with personal experiences and feelings similar to those in the novel. For the first time since David had come to this class, he was participating—listening and sharing—and he was involved with his peers as they responded to the novel. David was beginning to become a part of the community, and he seemed to be bonding through reading and responding to literature.

Amy, knowledgeable as she was about adolescent literature, made frequent suggestions about books she thought her students might like to read during their Sustained Silent Reading period. David was enjoying *The Outsiders* so much that Amy suggested that he read other books by Hinton, such as *That Was Then, This Was Now*, and *Tex*, a first step in broadening his interests. And David did begin reading more on his own. He supplemented class novels by reading others on the same topic. For instance, David read *A Light in the Forest* while the class was reading *The Sign of the Beaver*. Even though *A Light in the Forest* was a more difficult and more sophisticated novel to read, the background that David learned in class as part of Amy's integrated unit on Native Americans for social studies helped him read it on his own.

Since David had yet to initiate discussion about his reactions to his independent reading, Amy decided that she would have him begin to respond and react in a dialogue journal. David began the dialogue journal with the novel *Maniac Magee* by Jerry Spinelli. This journal would be shared with his teacher, who would respond as another reader might.

David's reactions were short but powerful. Unlike many students who are new to journaling, David did not summarize what he had read; instead, he reacted very much as a reader would when speaking with someone else about a significant part of a book. David responded in his writing to the part in each chapter that struck him as most important, sometimes because he could identify with what was happening and sometimes because he wanted to analyze the characters' actions. In the following entry, David reacts to Maniac's early morning runs, drawing a profound conclusion about the character's actions:

> Maniac has no where to go. He goes to the zoo, sleeps there a couple of nights. In the mornings he walks around town. He called these times his special time with the town. He looks everywhere except the P&W trolley in which his parents died on. I feel that he loves the morning so much because there is no division, no barriers between whites and blacks. I feel sorry for Jeffrey Lionel Magee.

When I (Kathleen) read this entry I was struck by the depth of David's thinking. There is an underlying theme of racial tension and prejudice in the novel, but nowhere did the author state that Maniac's running was a time to see the town as a whole, free of the racial tension that divided it. David saw this as a reader. When I read his interpretation, I realized that David had entered the novel, reacting and interpreting based on inferences made in the story.

David also used his journal to sort out what was happening in the novel. For example, when he wrote the following, it was evident that he was using writing as a mode of thinking:

> I don't really understand the first part. I think that Magee runs in the morning and Mars Barr knew that so he decided to run into Magee. In the second part I feel that Magee didn't realize what he was on [the tracks] and when he did he remembered his parents and just couldn't handle being there so he ran away from his feelings and down the street. I sorta know how he feels because my friend died in a car wreck and my parents had to force me to ride in a car when I didn't want to.

Over the subsequent months, David continued to enjoy writing in his dialogue journal. Whenever Amy or I responded and returned the journal to him, he quickly opened it, read the responses, and started to react. We were dialoguing in writing to what had been written, as two readers sharing a novel would.

David continued to share literature this way. When Amy told him about *Where the Red Fern Grows*, he was eager to read it independently and write about it in his journal. One of David's fondest personal memories was coon hunting with his grandfather, and as he read *Where the Red Fern Grows*, he connected the novel to his own experiences, reading it from cover to cover in just a few days. David got so "into" the book, consuming several chapters at a sitting, that his journal responses became less frequent, since he only wrote when he stopped reading. At first David apologized for not writing as often as he had before, but we assured him that it was best to write when he felt he wanted to, not because he thought he had to. David continued his journaling throughout the year—first with me and then with Amy. Following David's experience, several other students began using dialogue journals; Amy plans to introduce peer dialoguing next.

David's experiences with literature seemed to change his feelings about the class in general. At one point, I asked David about how this school compared to his old school, and he responded that "she [Amy] doesn't put the high people with the high people. She puts everyone together in a group." David was, of course, referring to the myth of homogeneity. He said he liked being grouped heterogeneously, and he felt that he was learning more in Amy's class. As he came to this realization, David's entire attitude toward school changed. He had become interested, attentive, and involved with what was going on in class.

In discussions with public school teachers, we find that they worry about how literature-based instruction will "work" in classes with students of varying abilities and capabilities. I often think of Amy's class, and students like David, a boy intellectually and socially very different from his classmates, who grew in literacy as he, his teacher, and his peers shared literature. What each received from the experience was personal, as it is with any reader, but each was able to share a great deal as well. Classmates of varying abilities supported each other, listened to each other, and reacted personally to what was happening in each of the novels they read. Each reading was an individual experience that took place in a community of readers, and because reading in this class surpassed skills, literal interpretations, and answering teacher questions, each individual student was able to grow.

In the spring, David was mainstreamed to the junior high school for math and social studies. I followed his progress and received reports from Amy that he was doing very well in the public school, making grades of A's and B's. I sometimes had the opportunity to watch and listen to him when he returned to Amy's classroom with reports of what was going on in the public school. No longer did he feel that the work in Amy's class was easy. In fact, he often turned to her and his peers for advice and help on projects he was doing in his junior high school classes. He knew how to approach a project—how to research a subject, how to use references, and how to write expository pieces—all things he had learned in Amy's class. He proudly but shyly shared his successes with his classmates as Amy read aloud the glowing progress reports that he brought back to class. David thanked his classmates as they cheered, and I remembered that sullen, withdrawn boy I had seen a year before, comparing him to the David I now saw as part of a community of learners who support each other. As a learner, David had a better idea of who he was and where he was going.

School-Wide Alternatives to Tracking

Recent research has pointed to the negative effects of tracking, especially for those students caught in the lower tracks (Kerckhoff, 1986; Oakes, 1985; Trimble & Sinclair, 1987). When Wendell Schwartz and Dan Galloway (1992), teachers at Adlai Stevenson High School in Illinois, looked at their school's ability-grouping practices, they and their colleagues found that the achievement of the students placed in the higher-level groups was high while the students in the lower-level classes never seemed to raise their level of performance and the program of instruction had become what some could only call "watered down." Not surprisingly, achievement seemed proportionate to motivation: Students in the lower-level classes were less motivated than students in the higher-level classes. But the most damning finding challenging ability grouping was that movement between tracks was infrequent and that students, once placed in lower-level groups, remained in lower-level groups year after year. Obviously, ability grouping seemed indefensible, given its rationale that "the academic needs of all students will be better met when the core subjects are taught to groups of students with similar capabilities or groups of students demonstrating prior levels of achievement" (p.9). Not only did ability grouping do little to address individual needs or cope with individual differences, it failed to promote success for the lower-level students. Instead, "it was perpetuating their lower-level status" (p. 9).

The teachers in the English department at Adlai Stevenson decided to try an alternative to tracking, one that would "promote greater success for the lower-track students while still maintaining . . . a very successful and large honors program for its higher-achieving students," those who were succeeding in the existing program (pp. 9–10). In 1989–90, the lower-level groups were eliminated in all junior-year English classes. Students who normally would have been placed in these tracks were placed instead in college preparatory level classes. The upper-level courses (Honors and Advanced Placement) remained as they had been. Although the alternative did not eliminate tracking, it was a start. The biggest change was in the curriculum—no more "watered down" versions of English. Instead, all students were given opportunities to read, write, and react to the same curriculum with positive expectations for all. In addition, extensive support services were offered to assist students during their study hall periods. These services consisted of mandated tutorials in composition and reading for students who needed such support and continued until such time as they were able to function successfully without such support. The tutorials were conducted by teachers who were assigned to the reading/writing center in lieu of study-hall duty. Although the tutoring sessions began by being mandatory, students frequently continued receiving instruction in the reading/writing center voluntarily.

By the end of the first semester, 80 percent of the students in these classes passed their English course with a grade of C or better, even though the course was more difficult than previous courses, involved more work, and had higher expectations. These students were able to function successfully with their peers in a positive environment, one challenging them but supporting them as well. They knew that their teachers believed in them, and they were able to accomplish more than they ever had in previous "basic" or "nonacademic" courses.

Although Stevenson's program was conceived as an English program, it was supported by teachers from other disciplines, especially in courses where reading and writing are central to the learning process. As the program progressed, tutors were enlisted from subject areas other than English, and teachers from these disciplines assisted students with content-related issues.

If students are not tracked, then teachers must use assessment strategies in order to know their students and meet their needs. By eliminating the lower tracks from their programs, teachers at Stevenson High School were able to directly address the needs of their students, providing opportunities for all—regardless of ability—to grow. When given the chance, instead of being told what they are incapable of doing by labeling them "lower track," "basic," or "remedial," students prove what they can do. All students make strides when they're working in authentic and meaningful language situations, as the examples from classroom situations have shown.

For Further Exploration

1. Visit a high school where they track students. How are students assigned to groups? How is their progress monitored? Interview teachers from each track. How do these teachers view tracking? What are their expectations for their students? How do their views on tracking compare with their philosophical stance for teaching and learning?

2. Find out what support services are available for students in an area high school. How are these services provided? Is there a resource room? If so, who is assigned there? Is there a remedial reading program? If so, what is the curriculum in this program and how are students assigned? Is there a writing lab? Who uses this lab? What other support services are in the school?

3. Interview high school students to find out their views of themselves as learners and their opinions about school. As part of the interview, try to find out what track these students are in. Does

their placement in tracks seem to affect their opinions about their abilities and their attitudes toward school?

4. Talk with a high school guidance counselor. How are students assigned to groups or tracks in that school? If assignment is based on test scores, what tests are given? Is any other criteria used for placement? Ask the guidance counselor about his or her opinion of tracking.

5. Interview a parent of a student who has had academic difficulty in school. When did this begin? How was the problem diagnosed? How was the student supported by the school system through the years? How does the student feel about school? About him or herself? Ask the parent how he or she feels about the education their son or daughter has gotten in school. What do they like and/or dislike?

Related Readings for Further Thought and Exploration

Five, C. (1991). *Special voices*. Portsmouth, NH: Heinemann.
Contains stories of students with special needs and the effect that a supportive classroom community has on these students' academic and personal growth. Although the examples are of elementary children, the situations apply to students in many schools at any grade level.

Rose, M. (1989). *Lives on the boundary: The struggles and achievements of America's underprepared*. New York: The Free Press.
Challenges educators to reexamine their assumptions about the adults and children labeled "at risk." Using personal experiences from his own journey from a Los Angeles ghetto to a major university, Rose contends that it is the barriers educators set up that prevent students from learning and offers a vision for truly democratic teaching.

Stires, S. (1991). *With promise: Redefining reading and writing for special students*. Portsmouth, NH: Heinemann.
Describes how classroom teachers and "special" teachers in elementary and middle school work together to support "at-risk" students.

Taylor, D. (1991). *Learning denied*. Portsmouth, NH: Heinemann.
Illustrates how labeling students in schools not only is detrimental to academic growth but fails to reflect a true profile of the child as a learner. This book should be required reading for all teachers at every grade level.

Chapter Eight

Program Versus Philosophy
Technology in the Context of a Whole Language Philosophy

Politicians, bureaucrats, administrators, and even parents will press for the expanded use of computers in education; they will continue to confuse economy with efficiency. Uncertain or lazy teachers who cannot think of more productive ways of using computers will open the classroom doors to the programs. They will admit the agent of their own destruction.

—Frank Smith

Questions for Thought/Journal Entries

1. Why do you think teachers, parents, school board members, and community leaders are pushing for computers in the classroom?

2. Why was there so much negative attention given to the introduction of an independent morning television news program, Channel One, into the schools?

3. What does the term *computer literate* mean to you?

4. Some advocates of computers are speaking of the virtual classroom, a classroom without physical location, one created by virtue of teachers and students being linked on a network. How would you feel "taking a class" at home, linked to other students at their home computers, all connected to a teacher at a computer somewhere else? How would you feel "teaching" such a class?

5. At one time audio-visuals in the classroom meant using a film-strip or overhead projector, playing a record, or showing a film. Today computers have the capability of combining text, graphics, and sound on screen, displaying the presentation according to the interactive selections made by the teacher or the students. Explore your initial reactions to this technological advance.

Introduction

Teachers, parents, school board members, and community leaders are absolutely convinced that students need to be computer literate if they are going to enter the Twenty-first Century. These groups are equally unsure what exactly being computer literate means. This chapter will explore the uses and abuses of technology in the classroom, considering the implications of programmed learning and examining how a whole language philosophy provides a theoretical context for computers in the classroom.

Programming the Curriculum

Parents, school board members, administrators, and community leaders want the best for their schools and the students in those schools. They have strong convictions about what should and should not be taught, how it should and should not be taught, and who should and should not be doing the teaching. Unfortunately, those convictions are shaped by numerous contradictory forces. At the moment, these groups have an instinctive desire for education to be technologically current, at the same time that they concede their own ignorance about what it takes to have currency. They are willing to spend extraordinary amounts from school budgets to employ experts—consultants from the business world—to give their schools the edge. Yet, the push for computers in the classroom is symptomatic of organizing a curriculum without having a theoretical understanding as the guide.

Instead of simply looking at the computer in the classroom, we would present the discussion in its broader sense—program versus philosophy.

One of the newest introductions of technology into the classroom has not been computer technology, but television. Many of us remember as students being herded into a gymnasium or auditorium to watch the latest triumph of the NASA space program on a small screen television. Others of us remember schools using television in the curriculum for years, tuning in the Public Broadcasting Network programs and showing pre-recorded videotapes of classic programs, network specials, and serious movies. Now, a private corporation has funded the wiring of schools across the country to broadcast a morning news show for high school students, Channel One. To many, a morning news program seemed a natural extension of the possibilities of education through broadcasting. Instead, the technology was met with controversy. For some reason, the introduction of Channel One hit a nerve. Parents complained about the two minutes of commercials targeted for teens. Community leaders argued that the news was being constructed by private industry, corporations outside the regulations and influence of the FCC. Teachers saw their role being usurped by the television commentators, their curriculum being co-opted by others outside of their community. Union leaders worried about television sets beaming a national curriculum into every classroom in the country, making the "live" teacher obsolete. Some saw Channel One as the beginning of a brainwashing campaign by the opposition—the communists, the liberals, the fundamentalists, the conservatives, or the facists. Others saw Channel One as a seductive advertising campaign, akin to what MTV might do if it ran the news department of CBS.

It seems to us that the real danger of Channel One is the introduction of a portion of the curriculum that is outside the control of the teachers and the students. On any given morning, no one—not the teachers, the students, the administration, or the parents—knows what the class will watch. This sort of activity flies in the face of a curriculum that is mandated by every agency from the federal and state governments to the local school board. The issue is control. Who controls the curriculum?

Presently, the curriculum is controlled by the textbook publishers, the audio-visual producers, the test-making corporations, and the lobbyists who influence the regulatory agencies. Textbook corporations not only control the written content of the textbooks but shape the curriculum by offering teacher-proof manuals, providing behavioral objectives, Madeline Hunter motivations, lesson plans, activities, and test questions with answer keys.

A-V makers offer supplements to the curriculum that reduce complex events and issues to a sequenced program trivializing education. Students watch a sound and vision presentation, less sophisticated than television, in a darkened room, their eyes focused on the screen in the front, unable to take notes or interact with classmates, their teacher reduced to the role of projectionist, turning the strip according to the chimed notes.

Test makers control the curriculum because it is they who validate whether learning has taken place. School districts judge their teachers just as parents judge their children—according to a test. When a test is given, everyone teaches to the test, hoping for high marks and the rewards that come from a job well done. When a test is given, a teacher knows what must be covered; therefore, those who construct the test, construct the curriculum.

Lobbyists who influence the regulatory agencies and the other groups already mentioned—textbook publishers, a-v producers, test makers—control what will be taught or not taught. Groups like the Eagle Foundation lobby to restrict the use of portfolios, the use of journals, the content of the curriculum (should evolution be taught as a competing theory to creationism, if at all?), and the teaching of values (should students respect everyone regardless of their race, heritage, lifestyle, etc. and should these things be discussed in classrooms?). In this light, Channel One hardly seems a threat to the objectivity of the curriculum.

Technology is simply the latest contender for the control of the curriculum. The danger to the curriculum is allowing others to program our classrooms, including those who control the technology. A whole language philosophy can inform our use of computers to enhance the teaching of composition and provide cautions against their misuse.

Computer-assisted instruction at one time promoted drill-for-skill programs and recently idea-processors, spell-checkers, and style-checkers, creating on-line versions of five-paragraph essays, focusing attention on error detection. When computers are introduced in a classroom, what happens is determined by teaching style, student writing activities, and classroom climate. The technology tends to draw attention to itself, making the machine the center of the lessons, forcing students to learn how to operate the system, learn a new vocabulary, and learn a new way of performing old tasks. But computers are not a single entity. A computer is a tool to write with—an electronic pen or typewriter—yet it's much more than a writing instrument. A computer is a media tool to deliver instruction; it's a communications tool like a telephone; and, it's a storage device like a book. A computer is not just one thing, so an analysis of computer technology has to be multi-dimensional. We will examine these four aspects of computers, looking at how they are used for writing, instruction, communications, and storage.

Technology for Writing

Many teachers understand the value the computer has for writing, echoing the feelings of one of our colleagues who said, "Word processing increases fluency and improves revision strategies (not to mention enhancing keyboard skills); I hope more students learn it."

In general, students have embraced the technology, with each year's class knowing more than their predecessors about computers. One first-year college student, discussing word processing in the course of an in-class free-writing focused on individual writing histories, wrote, "I didn't like writing too much in high school.... [Word processing] is great! ... The more you use it, the easier it gets." The most convincing argument that word processing does more than function as an electronic typewriter is offered by a student who writes, "I enjoy writing with the word processor because I am able to sit at the computer and try out different ideas in . . . my writing." Word processing encourages risk-taking. Another wrote, "In high school, I did just enough to get by. [Word processing] makes writing easier because you can erase easily and change your mind without having to start a new page." Revision is encouraged by computers; a fourth student explains, "Word processing makes it much simpler to change things around and make adjustments without retyping the whole paper. It's made a big difference." Our sense is that reluctant writers become writers by writing, a change that word processing encourages.

Technology for Instruction

Using technology in the classroom requires that teachers take instructional time in the classroom to teach students how to use a simple word-processing program, typically a two- or three-class orientation. After that, most students are able to do their work on the computer; however, some teachers feel that the increased amount of writing promoted by the computer is not in itself enough to improve writing. Teachers feel that they need software. Intuitively realizing that students' writing won't change unless given specific strategies for examining their writing in new ways, teachers seem to be searching for the perfect software.

It is important, however, to look at how software technology views language learning, remembering that, in a whole language context, students learn to read while they are writing, and they learn about writing by reading. Some software programs offer to analyze and check writing conventions with computerized spell checkers, style checkers, sentence parsers, and on-line handbooks. These programs put undue emphasis on correctness rather than on meaning, and considering the dubious accuracy of the programs, give students either a false sense of security ("I've checked it, . . ." they say) or a heightened anxiety about their abilities ("The computer flagged something as wrong, and since I don't know how to fix it, I'll simply delete it," they say). Whole language teachers agree that spelling is important at some point; nevertheless, they believe that spell checkers can give the wrong message—that revision means checking one's spelling—and style checkers, emphasizing stylistic features (sentence length, repetition of words, reading levels, percentages of certain parts of speech), give another wrong impression—that good writing means approximating the norms. On-line handbooks are no better than their textbook versions; although more convenient, on-line handbooks not only emphasize correctness but give confusing advice, often of value only to someone who already understands the rule being alluded to.

Much of the software on the market is impressive in its ability to calculate, offer branching alternatives, and present eye-catching graphics, but it is disappointing in its content—phonics for elementary school children and five-paragraph essays for older students. Some, including Michael Apple (1989) and Frank Smith (1988a;1988b), object that the curriculum is being usurped by software developers, despite many companies' advertising claims that their software has been developed with the "help" of "active teachers." Technological corporations will continue to offer unsatisfactory software—endorsed by those who should know better—as long as "uncertain or apprehensive teachers are . . . content to hand over the task of constructing programs to experienced software producers" (Smith, 1988a, p. 83).

What is often referred to as integrated software, computer programs that address the whole writing process—WRITER'S HELPER (William Wresch, Conduit) for example—are usually theoretically sound, but they can be misused by being applied in a lock-step fashion. Some packages force a student to complete its prewriting exercise before allowing the writer to start on a draft. Some programs turn the prewriting exercise into a five-paragraph theme. Such applications take the fire out of the writing. Even if the technology allows a student to move around at will, the student might not be aware of the options and react to the sequence as just another algorithm— first this, then that. A whole language teacher must present the integrated exercises as demonstrations of possibilities and encourage experimentation and risk-taking.

Yet a computer with a good word-processing program can also deliver instruction, providing individualized instruction through lesson files created by the instructor and read by the student like other text files. Lesson files are a planned sequence of activities, presented screen-by-screen, having the advantage of allowing students to return to previous screens to revise or modify answers. The lesson files contain prompts to writing, offering a myriad of writing activities—focusing on paragraphing, prewriting, editing, and more—and suggesting a variety of writing tasks. Lesson files operate as word-processing text files, so they can be created by a teacher with an elementary knowledge of word processing, making it much more realistic than creating programs written in computer languages. For example, many teachers assign some form of an autobiographical essay. This can become a computer-assisted lesson. Figure 8–1 shows a lesson file, called "Memory," created by Rebecca Laubach, a ninth/tenth-grade teacher at Mars Area High School, with no programming knowledge and nothing more than a word-processing program (Strickland, 1988). When one of her students loads the file, the first of seven screens appears, and the student simply reads the file and responds using the keyboard wherever appropriate. A full treatment of lesson files—how to create them and how to use them—may be found in Dawn and Ray Rodrigues's (1986) *Teaching Writing with a Word Processor*, an NCTE/Theory & Research into Practice booklet.

Hypermedia and Reading

I (Kathleen) have been "kid-watching," to use Yetta Goodman's term, a group of junior-high aged, emotionally disturbed children. One student told me, "I used to think reading was words, but now I know reading is stories." (Strickland, 1993, p. 195). The point was not lost on us: this student had previously seen books as containing symbols, but in an epiphany, his literacy had changed. He became print literate. Those symbols on the page—the black on blank, as Jacques Derrida (1981) says—are not meanings to be decoded; they become meaningful only in the act of reading. Reading takes place behind the eye (Smith, 1988c). By analogy, the computer screen contains symbols that can be manipulated, compared, and transferred, but they are not meaningful until a reader interacts with the symbols. A whole language perspective on technology rejects any use of the computer that attempts to co-opt the meaning-making function of the user. Yet, that is precisely the danger inherent in the latest technology, hypermedia.

Hypermedia or multimedia computer programs combine text, graphics, and images for interactive teaching that takes advantage of digitized sound, data-driven animation, and full-motion video interface. The software creates linked files, which can be selected from pop-up/pull-down menus or "triggered" by clicking hot-spots, on-screen buttons, offering truly interactive computer-assisted instruction. For example, hypermedia programs are being constructed to offer a more sense-oriented experience of literary classics. A "Great

Figure 8–1

Computer Screen Representation of "Memory" Lesson File

Screen 1   Memory

THIS IS YOUR LIFE

(Type your name here)

AS YOU MOVE THROUGH THIS LESSON, TRY TO CENTER EACH
SET OF DIRECTIONS ON THE SCREEN SO THAT YOU SEE ONLY
ONE SET OF DIRECTIONS OR ACTIVITIES AT A TIME

Screen 2   Memory

EVERYONE has unforgettable memories from CHILDHOOD.
These memories come from

- experiences at school,
- vacations with our families,
- time spent with friends,
- or just everyday life.

In this lesson, you are going to write about
events from YOUR PAST.

Screen 3   Memory

In the spaces provided below, complete as many of the
   following sentences as you can.

- The things that frightened me as a child were . . .
- My happiest memory is . . .
- My childhood was unusual because . . .
- I got into trouble when . . .
- When I was young I admired . . .
- My confidence showed when . . .
- My saddest memory is . . .

            When you've done as many as you can, move on.

Figure 8–1 (cont.)

Screen 4   Memory

Now you are going to E X P A N D

one of the sentences

you wrote into a paragraph.

Choose any sentence you want

and COPY/PASTE it below in Screen 5.

Screen 5   Memory

Copy your sentence here —>

Now, in a few more sentences,

EXPLAIN WHAT YOU SAID.

You can give two or three short examples

that illustrate your point, or

you can tell one long story.

Begin typing by placing the cursor

at the end of the sentence you copied above.

When you are finished move on to the next screen.

Screen 6   Memory

Now that you have something written,

you might want to revise it.

Go back and REREAD the paragraph you have just written.

While you are reading, ask yourself:

- Does my paragraph clearly express the idea I
  had in mind?

Figure 8–1 (cont.)

Screen 7   Memory

Trade seats with a classmate and read each other's memory.

  • Ask your classmate to point to places where
    someone who doesn't know you would have trou-
    ble understanding what you're saying and why
    you're saying it.

After trading, you may want to make some changes.

    Be sure to SAVE this file and get a PRINTOUT.

                                        End of ''Memory''

Book," *The Odyssey* perhaps, would be presented as text in an eye-pleasing large typescript in one portion of the computer screen, with a boxed portion for an appropriate illustration, say a drawing of Homer or one of the characters in the epic, and overlays providing other points of interest to sample. The illustration box might also act as a trigger-field that could play a full-motion video segment corresponding to the text—something from a PBS production or even a B-movie adventure film. A button on the screen could be triggered to hear a "reading" of the text given by a professional, an option allowing users to hear the text as their eyes follow along. Finally, all the important concepts, allusions, and references would have footnote buttons, locations that could be triggered to retrieve an explanation or corresponding information that the author of the interactive software thought would be helpful. The linked documents would themselves have boxes, buttons, and links ad infinitum. As a student "reads" the classic, the computer seems to offer a plethora of footnotes and a variety of experiences. Yet, we know that the ghost in the machine is a human agent who has structured the possible experiences—the student's university professor or an anonymous programmer working for a software corporation.

Our transactional theory of reading holds that linguistic or visual cues in the text trigger responses that create meaning. What happens when the trigger is pulled by the software programmer responsible for creating the links and supplying the content at the other end of the link? The imputation is that the software has been constructed in such a way as to attempt to embed the meaning of the text in the program—with boxes, buttons, and links—rather than to encourage a reader to bring meaning to the text. To give an example, imagine reading Edgar Allan Poe's "Annabel Lee." One student in the class might offer in a response journal or in a class discussion that the poem's line "my darling, my life and my bride" triggered an association with Billy Idol's song/video "White Wedding." Discussion could begin in a dialogue journal or class from this association. Contrast this personal interaction with text by imagining a student reading a hypermedia version of the poem. When the student clicks on a button at the end of the line quoted, the screen dissolves to an actual video clip of Billy Idol singing the chorus to "White Wedding." The screen might have just as reasonably dissolved to a video clip of the student's professor explaining the line as a reference to Poe's first sweetheart, Sarah Royster Shelton. The computer has, in effect, forced a reading on the student by encoding a meaning, one given added weight because of the technological presentation. The hypermedia reading, much more seductive than a classroom lecture, is an attempt to create "canned" schema in order to promote or privilege one reading of the text over another.

What is the point? The computer is merely a tool, yet it is not value neutral. The computer privileges information over understanding. We must consider the purpose for using the computer to deliver the text in the exciting world of hypermedia. If the purpose is to give the student information, then the computer has made great advances. If the purpose is to provide opportunities and situations where students can discover and experiment in order to create knowledge, then we may have just thwarted our desires. Allow an exploration of the subtlety a little further.

Whole language is concerned with the construction of meaning, valuing the role that the reader plays in the construction. With hypermedia, the world of text can open in two different ways. In one way, the linking possibilities are already made for the student reader to sample, what Michael Joyce (1988) terms the exploratory aspect of hypermedia; the possibilities are defined, however vast their number. Thus one reader's interpretation of significance, codified by the very creation of the buttons, has set the parameters for any exploration; the established readings have been validated as "correct" or possibly correct. Their pre-existence strips the reader of an active role in construction; the reader is simply a follower of paths. In this sense, the technology has created the electronic counterpart of the teacher's manual, the magic book that has the answers in the back. However, the second way the world opens with hypermedia is much more in

line with a whole language philosophy. In this way, the reader—
student as well as teacher—creates the links in order to establish the
buttons, what Michael Joyce (1988) terms the constructive aspect of
hypermedia. This second use of hypermedia capabilities would be
within a whole language context; no reading would be privileged
above another. This is to push risk-taking to the limit and requires
complete trust in students as meaning-makers.

In its defense, hypermedia has value in allowing the text to come
alive on-screen. When students read Martin Luther King's "I have a
dream" speech or "Letter from Birmingham Jail," they are able to
hear it read by King or a professional actor. While theoretically we
worry about what the buttons choose to offer as a brief biography of
King, a newspaper account of his famous march, or perhaps a television special covering the events surrounding his death—all autho-
rized and sanitized by whomever is in power—we recognize in
hypermedia a way to reach the reluctant reader. In the past, teachers
assigned readings and simply expected students to read the assignment and come to class prepared to take notes and answer "display
questions" about the work. Students who were unable to get through
it would simply skip the reading and hope to glean enough from the
lecture to pass the test. Teachers informed by a whole language philosophy support reading by using interactive video as a form of
shared reading, where students are able to follow along in the text as
they hear it read aloud, giving them the opportunity to read texts
they might not attempt otherwise.

Technology for Communication

It becomes clearer that the value of computers in a whole language
context depends, to a great degree, on how the teacher approaches
their use. Since learning is a social construct, computers should be
used in collaborative situations. This will take conscious effort, due
to classroom/lab designs, which work to heighten isolation. The
machine does not require social interaction; it draws the learner into
itself, not out. Regardless of the configuration of the computer lab,
students operate as though closed in a carrel, receiving assignments
sometimes given and even completed on disk, working on isolated
tasks with a worksheet mentality that tells them that they are free to
leave the lab when finished with the exercise.

Teachers must encourage students to talk to one another about
their learning, but this is learned behavior; students won't do so
spontaneously, unless it is encouraged as appropriate. Too often, the
help that students offer each other, documented in testimonials of

the computer's effectiveness, is help with technological problems and questions rather than help with learning/written expression problems. From their teachers and their years of schooling, students have learned to ignore the community aspect of learning. Students are judged by their performance as isolated individuals, receiving grades at the end of every semester for every course they take, an evaluation based upon performance in competition with others in the class. Students are told to hand in work that is their own, and those who receive help from another risk being accused of plagiarism or cheating. No wonder students sense that it may be okay to tell classmates how to do something on the computer but not how to express what they are trying to say.

Still, knowledge is socially constructed; everything we know or believe is negotiated and validated in community. In the traditional school community, the teacher is the final arbiter of meaning. In a teacher-centered classroom, students must find the answers and reach the conclusions that the teacher maintains as correct. In a student-centered classroom, the teacher is only one more voice within a community of learners—the meaning of a poem, the value of an essay, even the causes of the Second World War are arrived at and agreed upon by those present in the discussion. Learning is organic, shaped by contradictions, growing with the viewpoints and arguments being offered.

Learning in a community is fostered by the computer lab when there is time in class to give and receive feedback from other learners, time to make immediate changes to work in progress and to risk trying new things, and time to ask advice of a teacher who is also a learner. The computer lab is a special workspace where classmates working at terminals are accessible and their work is shareable. The computer lab stands in contrast to the desks and rows of a traditional classroom, constructed to isolate learners and focus attention to the front of the room, the location where the teacher is found. In a traditional classroom, regardless of whether desks are rearranged into small groups, sharing one's work with more than one person is difficult and even that requires handing over the physical copy to another person. In the computer lab, teachers can allow two or three people to sit around a classmate's screen and simultaneously read what has been written. If the lab is networked, the work can be sent to as many terminals in the room as desired (or elsewhere for that matter), all the while retaining the original on-screen.

For example, Laura might send a draft of her paper on the environment, a file named OZONE.DOC to her friend, Kayla (physically or over a network). After reading Laura's original text, Kayla can simply change the name to OZONE.TWO (or anything else) and begin to alter the original text, insert notes to Laura within the text, or write a letter to Laura giving her responses. Once finished, Kayla returns the new file (OZONE.TWO) to Laura, providing her with the feedback all learners require while allowing Laura, since she still has her original (OZONE.DOC), to maintain responsibility for and authority over her writing.

The computer affords teachers a place for two or more people to hold writers' conferences, using the same screen or conversing over a network. If Kayla were sitting as part of a group around the same screen, she could point to sections of the writing on the screen and make suggestions, trying them out in front of Laura and anyone else gathered around, a type of interactive feedback that is nearly impossible to achieve in a regular classroom setting.

Computers can also provide the computer conference as a forum for academic discourse outside the classroom. The computer conference uses a communal computer disk as a place to hold discussions, student-centered academic forums outside the control of a teacher. The computer offers disk space for the discussion; students send their written comments to be saved as part of a shared file. Thus, computer files become a place to hold public discussions of issues of concern to those involved in the conference. The computer allows time for students to consider, prepare, and work out thoughts before entering their contribution to the discussion taking place on a computer bulletin board or conference. Computer conferences offer equality because those reading the file lack the external clues about identity that color our perceptions—gender, age, and race. Computer conferences are less restrictive because students need not compete in academic discussions for attention of the teacher in order to be recognized and need not follow formal rules of classroom behavior. Computer conferences promote the activity of learning rather than the passivity of "being taught."

Teachers who encourage using a computer in this type of community teach that time spent in a collaborative effort—learning by interaction with other learners—is as valuable, maybe more valuable, as getting individual work done or getting the assignment finished.

Technology for Storage

Computers are not only tools for writing, for delivering instruction, and for carrying on conversations, they are also a means of storage, a radically different media than any other device teachers have considered previously. When students are finished working on a text, the computer stores the file on a magnetic disk. The file-on-disk contains the essence of the work in digital code, hidden from reading until called up on-screen again or printed in hard copy, a typescript of the work on paper. However, printing hard copy is no longer simply a matter of dot-matrix print. Most computer labs have access to laser printers, and some students even have desk-top publishing at their fingertips. We have seen students reprint their essays five or six times to get it to look right on the paper. Whole language teachers have to convince students to relax their concern for the look of the material and concentrate on the meaning, encouraging them to fiddle with text on-screen at various levels—word, sentence, paragraph—printing it to read again, and going back to write more. Unless whole language teachers model the process, students will continue to be seduced by appearance.

Over and above storing individual files on disk, computers have the ability to store linked files, producing a digital compilation. Whole language teachers will be able to use this capability to transform the reductionist grades of the report card into a hypermedia portfolio for individual assessment of students. Computers are capable of storing text (drafts, reports, projects), sound (speeches, in-class reports, readings), and image data (photographs, drawings, handwritten samples) in hypertext stacks. Instead of a written transcript, indicating courses and grades for each level, teachers, parents, and the students themselves would have access to a cumulative portrait of themselves in digital code.

Conclusion

Whole language teachers would hardly consider configuring a classroom where the learner receives information from an authority figure, manipulates the information according to a predetermined set of directions, and then receives feedback as to how adroitly the information was assimilated and returned. Yet this context for using computers continues because that's what a computer does; it's an information delivery system. Whole language teachers argue that information is not understanding; information is not education; information is not learning. Whole language is concerned with understanding, with learning, and with making meaning rather than with the retrieval of information. Whole language teachers maintain that students have to do something with the information, an aspect missing from many approaches to using computers to teach language, reading, and writing. In such a case, the teacher offers questions, artifacts, problems, situations, new information, and the students must formulate interpretations. The teacher can then validate those interpretations or offer new information to modify them (and the teacher's interpretation can be modified and validated as well). If we are more and more convinced of the rightness of a whole language classroom, then we cannot have students perform software activities, which by their nature are predetermined, and expect learning to take place.

Instead, a whole language classroom with computers is language rich, looking at language as exciting and dynamic, a means of bringing groups together, fostering collaborative learning and communication between and among discourse communities. We might advise teachers to simply resist engaging in educationally unsound practices simply because the technology makes them easy to do.

For Further Exploration

1. Visit a computer lab and pay attention to the social interaction. Are students working alone at their terminals? Do they talk to those around them? What is the talk about—the subject matter or technical concerns?

2. Visit a school that uses computers in the classroom. Keep notes on what type of programs the students use. Notice whether the students seem involved in the activity or are merely walking through the program.

3. Interview a teacher who seems involved with computers. Ask what he or she hopes the computer will do for the students. Interview a teacher who doesn't make use of computers. Ask why he or she doesn't seem to take advantage of the technology.

4. Ask to use a hypermedia program if you are in a school that is equipped for interactive software. Try the program as a student might, clicking the buttons that seem appropriate, taking the paths that students might choose. Consider the choices that are being offered and the information that is being delivered. Whose point of view are you getting? Is there any opportunity for you to make an active construction?

5. The next time you hear a parent express the cliché that students need to know computers, ask the parent to explain why. Try to get the discussion beyond merely agreeing that computers seem to be influencing every aspect of the business world.

Related Readings for Further Thought and Exploration

Handa, C. (Ed.). (1990). *Computers and community: Teaching composition in the twenty-first century.* Portsmouth, NH: Boynton/Cook.

Examines the social and pedagogical implications of teaching with computers in a networked environment.

Hawisher, G. E., & LeBlanc, P. (Eds.). (1992). *Re-imagining computers and composition: Teaching and research in the virtual age.* Portsmouth, NH: Boynton/Cook.
Explores the changes that virtual technologies, networking and hypermedia, for example, will bring to our notions of teaching composition.

Hawisher, G. E., & Selfe, C. L. (Eds.). (1991). *Evolving perspectives on computers and composition studies: Questions for the 1990s.* Urbana, IL: National Council of Teachers of English.
Reviews the present state of computer use in writing instruction and anticipates future areas of concern, examining four broad categories: Scholarly Research, Classroom Contexts, Hypertext Applications, and Political Considerations.

Rodrigues, D., & Rodrigues, R. (1986). *Teaching writing with a word processor, grades 7-13.* Urbana, IL: ERIC/National Council of Teachers of English.
Offers theory supporting the use of computers and language learning as well as practical strategies for teaching writing with a computer.

Selfe, C. L., Rodrigues, D., & Oates, W. R. (Eds.). (1989). *Computers in English and the language arts.* Urbana, IL: National Council of Teachers of English.
Describes a dozen examples of teacher-preparation programs and inservice programs offered at high schools and colleges, and probes specific topics of interest, such as prewriting software, style-checkers, databases, and networks.

Chapter Nine

Whole Language— A Political Issue

As part of the more general move toward increased profes- sionalism that is at the heart of whole language, we whole language educators have also started to become more polit- ical. We are making political analyses and political state- ments where we made none before; we are recognizing the political nature of curriculum and acting as advocates for students and, at long last, for ourselves as professionals as well.

—Carole Edelsky

Questions for Thought/Journal Entries

1. Is education political? In what ways? Have the politics of educa- tion changed since you have been in school? In what ways and why?

2. How do you think parents react to whole language? Why? How can teachers and parents work together?

3. Who controls education; that is, who makes the decisions about what and how students should be taught? Is it teachers? Parents? Politicians? Students? Who *should* control education? Why?

4. Are schools value neutral? In what sense are the values taught in school determined by different political factions?

5. Should teachers be political? If so, in what ways and why?

Introduction

The Whole Language movement is part of a paradigm shift in education, a change in basic beliefs and assumptions that inform our view of the world. Yet understanding the philosophy of whole language and desiring to enact it in the classroom is not always enough. Education itself is political; when changes in philosophy change the way teachers and students view learning, those who do not understand often set up road blocks and barriers. This chapter will deal with the issue of political change in education and how teachers can work within the system to bring about change.

Whole Language—Why Not?

After several weeks of reading and discussion in class about whole language, our students will often ask a simple yet powerful question: "Since whole language makes so much sense, and research has shown that this is the way people learn best, why isn't the whole language philosophy the basis for instruction in all schools?"

Good question.

As more and more teachers embrace a whole language philosophy, teachers themselves are organizing local support groups, meeting weekly or monthly, to share ideas and concerns. In fact, national teacher-support groups, such as the Whole Language Umbrella, a confederation of support groups with membership in the thousands, have begun to hold conferences at numerous sites across the United States. School districts in every state announce themselves as "whole language" districts, ones in which principals, coordinators, and superintendents support teachers who are willing to take risks and implement student-centered, purposeful instruction. States such as California, Kentucky, and New York openly promote whole language and provide state support for the training of teachers and the reorganization of schools. Publications such as *Teachers Networking: The Whole Language Newsletter* (see "Related Readings" at the end of this chapter) and *The Whole Language Umbrella Newsletter* (Box 2029, Bloomington, IN 47402-2029) provide necessary professional links for their subscribers as well as informative articles.

Our students and many others get the impression that whole language is becoming the foundation for education across the country; in reality, however, many teachers and administrators are not only unwilling to learn about whole language but openly hostile toward such a change. Another complicating factor is well-intentioned teachers who call their methodology and programs "whole language" without understanding or embracing its underlying philosophy, thereby further confusing those unfamiliar with the term and what it means.

Although our students' question is simple and straightforward, the answer to their question is far from simple. Patrick Shannon (1991), in his article "Talking Back to Critics," sets out three distinct groups of "resisters to whole language" (p. 1). These groups include those who resist because they were taught differently and will not change since the traditional ways worked for them; those who resist because they reject the evidence of whole language research, considering authentic research as a strictly quantitative investigation, discounting other types of research that examine the affective domain; and those who resist because they regard learning and the function of schools in a way very different from whole language advocates.

The Old Ways Are the Best Ways—Why Change?

In most cases, it's human nature to be comfortable with that which is familiar; the idea of change is often frightening and overwhelming. Many people question whole language because it means a complete change in how they define learning, teaching, and school; it departs from the ways in which they were taught, from what they know, and from what they conceive school and education to be. They view school as a place where teachers are the authorities—where teachers know the answers and are responsible for passing on knowledge to their students, conceptions consistent with a transmission model of education. Furthermore, by extension, textbooks are also authorities, equivalent sources of information and knowledge, and learning is a matter of remembering what is contained in those texts. Such people believe that students should strive for "correctness," error being both unacceptable and a sign of weakness or failure. They believe in the "ladder of learning" metaphor: learning begins from the bottom, starting with what is most simple, and progresses sequentially rung by rung. Many people who were successful in school, educators included, credit this type of instruction for their success. "I learned this way," they contend, "and now I'm a principal . . . , or a teacher . . . , or a lawyer . . . , or a doctor . . . , or an accountant." As one principal put it, "The traditional ways have worked for lots of us. Why change? Why fix what isn't broken?"

And it is not only the successful students who are convinced of the magic of the traditional ways; adults who were not successful in school are equally convinced, blaming themselves for not trying hard enough, for not being bright enough, or for not having teachers who were smart enough. They rarely blame the system that taught them because, if they learned little else, they learned that their own inadequacies were responsible for their failure.

In sharp contrast to the traditional believers, teachers who advocate whole language are those who, having examined their own teaching or experiences, have realized that the traditional paradigm has not permitted students to develop the thinking skills and independent learning behaviors that are essential for lifelong learning. These whole language teachers were not forced to change; instead, they changed as a result of investigation into ways that would improve their teaching and would support all students. Educators who resist whole language fail to question why some of their students are not learning, choosing instead to blame the students for not fitting into the system. Whole language can't be forced upon these traditionalists. These people will remain unconvinced of the significance of whole language until they begin to ask questions and seek answers. Until then, they will be content with what they believe worked in the past; for them, the old ways are the best ways.

Twisted Research

Many in the educational community resist whole language because its philosophy is based on a set of beliefs about research and science that are very different from behaviorist or traditional beliefs. Some in this category agree "partially" with what advocates of whole language say, but the difference is that they do not look to the same type of research or scientific evidence to support their beliefs. Their definitions of reading, writing, learning, teaching, and research are fundamentally different from those of whole language advocates.

Debate is unlikely to change the point of view of those educators. They believe in what they know, and they're not going to change their minds. Many write or consult for the publishing companies that produce the texts based on traditional approaches, and thus politics and business cloud the issue concerning what type of research is to be believed.

Patrick Shannon (1991) offers the misrepresentation of whole language research by Steven Stahl (1990) as an example of this type of resistence. Stahl, Shannon says, distorts the whole language position when he quotes whole language researchers regarding the place of phonics in elementary whole language classrooms, a highly charged, emotional issue for those teaching reading in elementary schools. Stahl quotes Dorothy Watson (1989) as saying that phonics "... is incompatible with a whole language perspective on reading and is therefore rejected" (Shannon, 1991, p. 12). However, Watson actually wrote, "Phonics, as a prescribed skill and drill program rather than a cue to be used in conjunction with all the cues of language is incompatible . . ." (p. 134). Obviously Watson's words and meaning were distorted to suit Stahl's purpose.

An example of how political pressure shapes research is given by Kenneth Goodman (1992) in his article "Why Whole Language Is Today's Agenda in Education." Goodman traces the influence: "Congress ordered the U.S. Department of Education to do a study authenticating phonics as the official government reading methodology. The Department of Education passed the charge to the Center for the Study of Reading (threatening to cut their funding if they declined). The Center contracted with [Marilyn] Adams [(1990a), author of *Beginning to Read*] to write the actual book. Then they assigned Jean Osborn and her colleagues [Steven Stahl included] to write a digest of the book that the Center itself published (see Adams 1990b). These government-subsidized books are being widely promoted by publishers, right-wing groups, and professional associations" as research supporting traditional methods of teaching (p. 355). This is typical of how political pressure is exerted by governmental agencies, business corporations, political groups, and textbook publishers to control the research informing classrooms across the country.

Truth, Justice, and The American Way

For a long time, Americans pretended that their schools were in the business of teaching the truth—"Truth, Justice, and The American Way," if you will. We still remember the day our niece, Carrie, told us that she learned in school that there are no classes in America. We thought of the homeless, the welfare families, the chronically unemployed and began to debate the issue, but Carrie was adamant; apparently in her junior year they had been studying India and the caste system. Her school, despite economic and political realities, taught Carrie that all Americans are equal, but, Thomas Jefferson not withstanding, was it the truth? What is considered the "truth" is intimately connected to the values one holds, and yet, the understanding has always been that public schools, because they are public, are supposed to be value neutral, refraining from espousing or promoting one group's set of beliefs over another's (aside from a generic version of Christianity upon which this country was founded). However, schools have always embraced values that have colored the curriculum—competition, patriotism, individuality, and honesty among others; and the multicultural movement, seeking a broader representation of values—collaboration, ethnic pride, and cooperation, for example—is a reaction to the traditional curriculum. This reaction, in turn, has fed a third group of resisters to whole language who, we believe, are the most powerful. This group is comprised of religious fundamentalists and political conservatives who, using the facade of neutrality, try to organize schools around their personal values, which they claim are pro-family and pro-America.

Not too long ago, I (Kathleen) was called by the assistant superintendent of an area school district, one in which I had acted as a whole language consultant for teachers rewriting their district's Language Arts curriculum. The assistant superintendent was worried about a group of parents, upset by the proposed changes in the curriculum, who were planning to attend a school board meeting in order to voice their concerns. As the district's consultant, I was asked to attend to help the teachers address any questions that might come up at the meeting. Although I knew that the teachers were very knowledgeable about the philosophy of whole language and were themselves very capable of answering any questions, I was also aware that teachers are often underestimated in the political hierarchy of education. As a university professor, I would be regarded as more of an "expert," solely because of my position, even though the teachers and I worked together as colleagues and learned from each other.

The evening of the school board meeting I sat at a table with the assistant superintendent and two teachers who had served in the capacity of lead teachers. It was soon apparent that I was not there to educate anyone or to even answer any questions, as none were ever asked. My purpose was "window dressing"—I was present to show the board that the teachers had had guidance through the process. Two parents attended, supposedly representing many parents in the district, part of a group organized at a fundamentalist Christian Church, one that was outspoken about many social and political issues and one that might be characterized as representing the far right in its views. As these two people spoke, one a housewife and mother of six children, the other a construction worker and father of three, I was amazed at the amount of literature that they had brought with them. Both sat with thick folders before them and often referred to reports and "studies" that were published by educational experts such as Jeanne Chall and information that was disseminated by groups such as The Eagle Forum and Citizens for Excellence in Education, as well as by the Republican National Steering Committee. I listened for nearly a half hour as these two well-intentioned people, genuinely concerned about the education of their children, quoted from research that I knew was flawed and from propaganda based on misinformation and a fear of change. At one point, the father pointed out that such changes in education were the result of theories of a socialist named Dewey. These people were afraid that any change would destroy what they knew to be correct—the way they had been taught and the way they believed they had learned.

After the meeting, I met with these parents for another half hour. I provided them with material that I thought would explain the whole language philosophy and articles that briefly described transactional research. It was apparent, however, that their minds were made up. They were not at the meeting to be educated; they were there to protect their children against an evil that others had already convinced them existed. At the time I was polite, realizing a discussion was futile. As I drove home, angry and frustrated, I went over in my mind all I would have liked to have said but was not in a position to say. I had been an educator for twenty years, studied, taught, researched, and spent my entire life questioning and learning about how students learn. Although I respected the concern these parents had, I wanted to ask them how they could discredit all I had spent my life doing while they posed as educational authorities. I wanted to tell the construction worker that when I had an addition put on my home, I turned to experts for advice—architects and contractors, and I respected their knowledge and expertise. I worked along with them making decisions, but I admitted I didn't know anything about construction. These parents were not themselves educators, yet unlike their behavior toward any other profession, they and many other lay people believe they know about education simply because they attended school.

Resistance to whole language, as with any educational reform, is widespread and very powerful. Reactionary groups not only want to get rid of whole language but also attack, in the process, teachers and other educators who are working to help students. They are simplistic in what they want—traditional methods of instruction based on a behaviorist, bottom-up model of teaching and learning. Such demands encompass the environment of the classroom, the curriculum taught, the books allowed, and the culture and languages that are deemed acceptable.

Control of education doesn't stop with an occasional remark by a parent to a superintendent. Boards of education are comprised of lay persons, people in the community who too frequently win seats on the school board based on platforms promising taxes will not be raised rather than ones promising better learning environments. Of course, these boards are very responsive to the community, listening carefully to the opinions of community members, aware that their seats are elected and their positions are at the whim of the voters. If a few parents, representing even a small minority, are vocal enough in their objections to educational innovation, members of the school board will frequently refuse to support educators for fear of displeasing the community and attracting negative press coverage.

Not only are parents and school boards misinformed by the reactionary feeder groups but elected officials are also hopping on the bandwagon of protecting American education, unaware or misled in their criticism of whole language. Unfortunately the general public often believes what it hears, especially when spoken by their distinguished representatives to the U.S. Senate or Congress. For example, as reported in the Congressional Record, Congressman James E. Brennan of Maine said that, "whole language—look-say methods of reading instruction must be stopped dead in its tracks, if we truly want to cure the nation's illiteracy problem" (Shannon, 1991, p. 13). While it may be obvious, at least to those who understand whole language, that politicians such as Congressman Brennan have no idea what whole language really is, we can't help but worry about how the others in Congress, on school boards, and in neighborhood meetings will regard his words.

Similarly, Senator William L. Armstrong of Colorado gave the following rationale for the "reading instruction in phonics" rider he attached to the National Literacy Act of 1989: "For too long we have been unwilling to deal with the root cause of the problem of illiteracy in America and that is the flawed methods we have used to teach our children to read—namely look-say and whole language methods" (Shannon, 1991, p. 13). The National Literacy Act passed the U.S. Senate on February 6, 1990.

Are Congressman Brennan or Senator Armstrong experts in educational matters? Apparently not. Will their opinions turn up at school board meetings in small towns and large cities? We're afraid so. Part of the ongoing problem with the system of American education is that school boards, senators, congressmen, and governors—people with little or no training in education—make decisions about education, decisions about what and how children should be taught in schools. During Former President Bush's term in office, an Education Summit was held—a meeting at which there was not one teacher in attendance. The summit was attended by state governors, hardly experts in current research and theory. Their systematic exclusion of classroom teachers and teacher-researchers makes it obvious that they continue to regard teachers as nothing more than skilled technicians who carry out the directives of others. President Clinton nominated Richard Riley as Secretary of Education, a man who is a lawyer and former governor of South Carolina, a man whose classroom experience ended when he graduated from the University of South Carolina Law School in 1959. Imagine if President Clinton would have named Ken Goodman or Frank Smith as Secretary of Education.

Censorship: Power Through Control

Nowhere does the classroom teacher's lack of control in educational matters become more pronounced than in the constraints surrounding choice of reading material for assignments, discussions, and projects. In this country, we seem capable of drawing fine distinctions between book-burning, book-banning, and censorship. Book-burning is something anti-intellectual and very radical, the product of times of fear and ignorance. Book-burning is usually thought of as an event in the past, something in history books, taking place in less enlightened countries, such as the reactions and demonstrations in Germany during the 1940s. Book-banning is a slightly different variation; rather than burning a book in protest or torching it as a dramatic means of removal from the shelves, banning a book simply halts its publication or sale. Many famous authors have found their works banned, and the phrase, "banned in Boston," on the cover of a book formerly assured its sales. Although book-banning is no longer common among the adult public, a historical phenomena seldom even discussed among preservice or practicing teachers, the more benign form of book-burning or book-banning is more familiar—censorship.

Censorship is a common topic whenever adults and teens discuss rock music, television, movies, and of course, magazines and books. Conscientious parents check a movie's rating before allowing their children to attend. Those who do are frequently baffled by the system: "That was a PG-13?" murmurs the crowd leaving the theaters. Hardly anyone asks who is doing the rating. Television stations employ professional censors, although even their sensibilities are becoming less refined. Music packages are now labelled, due to the efforts of the Parents Music Resource Center headed by Tipper Gore. The "Warning: Explicit Lyrics" sticker is now such a sought-after label that some rap groups refuse to release their songs unless they are assured of offending someone.

Today, in many school districts, titles such as *To Kill a Mockingbird, Soul on Ice, Of Mice and Men, Forever,* and *The Color Purple* are not allowed in school libraries or in classrooms. Censorship decisions such as these are made locally, usually by school boards and by small groups of concerned citizens; often such decisions are made by people who haven't even read the books. Probst (1988) surmises that such "communities are willing to gamble that keeping children ignorant will keep them pure and safe" (p. 189). Advocates of censorship while maintaining that it is a way of protecting children rarely answer the nagging questions: Who makes the decision what to censor? Do we censor for a community or for an individual? What is the role of the school in censorship?

In the past, students in traditional classrooms read "The Classics," the works of the Western World respected and thought to be "good for students." Parents and their grandparents read Shakespeare, Poe, Dickens, and Homer; such classics of literature—the canon—were accepted as scholarly and appropriate. More recently, students and teachers sensed a need to include literature that fell outside the canon, works that dealt with contemporary life and human issues, such as *To Kill a Mockingbird*, *The Autobiography of Malcolm X*, *Catcher in the Rye*, and *Slaughterhouse Five*. Themes such as bigotry, human suffering, and personal identity could thus be presented in literature that students found relevant and identified with, themes similar to those same ones presented in the works of the canon. Nevertheless, teachers who used these works found that they were met with resistance from community and religious groups professing to be protecting students against literature deemed inappropriate.

Publications such as *What Are They Teaching Our Children?* by Mel and Norma Gabler (1985) and groups such as Educational Research Analysts, the Texas corporation, which the Gablers established, serve as frightening examples of how doctrinaire, conservative, and well organized these censorship groups can be. In the censorship plan, parents inspect the texts and literature that their children use in school, casting about for anti-family, anti-Christian, or anti-American material. Once items are identified, the parents are directed to mobilize a search-and-destroy mission to remove the materials from the schools and the shelves of the libraries. The effect that the Gablers and others have on education goes beyond individual schools or districts; their beliefs shape the actual scope, format, language, and illustrations in children's textbooks. These people identify what they consider to be "dangerous topics" that should be avoided when schools are adopting new textbooks. Since the Gablers' home state of Texas makes state-wide textbook adoptions for its schools, publishers anxious for the multimillion-dollar business pay close attention to the opinions the Gablers express when producing and marketing new textbooks. Since the publishers are not about to produce Texas-only textbooks, the textbooks used by children in every other state have been unduly influenced by the beliefs of the Gablers and other conservatives (Shannon, 1992, p. 66). If the amount and influence of censorship is a sign of the political times, the eighties and early nineties have been a time for conservative viewpoints and conservative political positions (Edelsky, 1992).

Censorship of literature and book-banning has become so organized that such actions often end up in court. In the fall of 1992, a county judge in Western Pennsylvania denied the request of a Pentecostal minister to ban a book from the curriculum of a local junior high school. The minister contended that the use of the book violated the constitutional separation of church and state because it promoted non-Christian beliefs. The book, *Dragonwings*, a Newbery-award-winning novel by Laurence Yep, tells the story of a young Chinese boy who immigrates to California in the 1900s. *Dragonwings* follows his struggles to adapt to a new culture and overcome his and others' prejudices. The book mentions Taoism and refers to the concept of reincarnation several times, the subject to which the minister objected. Judge Joseph Nickleach of Armstrong County Court said that his reading of the book and the testimony of the district's teachers and students led him to believe, according to the October 7, 1992, story in the *Allegheny Bulletin*, that "Neither the book nor the teachers who taught it expounded a particular religion as the only belief nor even a preferred belief. Nor did the book or the teachers credit or hinder the Christian faith or any other religion."

Although the teachers in this Western Pennsylvania district won, their victory was attributable to administrative support, which included spending $4,000 in legal fees. At other times, in other districts, administrators and boards of education back down from such a fight, letting the demands of small groups control what students are allowed to read and what teachers are allowed to teach. Book-banning and censorship are very much alive and efforts are often very organized. The same news story that reported the *Dragonwings* decision also mentioned a nationwide increase in the number of requests to ban books from classrooms and libraries, according to a survey taken by a civil-liberties group, People for the American Way. Whole language teachers, who represent a change, a shift from the traditional, have had to try to institute change at a point in time when change is feared and often blocked. What can whole language teachers do? Change depends very much on improved public relations and effective staff development.

The Importance of Public Relations

Often in education, teachers tend to justify the status-quo by blaming politicians, special-interest groups, boards of education, and parents for making decisions about the profession. That may often be the case, as the examples in this chapter suggest, but other than complaining, what are teachers doing about the decisions that they feel are ignorant and harmful? Traditionally, teachers have been reticent to educate the public about their profession, feeling, "We're the professionals; why should we have to explain ourselves?" The reality of the situation is that teaching is not like other professions—teachers are controlled and regulated by the public. Although whole language teachers may get angry with the interference of the public, as public school educators, they are public servants in the truest sense. If teachers have strong beliefs about what should be happening in schools, then they have to step out of the classrooms and educate the public about their beliefs, enlisting the public's help and support in order to move forward in education. Parents, concerned about the welfare of their children, want what is best for them. Teachers cannot simply counter that parents don't know what is best for their children; they need to begin to think of ways to educate the public about whole language. Teachers need to become political.

Some teachers have banded together to establish the Center for the Expansion of Language and Thought (CELT) (c/o Center for Establishing Dialogue in Teaching and Learning [CED], 325 E. Southern, Tempe, AZ 85282), an organization to support teachers helping each other address serious political problems. Comprised of whole language teachers, educators, and administrators, CELT was founded over a decade ago by Ken Goodman, Yetta Goodman, Dorothy Watson, and Jerry Harste, leaders who recognized the political implications of change. Through this organization, a Crisis Hotline has been established to help teachers, administrators, and professors who are attacked by those whose personal political agendas oppose whole language. The hotline offers help by providing: "information for educators, statements [which] educators can photocopy and distribute to parents, legislators, and the general public, and advice from someone who has suffered through a similar experience" (Edelsky, 1991, p. 4). The advice is provided by volunteers—teachers and administrators— who have had similar problems in their schools or districts and who are willing to share ideas and offer suggestions. In addition to specific problems that teachers identify, the topics addressed by the hotline include censorship of books and materials, campaigns to mandate skills programs, campaigns to end whole language, efforts to dismantle ungraded classrooms or untracked classrooms, efforts to do away with journals and writers' workshop, campaigns to end literature-based reader-response teaching. Elementary and secondary school teachers can call (602)–929–0929 to ask for printed information which can be duplicated and distributed; to ask for advice from

others who have faced similar challenges from the public, administrators, or school boards; and to volunteer to support others faced
with similar situations.

Even given the support of CELT and the Hotline, teachers must
become proactive instead of merely reactive. Other professions and
the business world have long recognized the importance of getting
positive messages to the community before a product, service, or
policy is implemented. Whole language teachers must think of ways
of getting their message to the community, supplying people with
accurate information to understand what teachers are doing, providing knowledge before other groups send misinformation through
confusing, even frightening messages.

One way to do this is to let the public see the product of whole
language teachers' efforts at making learning meaningful for students. John Ferguson, an English teacher at Murphy Junior High
School in Stony Brook, New York, pondered the various ways the
public celebrates student achievement. Athletic departments have
traditionally sponsored sports banquets for students, faculty, and
parents, presenting awards for student athletic performance and
accomplishments. Such events are frequently covered by the local
news media. The music teachers have recitals; the art teachers have
shows; the choir directors have concerts. Taking the lead from his
colleagues in physical education and the performing arts, John and
others in the English Department at Murphy Junior High instituted a
writing contest open to all students at the school. Numerous divi-
sions and categories insured a multitude and variety of winning
entries. As a celebration of accomplishment, an awards ceremony
and writers' banquet was held, with the winning entries collected in
a professionally printed magazine distributed to those attending and
donated in class sets so that each teacher might be able to use student writing as part of the curriculum.

The writers' banquet itself was an occasion. Parents, community
leaders, and educators were invited, and the honored students were
distinguished by receiving medals as their awards. Guest speakers
were invited, and over the years nationally known authors such as
M.E. Kerr and Gordon Kerman have participated. The banquets were
initially funded through monies from a grant, and even when money
became a problem the idea lived on by down-sizing the banquet to
an awards ceremony with dessert. The important thing for John and
the English faculty is that the students receive recognition for learning and the public sees tangible evidence of classrooms where students view writing as important and meaningful. Similarly, Kathy
Simmons, who teaches English at Hempfield Senior High School in
Pennsylvania, gives her students a chance to share what they're

learning. All the students in Kathy's classes contribute to the class magazine. They work in groups, choose their favorite pieces of writing, and prepare them for publication. All students also submit a piece for a national magazine, working together in their groups to help each other revise, assess, and choose what they will submit. Every student in her class also submits to *Balderdash*, the Hempfield literary magazine. These publications, whether class, high school, or national magazines, let parents, other teachers, and community members know what students such as these are accomplishing in our classrooms.

Being a teacher is never easy, yet those who have transformed their views about teaching and learning, who work as facilitators in student-centered classrooms, are the first to say that teaching has never been as exciting or rewarding. Whole language teachers find many ways to share the excitement. In addition to holding a writers' banquet or sponsoring a class publication, teachers and students can write newsletters to be sent home regularly, celebrating the achievements and activities in class. One teacher, Carol Jago of Santa Monica High School in California, discovered that local newspapers are always anxious for well-written contributions; she now writes a weekly column devoted to thoughtful reflection on parenting and education. In addition to writing articles for local newspapers, teachers and students can construct displays for exhibition in shopping malls and banks and create video presentations to air on television stations during the local access time reserved for community broadcasts. Whole language teachers are always thinking of ways to include the community in their celebration of what students *can* do.

Becoming a Whole Language Teacher— Effective Staff Development

Admittedly, it's difficult to be the only whole language teacher in a grade-level or in a school, but it's even more difficult to change an entire school. As a philosophy, not a methodology, whole language cannot be mandated, imposed, or forced on those who are unwilling or uninformed. Whole language cannot be packaged; it cannot be adopted as a product. Whole language is a grassroots movement—it is teachers helping and supporting other teachers, the key to its implementation. Districts who have been successful in instituting change have done so by empowering teachers and enabling them to assume leadership roles. Talented and informed classroom teachers need to be identified as leaders and used as coaches, models, lead teachers, and district facilitators to insure the involvement of all teachers. When teachers are recognized as experts in their field, as professionals who know best how to design and implement curriculum, then they must be involved in decisions to hire new teachers, plan evaluation procedures, and purchase equipment and supplies. These leaders will need time to be reflective, to mentor and network with others, and to be involved in decision making. Teachers must be given time, training, and support by administrators and even state coordinators if whole language is to be instituted in a school or in a district. A commitment to change means more than one day of in-service every couple of months.

Staff development is another area in which whole language teachers can work proactively for change, helping teachers learn. Change is never easy and teachers need to be provided with support throughout the process. Such support can take the form of in-service programs, mentoring relationships, coaching, lead teacher modeling, and administrative encouragement. Ideally, everyone will be involved in change. School personnel need to work as teams of professionals. Instead of seeing themselves as "bosses," administrators need to be leaders, facilitators, and coaches, participating actively in teaching and educating as well as administering. Not only should teachers be encouraged to attend professional conferences but district support and funds should be allocated to make professional growth a recognized and encouraged opportunity. If education is to move forward, then whole language teachers must be supported while other teachers are educated and trained in the philosophy.

Change requires a commitment of time. It's foolhardy to expect transformation in a short time and to mandate new programs before teachers are properly prepared. Regie Routman (1991) believes staff development should be ongoing and regular, provided for those who participate voluntarily, and coinciding with a timeline for implementing change, such as a three- to five-year plan. Meaningful change cannot happen without planning, support, and reasonable timelines, established with the participation of the classroom teachers. Otherwise reform will fail, and when it does, districts will retreat to what was safe and traditional.

In addition to a commitment of planning, support, and time, teachers need to understand the psychology of effective staff development (Bruce & Showers, 1980). Change needs to be based in theory and research, the result of those involved in curricular change doing their homework—reading professional literature and research and attending conferences and workshops. Many teachers believe they need practical tips or ideas for what to do on Monday. What they really need is theory, a set of beliefs so they can design a meaningful framework for their week. Teachers and administrators need to be aware of how people learn before they can decide the best way to teach. Even when teachers in a district are open to theory when it's explained by "experts," those who have researched, published, and are well known in their field, the development of theory itself is ongoing and something that can't be accomplished during one or two inservice days. We have heard administrators say, "Oh, our teachers have been inserviced in whole language, so we are ready for portfolios," when in reality the teachers sat for a two-hour presentation conducted for several hundred teachers in a large auditorium. It's possible to present theory in a large group lecture, but follow-up is needed for acceptance and understanding of this theory.

Furthermore, to understand the application of the theory, teachers need to see a demonstration—a "how-to-do-it" that includes modeling strategies. A cost-effective way to do this is for teachers to demonstrate to and for each other. Of course, the atmosphere of the school must be such that it promotes and supports risk-taking among the teachers. One local school district I (Kathleen) have been working with started a lead-teacher program several years ago on a voluntary basis, and teachers who attended workshops and conferences returned to the district and modeled what they had learned in other teachers' classrooms. Of course, such demonstration must be voluntary on everyone's part.

Videotapes also bring others' ideas into staff development. Professionally produced videos, providing demonstrations of teachers using whole language strategies, may be rented or purchased from publishing companies to let other teachers see "how it is done." Schools can even produce home- grown demonstrations by videotaping teachers willing to model their teaching, thereby sharing their experiences with colleagues. Teachers might also be reminded that when one is a whole language teacher, there is no one, correct way to teach, especially when meeting the needs of students is the foremost concern. After any demonstration, whether live or on videotape, it's important to allow time for questions or discussion, so that teachers understand that they are not being shown "The Way" but are being given suggestions and strategies for teaching based on the theory that has been presented.

Demonstration presupposes practice. Whole language teachers can help each other, finding ways within the traditional schedule to work together, even if only a few teachers in a building are interested. They can support each other through team teaching and coaching, even if they have to use their planning periods in order to work together.

Classroom teachers need feedback, ongoing and constructive opportunities not limited to formal yearly observations. Feedback must be a cooperative situation, one in which the teacher and the observer discuss what happened in class so that the teacher can self-assess, developing goals and suggestions rather than having such suggestions imposed by the observer. Student teachers actually have an advantage with practice under simulated conditions because they often work with small groups before trying to manage a whole class. They also receive support from a mentor who provides immediate feedback, suggestions, and encouragement.

Teachers at every stage of development need support, assistance, and companionship; that is, they need to talk to other teachers who hold the same beliefs and goals. Feedback from peers is constructive and useful only in an atmosphere of mutual trust and respect. Whole language teachers have found ways to do this both in and out of school by holding informal yet structured meetings before or after school and meeting with teachers from within or across districts in whole language networking groups, meetings where they discuss ideas and ask questions. To learn and grow as a teacher, it is important to have a friend, confidant, cheerleader, and coach. Becoming a teacher is a lifelong activity.

For Further Exploration

1. Interview a teacher who is teaching according to a whole language philosophy. What are the reactions from other teachers to what he or she is doing? From administration? From parents? How do these reactions influence what this teacher is doing?

2. Talk with a superintendent or principal in a district that is going through a change toward whole language. How was this change begun and for what reasons? What roles are the teachers playing in this change? How have parents and the community been involved?

3. Talk to teachers about inservice opportunities in their districts. What opportunities are provided for teachers to grow as professionals? How do teachers work together?

4. Ask a whole language teacher how he or she became a whole language teacher. How do such teachers function in a school where most teachers are traditional? Are these teachers encouraged to grow and how do they support each other?

5. Check with a local librarian, school librarian, or whole language teacher who uses literature in the classroom. Have these people had problems with censorship? How are such problems handled? What is the role of the teacher? Who censors books? Are there any other areas of censorship in schools besides classroom novels?

Related Readings for Further Thought and Exploration

Edelsky, C. (1991). *With literacy and justice for all: Rethinking the social in language and education.* New York: The Falmer Press. *Ties together sociolinguistics, bilingual education, whole language, and critical pedagogy through a collection of essays from the perspective of classroom teachers and teacher-researchers.*

Oboler, E. (1981). *Defending intellectual freedom: The library and the censor.* New York: Wilson. *Confronts the issue of censorship and book-banning, one that whole language teachers often face. This book looks at the issue of censorship from the viewpoint of democracy and freedom, and it may prove helpful to teachers and administrators facing a censorship problem.*

Shannon, P. (1992). *Becoming political: Readings and writings in the politics of literacy education.* Portsmouth, NH: Heinemann. *Offers a collection of writings from North America's most celebrated researchers and teachers who tell how race, social class, gender, and language affect schools, students, teachers, and learning.*

Smith, F. (1988). *Insult to intelligence: The bureaucratic invasion of our classrooms.* Portsmouth, NH: Heinemann. *Distinquishes between how children learn and how they are often taught. This book, guaranteed to promote discussion, is applicable to every grade level and content area.*

Teachers Networking: The Whole Language Newsletter. Katonah, NY: Richard C. Owen Publishers. *Addresses problems faced by whole language teachers, ideas for the classroom, stories of children's and teachers' successes, and announcements of whole language meetings. This newsletter is published four times a year and reports information from teachers, researchers, and noted authors on whole language.*

Contemporary Classroom Literature Cited

The Autobiography of Malcolm X by Malcolm X as told to Alex Haley. New York: Ballantine Books, 1987.

Barefoot Gen: The Day After by Keiji Nakazawa. Philadelphia,PA: New Society Publishers, 1988.

The Boys' War by Davis Paxton. Winston-Salem, NC: John F. Blair, 1990.

Catcher in the Rye by J. D. Salinger. New York: Bantam, 1984.

Charlie Skeedaddle by Patricia Beatty. New York: William Morrow, 1987.

The Color Purple by Alice Walker. New York: Pocket Books, 1988.

Daddy-Long-Legs by Jean Webster. New York: Scholastic, 1991.

A Day No Pigs Would Die by Robert Newton Peck. New York: Dell, 1979.

Diary of a Young Girl by Anne Frank. New York: Pocket Books, 1990.

Dragonwings by Laurence Yep. New York: Harper Collins, 1977.

Forever by Judy Blume. New York: Bradbury Press, 1982.

Francesca by Roger Scruton. North Pomfret, VT: Trafalgar, 1991.

The Great Gatsby by F. Scott Fitzgerald. New York: Macmillan, 1988.

Harriet Tubman: Wanted Dead or Alive. The True Story of Harriet Tubman by Ann McGovern. New York: Scholastic, 1965.

Kaffir Boy in America by Mark Mathabane. New York: Macmillan, 1990.

A Light in the Forest by Conrad Richter. New York: Bantam, 1990.

Looking the Tiger in the Eye: Confronting the Nuclear Threat by Carl Feldbaum and Ronald Bee. New York: Harper and Row, 1988.

Lord of the Flies by William Golding. New York: Putnam, 1959.

Maniac Magee by Jerry Spinelli. New York: Little, Brown, 1990.

Manzanar by John Armor and Peter Wright. New York: Random House, 1989.

Member of the Wedding by Carson McCullers. New York: Bantam, 1985.

Night by Elie Wiesel. New York, Bantam, 1982.

Of Mice and Men by John Steinbeck. New York: Bantam, 1983.

Old Yeller by Fred Gipson. New York: Harper Collins, 1990.

The Outsiders by S. E. Hinton. Boston: G. K. Hall, 1989.

The Pearl by John Steinbeck. New York: Bantam, 1986.

The Red Pony by John Steinbeck. New York: Viking, 1989.

Roll of Thunder, Hear My Cry by Mildred Taylor. New York: Bantam, 1984.

Rosencrantz and Guildenstern Are Dead by Tom Stoppard. New York: Grove/ Weidenfeld, 1987.

The Sign of the Beaver by Elizabeth George Speare. New York: Dell, 1984.

Slaughterhouse Five by Kurt Vonnegut, Jr. New York: Dell, 1978.

Soul on Ice by Eldridge Cleaver. New York: Dell, 1992.

Sounder by William H. Armstrong. New York: Harper Collins, 1969.

The Stone Angel by Margaret Laurence. New York: Bantam, 1981.

Streetcar Named Desire by Tennessee Williams. New York: New American Library/Dutton, 1986.

Tex by S. E. Hinton. New York: Dell, 1989.

That Was Then, This Was Now by S. E. Hinton. New York: Dell, 1989.

Their Eyes Were Watching God by Zora Neale Hurston. New York: Harper Collins, 1990.

To Kill a Mockingbird by Harper Lee. New York: Warner, 1988.

Where the Red Fern Grows by Wilson Rawls. New York: Bantam, 1974.

References

Adams, M. J. (1990a). Beginning to read: Thinking and learning about print. Cambridge, MA: MIT Press.

————. (1990b). Beginning to read: Thinking and learning about print. A summary. S. A. Stahl, J. Osborn, & F. Lehr (Eds.). Urbana, IL: Center for the Study of Reading/ The Reading Research and Education Center.

Anderson, R., Hiebert, E., Scott, J., & Wilkinson, I. (1984). *Becoming a nation of readers: The report of the commission on reading.* Urbana, IL: National Council of Teachers of English.

Anderson, R., Reynolds, R.E., Schallert, D. L., & Goetz, T. E., (1977). Frameworks for understanding discourse. *American Educational Journal, 14,* 367–381.

Apple, M. W. (1989). Teaching and technology. In L. Weis, P. G. Altbach, G. P. Kelly, H. G. Petrie, & S. Slaughter (Eds.), *Crises in teaching: Perspectives on current reforms* (pp. 227–251). Albany, NY: SUNY Press.

Applebee, A. (1974). *Tradition and reform in the teaching of English: A history.* Urbana,IL: National Council of Teachers of English.

————. (1981). *Writing in the secondary school: English and the content areas.* Urbana, IL: National Council of Teachers of English.

Atwell, N. (1987). *In the middle: Writing, reading, and learning with adolescents.* Portsmouth, NH: Boynton/Cook.

————. (1988). A special writer at work. In T. Newkirk & N. Atwell (Eds.) *Understanding writing: Ways of observing, learning, and teaching K–8.* Portsmouth, NH: Heinemann.

Bencich, C. (1991, May). Tracking or sidetracking? *English Leadership Quarterly.* pp. 7–8.

Berthoff, A. E. (1979). *Forming, thinking, writing: The composing imagination.* New York: Hayden.

Birnbaum, J.C. (1982). The reading and composing behavior of selected fourth- and seventh-grade students. *Research in the Teaching of English, 16*(3), 241–261.

Bleich, D. (1975). *Readings and feelings: An introduction to subjective criticism.* Urbana, IL: National Council of Teachers of English.

————. (1978). *Subjective criticism.* Baltimore: Johns Hopkins University Press.

Bloom, B. (1956). *Taxonomy of educational objectives: Handbook I: Cognitive domain.* New York: McKay.

Bradley, S., Beatty, R. C., Long, E. H. (1967). *American tradition in literature* (Vol. 2). New York: W. W. Norton.

Britton, J., et al. (1975). *The development of writing abilities 11–18.* New York: Macmillan.

Broughton, E. (1992). *A mother's view of whole language.* Unpublished manuscript. Mesa State College, Grand Junction, CO.

Bruce, J., & Showers, B. (1980). Improving inservice training: The messages of research. *Educational Leadership,* 379–385.

Cambourne, B. (1989). *The whole story.* Sydney, NSW, Australia: Ashton-Scholastic.

Carrier, J. G. (1983). Masking the social in educational knowledge: The case of learning disability theory. *American Journal of Sociology, 88,* 948–974.

Cazden, C. (1988). *Classroom discourse: The language of teaching and learning.* Portsmouth, NH: Heinemann.

Chambers, R. (1992). *Reader response in action, for freshmen and seniors.* Unpublished manuscript. Grand River Collegiate Institute, Kitchner, Ontario.

Chomsky, N. (1957). *Syntactic structures.* The Hague: Mouton.

Coles, G. S. (1978). The learning disabilities test battery: Empirical and social issues. *Harvard Educational Review, 48,* 313–340.

Cosgrove, C. (1991, May). Unmasking psycho/biological labels for language acts. *English Leadership Quarterly.* pp. 2–5.

Derrida, J. (1981). *Dissemination.* (B. Johnson, Trans.) Chicago: University of Chicago.

Dewey, J. (1916). *Democracy in education.* New York: Macmillan.

Dixon, J. (1967). *Growth through English.* London: Oxford University Press.

Dolly, M. R. (1992). *A learning disabled student in advanced composition: Three perspectives.* Unpublished manuscript. Frostburg State University, MD.

Dreyer, D. Y. (1992). *Responding to peers: The language of native and nonnative speakers in writing groups.* Unpublished doctoral dissertation. Indiana University of Pennsylvania.

Edelsky, C. (1991). The crisis hotline: Professionalism in action. *Teachers Networking: The Whole Language Newsletter, 10,* 4–5.

————. (1992). The psycholinguistic guessing game: A political-historical retrospective. Paper presented at the Annual Convention of the National Council of Teachers of English, Louisville.

Eisner, E. (1992, October). The reality of reform. *English Leadership Quarterly.* pp. 2–5.

Elbow, P. (1973). *Writing without teachers.* New York: Oxford University Press.

Emig, J. (1971). *The composing process of twelfth graders.* Urbana, IL: National Council of Teachers of English.

――――― . (1977, May). Writing as a mode of learning. *College Composition and Communication*, pp. 122–128.

――――― . (1978). Hand, eye, brain: Some "basics" in writing. In C. R. Cooper & L. Odell (Eds.) *Research on composing: Points of departure.* Urbana, IL: National Council of Teachers of English.

Evangelauf, J. (1990). Reliance on multiple-choice tests said to harm minorities and hinder reform; panel seeks a new regulatory agency. *The Chronicle of Higher Education, 37*, A1.

Fish, S. (1980). *Is there a text in this class?.* Cambridge, MA: Harvard University Press.

Flower, L., & Hayes, J. (1980). Identifying the organization of the writing process. In L. Gregg & E. Steinberg (Eds.) *Cognitive processes in writing* (pp. 9–10). Hillsdale, NJ: Lawrence Erlbaum.

Franklin, B. M. (1987). Introduction: Learning disability and the need for dissenting essays. In B.M. Franklin (Ed.) *Learning disability: Dissenting essays* (pp. 1–12). London: The Falmer Press.

Freire, P. (1970). *Pedagogy of the oppressed.* New York: Herder and Herder.

Fulwiler, T. (1987). *The journal book.* Portsmouth, NH: Boynton/Cook.

Gabler, M., & Gabler, N. (1985). *What are they teaching our children?* Wheaton, IL: Victor.

Golub, J. (1993, May). The voices we hear. *English Leadership Quarterly*, pp. 2–5.

Good, T. (1981). Teacher expectations and student perceptions: A decade of research. *Educational Leadership, 38*, 415–421.

Goodlad, J. (1984). *A place called school.* New York: McGraw-Hill.

Goodman, K. (1969). Analysis of oral reading miscues: Applied Psycholinguistics. *Reading Research Quarterly, 5*, 9–30.

――――― . (1979). The know-more and the know-nothing movements in reading: A personal response. *Language Arts, 56*, 657–63.

――――― . (1987). Reading and writing: A psycholinguistic view. In K. Goodman, E. B. Smith, R. Meredith, and Y. Goodman (Eds.), *Language and thinking in school: A whole-language curriculum* (pp. 265–83). Katonah, NY: Richard C. Owen.

――――― . (1992). Why whole language is today's agenda in education. *Language Arts, 69*, 354–363.

Goodman, Y. (1978). Kid watching: An alternative to testing. *National Elementary Principals Journal, 57*, 41–45.

Graves, D. (1983). *Writing: Teachers and children at work.* Portsmouth, NH: Heinemann.

Greenbaum, V. (1990, December). Some are more equal than others. *English Journal*, p. 68.

Gronlund, N. (1985). *Measurement and evaluation in teaching* (5th ed.). New York: Macmillan.

Grossman, P. (1989). A study in contrast: Sources of pedagogical content knowledge for secondary English. *Journal of Teacher Education, 40*(5), 24–31.

Hairston, M. (1982). The winds of change: Thomas Kuhn and the revolution in the teaching of writing. *College Composition and Communication, 33,* 76–88.

Hall, W. (1987). *The emergence of literacy.* Portsmouth, NH: Heinemann.

Hansen, J. (1987). *When writers read.* Portsmouth, NH: Heinemann.

Harker, W. J. (1987). Literary theory and the reading process: A meeting of perspectives. *Written Communication, 4,* 235–252.

Harp, B. (1991). Principles of assessment and evaluation in whole language classrooms. In B. Harp (Ed.) *Assessment and evaluation in whole language programs.* Norwood, MA: Christopher-Gordon.

Harste, J., Woodward, V., & Burke, C. (1984). Examining our assumptions: A transactional view of literacy and learning. *Research in the Teaching of English, 18,* 84–108.

Hartwell, P. (1981). *Writers as readers.* (ERIC Document Reproduction Service No. ED 199 701).

Hatfield, P. (1990, March). From the other side of the tracking. *English Journal,* p. 75.

Hickman, J., & Cullinan, B. (1989). *Children's literature in the classroom: Weaving Charlotte's web.* Norwood, MA: Christopher-Gordon.

Hirsch, E. D. (1987). *Cultural literacy.* Boston: Houghton Mifflin.

Hodges, R. (1977). In Adam's fall: A brief history of spelling instruction in the United States. In H. Robinson (Ed.) *Reading and writing instruction in the United States: Historical trends* (pp. 1–16). Newark, DE: International Reading Association.

Holdaway, D. (1979). *Foundations of Literacy.* Portsmouth, NH: Heinemann.

Huck, C. (1977). Literature as the content of reading. *Theory into Practice, 16,* 363–371.

Isher, W. (1978). *The act of reading: A history of aesthetic response.* Baltimore, MD: Johns Hopkins University Press.

Jago, C. (1992, February). No more objective tests, ever. *English Leadership Quarterly.* pp. 4–6.

Joyce, M. (1988, November). Siren shapes: Exploratory and constructive hypertexts. *Academic Computing.* pp. 10–42.

Kelly-Garris, K. (1993). *Writing workshop at Penn-Trafford High School.* Unpublished manuscript. Harrison City, PA.

Kent, J., & Trevisani, T. Jr. (1989, October). Linking professional development to curricular change. *CSSEDC Quarterly.* pp. 3–4.

Kerckhoff, A.C. (1986). Effects of ability grouping in British secondary schools. *American Sociological Review, 51,* 842–58.

Kessler, K. (1992). *Peer dialogue journals: An ethnographic study of shared reader response to holocaust literature.* Unpublished doctoral dissertation. Indiana University of Pennsylvania.

King-Shaver, B. (1991, February). Whole language: Implications for secondary classrooms. *English Leadership Quarterly.* pp. 4–5.

Knoblauch, C. H., & Brannon, L. (1983). Writing as learning through the curriculum. *College English, 45,* 465–474.

Kuhn, T. (1963). *The structure of scientific revolutions.* Chicago: University of Chicago Press.

Laubach, R. (1990, December). Learning to Trust. *English Leadership Quarterly.* pp. 3–4.

Ljung, E. J. (1990, December). Tracking: A rebuttal. *English Journal,* p. 70.

Macrorie, K. (1984). *Writing to be read* (3rd ed.). Portsmouth, NH: Heinemann.

Mandler, G. (1985). *Cognitive psychology: An essay in cognitive science.* Hillsdale, NJ: Lawrence Erlbaum.

Miller, S. (1991, May). Room to talk: Opening possibilities with the at-risk. *English Leadership Quarterly.* pp. 10–11.

Moffett, J. (1981). *Active voice: A writing program across the curriculum.* Portsmouth, NH: Heinemann.

———. (1983). *Teaching the universe of discourse.* Boston: Houghton Mifflin.

Morine-Dershimer, G. (1985). *Talking, listening, and learning in elementary classrooms.* New York: Longman.

Murdick, W. (1992). *Writing learning across the curriculum: Examples from journal writing in college art classes.* Unpublished manuscript. California University of Pennsylvania.

Murray, D. (1978). Internal revision: A process of discovery. In C. Cooper & L. Odell (Eds.) *Research on composing: Points of departure.* Urbana, IL: National Council of Teachers of English.

Oakes, J. (1985). Keeping track: How schools structure inequality. New Haven: Yale University Press.

Oliver, E. (1992). *Contemporary literature, heterogeneous style.* Unpublished manuscript. Washington State University, Pullman, WA.

Page, W., & Pinnell, G. S. (1979). *Teaching reading Comprehension.* Urbana, IL: National Council of Teachers of English.

Perl, S. (1979). The composing process of unskilled college writers. *Research in the Teaching of English, 13,* 317–36.

Piaget, J. (1971). *Psychology and epistemology.* Translated by A. Rosin. New York: Grossman.

Probst, R. (1988). *Response and analysis: Teaching literature in junior and senior high school.* Portsmouth, NH: Boynton/Cook.

——— . (1992). Five kinds of literary knowing. In J. Langer (Ed.) *Literature Instruction* (pp. 54-77). Urbana, IL: National Council of Teachers of English.

Purves, A. C., & Beach, R. (1972). *Literature and the reader: Research in response to literature, reading interests, and the teaching of literature.* Urbana, IL: National Council of Teachers of English.

Reigstad, T., & McAndrew, D. (1984). *Training tutors for writing conferences.* Urbana, IL: National Council of Teachers of English.

Rider, J. (1992). *I need a psychologist in my classroom.* Unpublished manuscript. Mesa State College, Grand Junction, CO.

Rodrigues, D., & Rodrigues, R. (1986). *Teaching writing with a word processor, grades 7–13.* Urbana, IL: ERIC/National Council of Teachers of English.

Rosenblatt, L. (1938). *Literature as exploration.* New York: Appleton-Century.

——— . (1976). *Literature as exploration* (3rd ed.). New York: Noble and Noble.

——— . (1978). *The reader, the text, the poem: The transactional theory of the literary work.* Carbondale, IL: Southern Illinois University.

Routman, R. (1991). *Invitations: Changing as teachers and learners K–12.* Portsmouth, NH: Heinemann.

Rumelhart, D. E. (1980). The building blocks of cognition. In R.J. Spiro, B.C. Bruce, & W.F. Brewer (Eds.) *Theoretical issues in reading comprehension* (pp.33–58). Hillsdale, NJ: Lawrence Erlbaum.

St. Michel, T. (1992). *The first six minutes.* Unpublished manuscript. South Mountain High School, Phoenix, AZ.

Schwartz, W., & Galloway, D. (1992, February). Eliminating the negative effects of ability grouping on low-achieving students. *English Leadership Quarterly.* pp. 9–10.

Shannon, P. (1991). Talking back to critics. *Teachers Networking: The Whole Language Newsletter, 10*(3), 1, 12–14.

——— . (1992). *Becoming political: Readings and writings in the politics of literacy education.* Portsmouth, NH: Heinemann.

Shaughnessy, M. (1977). *Errors and expectations.* New York: Oxford University Press.

Simon, H. (1974). How big is a chunk? *Science, 183,* 482–488.

Skinner, B. F. (1953). *Science and human behavior.* New York: Macmillan.

Smith, F. (1988a). *Insult to intelligence: The bureaucratic invasion of our classrooms.* Portsmouth, NH: Heinemann.

——— . (1988b). *Joining the literacy club: Further essays into education.* Portsmouth, NH: Heinemann.

————. (1988c). *Understanding reading* (4th ed.). Hillsdale, NJ: Lawrence Erlbaum.

Squire, J. (1983). Composing and comprehending: Two sides of the same basic process. *Language Arts, 60* (5), 581–589.

Stahl, S. (1990). Riding the pendulum, *Review of Educational Research, 60,* 141–151.

Strickland, J. (1988, February). The reluctant writer and word processing, *CSSEDC Quarterly.* pp. 4–5.

Strickland, K. (1991). *Changes in Perspectives: Student Teachers' Development of a Reading Instruction Philosophy* (ERIC Document Reproduction Service No. ED 331 037).

————. (1993). *A microethnography of literature-based reading and writing instruction in a whole language classroom with "at-risk" adolescents.* Unpublished doctoral dissertation, Indiana University of Pennsylvania.

Swope, J. W. (1991, October). When whole language learners reach us: Challenges for a changing secondary literature classroom. *English Leadership Quarterly.* pp. 6–7.

Taylor, D. (1991). *Learning denied.* Portsmouth, NH: Heinemann.

Taylor, S. (1971). *The dynamic activity of reading: A model of the process.* Bulletin No. 9. Huntington, NY: Educational Laboratories, Inc.

Tchudi, S. (1985). *Language, schooling and society.* Portsmouth, NH: Boynton/Cook.

Teichmann, S. G. (1993). Tales of two teachers, *English Leadership Quarterly,* forthcoming.

Thompson, E. H. (1991, October). Tying reader response to group interaction in literature classrooms, *English Leadership Quarterly.* pp. 9–10.

Tierney, R., Carter, M., & Desai, L. (1991). *Portfolio assessment in the reading-writing classroom.* Norwood, MA: Christopher-Gordon.

Tierney, R. J., & Leys, M. (1986). What is the value of connecting reading and writing? In B.T. Peterson (Ed.) *Convergences: Transactions in reading and writing* (pp. 15–29). Urbana, IL: National Council of Teachers of English.

Tinker, M. (1965). *Bases for effective reading.* Minneapolis: University of Minnesota Press.

Trimble, K. D., & Sinclair, R.L. (1987). On the wrong track: Ability grouping and the threat to equity. *Equity and Excellence, 22,* 15–21.

Tucker, E. C. (1991, October). Mr. C. didn't do it this way. *English Leadership Quarterly.* pp. 10–11.

Vacca, R., & Vacca, J. A. (1989). *Content area reading* (3rd ed.). Glenview, IL: Scott, Foresman.

Valencia, S. (1990). A portfolio approach to classroom reading assessment: The whys, whats, and hows. *The Reading Teacher, 43*(4), 338–340.

Vygotsky, L. (1978). *Mind and society.* M. Cole, V. J. Steiner, S. Scribner, &

E. Souberman (Eds.). Cambridge, MA: Harvard University Press.

Watson, D. J. (1989). Defining and describing whole language. *Elementary School Journal, 90,* 129–142.

Weaver, C. (1988). *Reading process and practice: From sociopsycholinguistics to whole language.* Portsmouth, NH: Heinemann.

————. (1990). *Understanding whole language: From principles to practice.* Portsmouth, NH: Heinemann.

Wells, G. (1986). *The meaning makers: Children learning language and using language to learn.* Portsmouth, NH: Heinemann.

Wieland, S. (1990, December). Leading classroom discussions. *English Leadership Quarterly.* pp. 1–3.

————. (1991, February). Student writers set their own goals. *English Leadership Quarterly.* pp. 8–11.

Williams, W. F. (1991, October). Teaching literature, canon formation, and multiculturalism. *English Leadership Quarterly.* pp. 2–3.

Young, R. (1978). Paradigms and problems: Needed research in rhetorical invention. In C.R. Cooper & L. Odell (Eds.). *Research on composing* (pp. 29–47). Urbana, IL: National Council of Teachers of English.

Zemelman, S., & Daniels, H. (1988). *A community of writers: Teaching writing in the junior and senior high school.* Portsmouth, NH: Heinemann.

Acknowledgments

(Continued from page iv)

Excerpts from "Tales of Two Teachers" by Sandra Gail Teichmann. In *English Leadership Quarterly*, forthcoming. Reprinted by permission of the author.

Excerpts from "Student Writers Set Their Own Goals" by Sharon Wieland. In *English Leadership Quarterly*, February 1991. Reprinted by permission of the author.

Excerpts from "Writing Workshop at Penn-Trafford High School" by Kathy Kelly-Garris. Unpublished manuscript, 1993. Reprinted by permission of the author.

Figure 2–1: Reprinted by permission of Nancie Atwell: *In the Middle: Writing, Reading and Learning with Adolescents* (Boynton/Cook Publishers, Inc., Portsmouth, NH, 1987).

"Stopping by Woods on a Snowy Evening" by Robert Frost, from *The Poetry of Robert Frost* edited by Edward Connery Lathem. Copyright ©1923, © 1969 by Holt, Rinehart and Winston. Copyright © 1951 by Robert Frost. Reprinted by permission of Henry Holt and Co., Inc.

Excerpts from "Mr. C. Didn't Do It This Way" by E. Carolyn Tucker. In *English Leadership Quarterly*, October 1991. Reprinted by permission of the author.

Excerpts from "Reader Response in Action, for Freshmen and Seniors" by Rick Chambers. Unpublished manuscript, 1992. Reprinted by permission of the author.

Excerpts from "Tying Reader Response to Group Interaction in Literature Classrooms" by Edgar H. Thompson. In *English Leadership Quarterly*, October 1991. Reprinted by permission of the author.

Excerpts from "Teaching Literature, Canon Formation, and Multiculturalism" by William F. Williams. In *English Leadership Quarterly*, October 1991. Reprinted by permission of the author.

Excerpts from "Leading Classroom Discussions" by Sharon Wieland. In *English Leadership Quarterly*, December 1990. Reprinted by permission of the author.

Excerpts from "Room to Talk: Opening Possibilities with the At-Risk" by Suzanne Miller. In *English Leadership Quarterly*, May 1991. Reprinted by permission of the author.

Figure 4–1: Reprinted by permission of Steven Zemelman and Harvey Daniels: *A Community of Writers: Teaching Writing in the Junior and Senior High School* (Heinemann, a division of Reed Publishing (USA) Inc., Portsmouth, NH, 1988).

Figure 4–2: Tutor Critique Sheet from *Training Tutors for Writing Conferences* by Tom Reigstad and Donald McAndrew. Published by ERIC/NCTE, 1984. Reprinted by permission of Donald McAndrew.

"Innocence" from *Selected Poems 1950–1975* by Thom Gunn. Copyright © 1979 by Thom Gunn. Reprinted by permission of Farrar, Straus and Giroux, Inc., New York, and by Faber and Faber Ltd, London.

Excerpts from "Writing Learning Across the Curriculum: Examples from Journal Writing in College Art Classes" by William Murdick. Unpublished manuscript, 1992. Reprinted by permission of the author.

Excerpts from "The Reality of Reform" by Elliot Eisner. In *English Leadership Quarterly*, October 1992. Reprinted by permission of the author.

Excerpts from unpublished teacher notebook by Amy Walker. Reprinted by permission of the author.

Excerpts from "Tracking or Sidetracking?" by Carole Bencich. In *English Leadership Quarterly*, May 1991. Reprinted by permission of the author.

Excerpts from "A Learning Disabled Student in Advanced Composition: Three Perspectives" by Martha R. Dolly. Unpublished manuscript, 1992. Reprinted by permission of the author.

Figure 8-1: "Memory" lesson file by Rebecca Laubach. From "The Reluctant Writer and Word Processing" by James Strickland. *CSSEDC Quarterly*, February 1988. Reprinted by permission of the authors.

Every effort has been made to contact the copyright holders for permission to reprint borrowed material. We regret any oversights and would be happy to rectify them in future printings of this work.

Index